Teaching and Researching Reading

APPLIED LINGUISTICS IN ACTION

General Editors:

Christopher N. Candlin and David R. Hall

Books published in this series include:

Teaching and Researching Reading

William Grabe and Fredricka L. Stoller

An imprint of **Pearson Education**

Harlow, England · London · New York · Reading, Massachusetts · San Francisco
Toronto · Don Mills, Ontario · Sydney · Tokyo · Singapore · Hong Kong · Seoul
Taipei · Cape Town · Madrid · Mexico City · Amsterdam · Munich · Paris · Milan

Pearson Education Limited
Edinburgh Gate
Harlow, Essex CM20 2JE
England

and Associated Companies throughout the world

Visit us on the World Wide Web at:
www.pearsoned.co.uk

First published in Great Britain in 2002

© Pearson Education, 2002

The right of William Grabe and Fredricka L. Stoller to be
identified as Authors of this Work has been asserted by them
in accordance with the Copyright, Designs and Patents Act 1988.

ISBN 978-0-582-36995-5

British Library Cataloguing in Publication Data
A CIP catalogue record for this book can be obtained from the British Library

10   9
07

Set in 11/13pt Janson by Graphicraft Limited, Hong Kong
Printed in Malaysia, LSP

The Publishers' policy is to use paper manufactured from sustainable forests.

Contents

General Editors' Preface

Applied Linguistics in Action, as its name suggests, is a Series which focuses on the issues and challenges to practitioners and researchers in a range of fields in Applied Linguistics and provides readers and users with the tools they need to carry out their own practice-related research.

The books in the Series provide readers with clear, up-to-date, access-ible and authoritative accounts of their chosen field within Applied Linguistics. Using the metaphor of a map of the landscape of the field, each book provides information on its main ideas and concepts, its scope, its competing issues, solved and unsolved questions. Armed with this authoritative but critical account, readers can explore for them-selves a range of exemplary practical applications of research into these issues and questions, before taking up the challenge of undertaking their own research, guided by the detailed and explicit research guides provided. Finally, each book has a section which is concurrently on the Series *web site* www.booksites.net/alia and which provides a rich array of chosen resources, information sources, further reading and com-mentary, as well as a key to the principal concepts of the field.

Questions that the books in this innovative Series ask are those familiar to all practitioners and researchers, whether very experienced, or new to the fields of Applied Linguistics.

- What does research tell us, what doesn't it tell us, and what should it tell us about the field? What is its geography? How is the field mapped and landscaped?
- How has research been carried out and applied and what interesting research possibilities does practice raise? What are the issues we need to explore and explain?

- What are the key researchable topics that practitioners can undertake? How can the research be turned into practical action?
- Where are the important resources that practitioners and researchers need? Who has the information? How can it be accessed?

Each book in the Series has been carefully designed to be as accessible as possible, with built-in features to enable readers to find what they want quickly and to home in on the key issues and themes that concern them. The structure is to move from practice to theory and research, and back to practice, in a cycle of development of understanding of the field in question. Books in the Series will be usable for the individual reader but also can serve as a basis for course design, or seminar discussion.

Each of the authors of books in the Series is an acknowledged authority, able to bring broad knowledge and experience to engage practitioners and researchers in following up their own ideas, working with them to build further on their own experience.

Applied Linguistics in Action is an **in action** Series. Its *web site* will keep you updated and regularly re-informed about the topics, fields and themes in which you are involved.

We hope that you will like and find useful the design, the content, and, above all, the support the books will give to your own practice and research!

Christopher N. Candlin and David R. Hall
General Editors

A Companion Web Site accompanies *Teaching and Researching Reading by* William Grabe and Fredricka L. Stoller

Visit the *Teaching and Researching Reading* Companion Web Site at www.booksites.net/grabe to find valuable teaching and learning material including:

- Links to valuable resources on the web
- Useful sources and resources relating to the study of Reading

www.booksites.net

Authors' Acknowledgements and Dedication

We'd like to thank Rose-Marie Weber for her careful reading of our manuscript and the suggestions for changes that she made; they significantly improved the volume. We'd also like to thank Chris Candlin and David Hall, ALIA series editors, for their guidance and ongoing feedback through several draft versions of the book. Their vision for this series, as a whole, helped us rethink a number of ideas and the volume is far better for their input. And, of course, we must thank our students at Northern Arizona University who have helped us think through reading from various perspectives over the years.

We'd like to dedicate this volume to our mothers:
Kathe Rositzke and Betty L. Stoller

Publisher's Acknowledgements

We are grateful to the following for permission to reproduce copyright material:

Figure 8.9 copyright 1988 by the North Central Regional Educational Laboratory. All rights reserved. Reprinted with permission.

While every effort has been made to trace the owners of copyright material, in a few cases this has proved impossible and we take this opportunity to offer our apologies to any copyright holders whose rights we have unwittingly infringed.

Introduction

Approximately 80 per cent of the world's population is reported to be able to read. While numbers on such a large scale can be misleading, it is safe to say that the majority of humans are able to read in their first languages at some basic level. An unknown percentage of these readers is also able to read, at varying ability levels, in one or more additional languages. The extent of basic literacy around the world should not be surprising because literacy is seen as necessary (but not sufficient) for improving earning potential and quality of life. At the same time, a bit of reflection reveals that reading, and literacy more generally, provides no special entry to a better standard of living. All we know is that, without it, opportunities for improving one's life are limited. As we enter a new century, productive and educated citizens will require even stronger literacy abilities (including both reading and writing) in increasingly larger numbers of societal settings. Likewise, the age of technology growth is likely to make greater, rather than lesser, demands on people's reading abilities.

The role of reading in society is actually quite complex, so a few comments are needed to situate the role of reading and student learning. A major goal for many educational institutions around the world is to promote greater literacy, and we often hear of efforts to eradicate illiteracy altogether. Many of us take this perspective for granted and seldom consider critically the role of literacy in societies around the world. In fact, the universal-eradication view is somewhat simplistic. As much as we would like to believe that all societies value the same educational goals, some people do not need literacy to function well in their societal contexts. Others achieve societal success with relatively minimal levels of literacy. Finally, literacy itself is not a singular no-tion that operates uniformly in all societies. There are many types of literacy abilities (e.g. reading, writing, reading and writing together, interpreting documents, working with multiple texts), much as there are many types of reading abilities and ways of reading. However, having made these comments, it is nevertheless true that the large majority of individuals need literacy to further their goals and better their lives.

Within this larger context, reading in second language (L2) settings continues to take on increasing importance. The overwhelming major-ity of societies and countries around the world are multilingual, and educated citizens are expected to function well in more than one lan-guage. L2 reading ability, particularly with English as the L2, is already in great demand as English continues to spread, not only as a global language but also as the language of science, technology and advanced research. Many people in multilingual settings need to read in an L2 at reasonably high levels of proficiency to achieve personal, occupational and professional goals. But reading proficiency in an L2 does not develop as completely or as 'easily' as it apparently does in one's first language (L1). (Actually, the development of L1 reading also takes a considerable amount of time, and it is one of the primary goals of K-6 education. As adults, we often overlook the intense time and resource commitments made by educational systems to teach L1 reading.) Seldom are L2 stu-dents given as much time to develop strong reading abilities, despite similarly demanding expectations for success.

We actually know relatively little about how people become good L2 readers, but we do know that there are significant differences between learning to read in L1 and L2 settings. It is also true that connections between research and reading instruction in L2 contexts are not well supported for a variety of reasons. In some cases, there are too many diverse types of L2 learners to generalise from the few existing studies that have been done well; in other cases, differing student L1s may limit general assertions from research; and, in yet other cases, great differences in L2 proficiency levels among student groups limit the generalisability of claims. Several of these issues in connecting research and teaching practice are explored throughout this volume.

Because there is not a single consensus view from L2 reading research, a major goal of this volume is to persuade teachers to carry out small-scale research projects on different aspects of reading that can strength-en the connection between research assertions and effective teaching practices. This building of linkages between research and teaching practices involves **action research**,[1] a form of teacher-initiated enquiry in which teachers look systematically and critically at their own classrooms to get an insider's view of the teaching and learning process. By means of action research, we can learn about our own teaching practices and improve student learning. The outcomes of action research can also influence more formal research, making the information flow a two-way enterprise.

Quote 1

A cornerstone of teacher research is that it is *pragmatic* and *action oriented*; that is, it involves reflecting on one's teaching and practice, inquiring about it, exploring it, and then taking action to improve or alter it. . . . We know from our own teacher research that engaging in classroom inquiry can transform an educator's views on teaching and learning.

Baumann and Duffy-Hester (2000, pp. 78, 80)

Reading research and reading instruction

The ability of teachers to benefit from formal research studies, and to inform research in turn (via action research), requires that teachers have a grasp of the fundamental issues that motivate researchers as they explore reading abilities and their development. Reading researchers have, themselves, developed mental images of the overall reading process (something like a conceptual map of the 'terrain' of reading) into which they incorporate new findings and assess the value of new claims. This sort of map is essential to understanding the competing assertions that researchers make about reading and their implications for teaching. And it is such a map that teachers will benefit from as they critically assess how students are learning and how students can learn more effectively through instructional innovations. The knowledge associated with these mental maps also offers teachers a way to evaluate the assertions made by others who are engaged in curriculum planning, course design and

---

[1] Words or phrases that are printed in bold throughout the volume are defined in the Glossary at the end of the book. In a number of cases, the terms in bold are not meant to be the key terms for the subsection, but only a cue to look at the glossary if more explanation is needed.

materials development or adaptation projects. Thus, a second major goal of this volume is to help teachers build their own maps of the reading research landscape and use this information for their own purposes.

The difficulty with building an effective concept map is that the field of reading has evolved remarkably in the past 20 years. The way that researchers now understand reading in L1 settings is quite different from the standard assumptions of 20 years ago and, for some practitioners, different even from their beliefs 5 years ago. So we see this volume as filling a need to highlight the major issues and research findings of the past decade, mapping out the 'territory' of reading as it is currently understood by reading researchers. To do so, we describe reading and reading instruction in ways that may not be entirely familiar to many applied linguists and L2 teachers, but there are strong arguments for these views of reading and reading instruction. These perspectives, we believe, will lead to more informed instruction, greater teacher awareness, more meaningful teacher enquiry and more effective learning for L2 students.

A preliminary notion of reading abilities

Reading can be thought of as a way to draw information from a text and to form an interpretation of that information. However, this 'definition' does not really tell us much about what happens when we read and how we comprehend a text. Actually, as the first chapter of the book shows, reading comprehension is remarkably complex, involving many processing skills that are coordinated in very efficient combinations. Because we also read for different purposes, there are many ways to read a text, further complicating any definition. Seen in this light, the ability to read is a remarkable type of expertise that most humans develop; it is not generally well understood, nor is its development widely recognised for the significant cognitive achievement that it is. We hope that readers of this volume develop a greater respect for the expertise required with any effort at reading comprehension. We also hope to share our fascination with research efforts that help clarify the abilities involved in reading comprehension and their development over time.

One of the logical places to begin a discussion of reading is to define this ability as it is used by the fluent L1 reader (as we do in Chapter 1). One needs to understand the skilled ability to explore how it is learned and what can be done to teach such abilities to learners. The same logic applies equally well whether the goal is to understand how a person learns to read in his or her L1, or L2 or, for that matter, L3. And while the path of development and the rate of progress may vary for different L2 readers, the end goal of highly skilled fluent reading looks quite similar for both L1 and L2 learners when advanced expertise emerges. At the same time, many research studies, as well as teaching and teacher-training resources, highlight the difficulties involved in describing the nature of reading abilities and how they are learned. These difficulties reveal the need for all of us to develop our own investigative practices in our classrooms. A principled set of ways to observe and analyse student learning will help us understand competing research claims and draw conclusions that will make us all more effective teachers.

Overview of the volume

This volume, composed of four major sections, is intended to build connections between research and instructional practices as well as help teachers formulate important questions about student learning and teaching practices, and to do so with appropriate methods for classroom enquiry. The book is divided into these sections:

Section I: Understanding L2 reading
Section II: Exploring research in reading
Section III: Researching reading in the classroom
Section IV: Resources

The first section, and its three chapters, presents an overview of reading theory as a guiding summary of the main ideas and issues that cover both L1 and L2 concerns. The purpose of Chapter 1 is not to provide a comprehensive treatment of the details, but rather to sketch an exploratory map of the reading domain and to indicate connections to promising instructional practices. This overview is followed, in Chapter 2, by a discussion of the differences between L1 and L2 reading. Chapter 3 explores dilemmas that emerge when students learn to read in an L2. These dilemmas suggest many questions for future L2 reading research as well as ideas for classroom exploration.

The second section, composed of two chapters, outlines key issues for reading research. Drawing on the survey of research in Section I, Chapter 4 highlights a number of key questions that have been explored effectively in L1 settings. Chapter 5 showcases a set of exemplary L2 reading research studies that illustrates different methods for conducting research.

The third section, made up of four chapters, outlines a range of manageable action research projects based on specific reading-related questions raised by research in the field and from concerns arising in real classroom settings. Chapter 6 provides guidelines for conducting meaningful action research and procedures for asking good questions appropriate to the classroom, collecting and analysing data, and arriving at fair and reasonable answers to the questions posed. The remaining chapters present detailed action research projects that model a variety of procedures for carrying out classroom-based research.

The final section of the book offers an array of resources for the teacher. These resources are intended to guide teacher enquiry so that classroom research can be located more easily within the larger world of reading research. Moreover, these resources should give teachers ideas for additional research questions that they themselves can ask about their own students and teaching.

The primary goal of this book is to help teachers add basic research enquiry to their expertise as teachers. Good teachers are well informed and able to assess critically the claims made by others in journals, teacher reference books and conference presentations. In particular, teachers can 'test' these claims through systematic observation, data collection, data analysis and critical reflection, using their own classrooms and students to understand learning processes and teaching practices better. Guided enquiry of this type may not lead to major research breakthroughs, but it will lead to a heightened awareness of the learning activities in L2 reading classrooms. Teachers will also be better able to evaluate and critique materials, curricular innovations and new teaching practices in the light of both a strong research foundation and personal experiences with classroom enquiry.

1 Understanding L2 reading

Chapter 1

The nature of reading abilities

This chapter sketches out an exploratory map of reading by providing the following:

- an initial definition of reading
- a discussion of purposes for reading
- a definition of fluent reading comprehension
- an explanation of how reading works
- an introduction to frequently cited models of reading

A common way to begin a discussion of reading is to provide a definition of the concept. However, this strategy, while important for clarifying later discussions, is not so easy. We noted in the introduction that it is possible to present a single-sentence definition of reading such as the following: 'Reading is the ability to draw meaning from the printed page and interpret this information appropriately.' However, without quibbling over the exact wording of such a definition, it is, nonetheless, insufficient as a way to understand the true nature of reading abilities. There are four important reasons why this simple definition is inadequate:

- First, it does not convey the idea that there are a number of ways to engage in reading. A reader has several possible purposes for reading, and each purpose emphasises a somewhat different combination of skills and strategies.
- Second, it does not emphasise the many criteria that define the nature of fluent reading abilities; it does not reveal the many skills,

processes and knowledge bases that act in combination, and often in parallel, to create the overall reading comprehension abilities that we commonly think of as reading.

- Third, it does not explain how reading is carried out as a cognitive process that operates under intense time constraints; yet, these very rapid time-processing constraints are essential to understanding how reading comprehension works for the fluent reader.
- Fourth, it does not highlight how the ability to draw meaning from a text and interpret this meaning varies in line with the second language (L2) proficiency of the reader.

These four issues are addressed in this chapter as a way to describe the nature of fluent reading abilities. The chapter closes with brief comments on various models of reading – models that synthesise what we know about reading and account for reading performance and reading development.

We would like to point out, at this time, that this chapter focuses primarily on the fluent first language (L1) reading process. One might ask why a book on L2 reading begins with a discussion of the fluent L1 reading process; there are a number of good reasons for adopting this strategy. First, far more research has been carried out on reading in L1 contexts (especially in English as an L1) than in L2 contexts. Second, students learning to become readers in L1 contexts usually achieve a reasonable level of fluency in reading comprehension abilities, but the same claim cannot be made for students learning to read in L2 contexts. Third, the ability to draw implications for instruction from research – including training studies that demonstrate the effectiveness of numerous instructional techniques and practices – is much more developed in L1 contexts than it is in L2 contexts. Fourth, reading instruction in L1 contexts has been a source of many instructional innovations that have not yet been explored extensively in L2 contexts, either at the level of research or at the level of practical implementation. These factors suggest that we can describe the reading abilities of students learning to read in their L1s quite well. Even if many L2 students will never become fluent L2 readers, they can be taught in ways that lead them in the right direction and help them make as much progress as possible. This direction toward a successful end-point is what L1 reading research can offer us.

Our position on the value of L1 reading research is not meant to suggest that we ignore the significant differences between L1 and L2 reading contexts; in fact, these differences are the subject of Chapters

2 and 3. However, at very advanced levels, L1 and L2 reading abilities tend to merge and appear to be quite similar. So, to understand the end-point of reading abilities, that of the fluent, critical reader, the research on L1 reading development offers us a much more complete understanding.

1.1 Purposes for reading

When we begin to read, we actually have a number of initial decisions to make, and we usually make these decisions very quickly, almost unconsciously in most cases. For example, when we pick up a newspaper, we usually read the front page with some combination of search processing, general reading comprehension and skimming. We read partly for information, but we also read with a goal to finish the newspaper fairly rapidly, since few people try to read every line of a newspaper. We may initially search the front page for a particular story that we expect to be there. If the headlines cue us in the right way, we may check quickly for the length of the article, and we may then read through a number of paragraphs for comprehension (appropriately influenced by the newspaper-story genre, a reporting of what, who, when, where, why and how). At some point, we will decide that we have enough information and will either stop reading the article or skim the remainder to be sure that we do not miss some surprisingly informative part.

In other settings, usually academic or professional ones, we sometimes synthesise information from multiple reading sources, from different parts of a long and complex text, or from a prose text and accompanying diagram or chart. Such reading is quite different from searching, skimming, or reading for general comprehension. In these circumstances, a more critical set of goals must be established for an effective synthesis: the reader needs to remember points of comparison or opposition, assess the relative importance of the information, and construct a framework in which the information will be organised.

Finally, and most commonly for L1 settings, people read for general comprehension (whether for information or for pleasure). Here we might read a novel, a short story, a newspaper article, or a report of some type to understand the information in the text, to be entertained and/or to use the information for a particular purpose. The overall goal is not to remember most of the specific details but to have a good grasp

Quote 1.1

There are purportedly five basic processes involved in reading text, or passages. . . . [W]hen someone is reading paragraphs in a book, for example, one of five basically different processes is likely to be involved. These processes, or reading gears, are called scanning (Gear 5), skimming (Gear 4), **rauding** (Gear 3), learning (Gear 2), and memorizing (Gear 1). . . .

The rauding process, Gear 3, is the process most readers use regularly. It is the type of reading that is most typical; it is normal reading, ordinary reading, natural reading or simple reading. It is the process that is used most often when adults are reading, something that is relatively easy for them to comprehend – that is, a magazine, a newspaper, a novel, a memo at work or a letter from a friend. Evidence that most of reading that goes on in the world involves rauding comes from Sharon (1973); he surveyed 5,067 adults in a national probability sample and found that less than 1% of their reading involved anything that was difficult to understand during their typical 2 hours of reading each day.

Carver (1997, pp. 5–6)

Quote 1.2

There is a considerable amount of experimental evidence in L2 reading that background knowledge can play the part envisioned for it in [reading] theory. Bernhardt (1991) gives an extensive list of studies, to which we refer the reader. The majority of studies she cites were successful in showing that readers' familiarity with content had a significant effect on their performance. However, in a number of cases no such effect has been found. . . . In spite of [some] inconclusive evidence, it seems to us undeniable that background knowledge has an effect on reading.

Urquhart and Weir (1998, pp. 63, 65)

of the main ideas and supporting ideas, and to relate those main ideas to **background knowledge** as appropriate.

All of these ways of reading, and a few others, have to be accounted for in a full explanation of reading. We believe that reading purposes can be classified under seven main headings (see Concept 1.1), while recognising that these headings are heuristics and many variations could be proposed. Each purpose for reading is explained further in the upcoming sections of the chapter.

Concept 1.1   **Purposes for reading**

1. Reading to search for simple information

2. Reading to skim quickly

3. Reading to learn from texts

4. Reading to integrate information

5. Reading to write (or search for information needed for writing)

6. Reading to critique texts

7. Reading for general comprehension

1.1.1   Reading to search for simple information and reading to skim

Reading to search for simple information is a common reading ability, though some researchers see it as a relatively independent cognitive process. It is used so often in reading tasks that it is probably best seen as a type of reading ability. In reading to search, we typically **scan** the text for a specific piece of information or a specific word. As an example, we usually search through a telephone directory to find key information, either an address or a phone number. In prose texts, we sometimes slow down to process the meaning of a sentence or two in search of clues that might indicate the right page, section, or chapter. Similarly, reading to **skim** (i.e. sampling segments of the text for a general understanding) is a common part of many reading tasks and a useful skill in its own right. It involves, in essence, a combination of strategies for guessing where important information might be in the text, and then using basic reading comprehension skills on those segments of the text until a general idea is formed.

1.1.2   Reading to learn from texts

Reading to learn typically occurs in academic and professional contexts in which a person needs to learn a considerable amount of information from a text. It requires abilities to

- remember main ideas as well as a number of details that elaborate the main and supporting ideas in the text
- recognise and build **rhetorical frames** that organise the information in the text
- link the text to the reader's knowledge base

Reading to learn is usually carried out at a reading rate somewhat slower than general reading comprehension (primarily due to rereading and reflection strategies to help remember information). In addition, it makes stronger **inferencing** demands than general comprehension to connect text information with background knowledge (e.g. connecting a character, event or concept to other known characters, events or concepts; or connecting possible causes to known events).

1.1.3   Reading to integrate information, write and critique texts

Reading to integrate information requires additional decisions about the relative importance of complementary, mutually supporting or conflicting information and the likely restructuring of a rhetorical frame to accommodate information from multiple sources. These skills inevitably require critical evaluation of the information being read so that the reader can decide what information to integrate and how to integrate it for the reader's goal. In this respect, both *reading to write* and *reading to critique texts* may be task variants of reading to integrate information. Both require abilities to compose, select, and critique information from a text. Both purposes represent common academic tasks that call upon the reading abilities needed to integrate information (Enright *et al.*, 2000; Perfetti, Rouet and Britt, 1999).

1.1.4   Reading for general comprehension

The notion of general reading comprehension has been intentionally saved for last in this discussion for two reasons. First, it is the most basic purpose for reading, underlying and supporting most other purposes for reading. Second, general reading comprehension is actually more complex than commonly assumed. (Note that the term 'general' does not mean 'simple' or 'easy'.) These assertions are treated in detail in the next two sections of this chapter. Reading for general comprehension, when accomplished by a skilled fluent reader, requires very rapid and automatic processing of words, strong skills in forming a general meaning representation of main ideas, and efficient coordination of many processes under very limited time constraints.

These abilities are often taken for granted by fluent readers because they usually occur automatically; that is, we make use of these abilities without giving them much thought if we are fluent readers. In L2 contexts, however, the difficulties that students have in becoming fluent readers of longer texts under time constraints reveal the complexities of reading for general comprehension. Because of its demands for processing efficiency, reading for general understanding may, at times, even be more difficult to master than reading to learn, an ability that is often assumed to be a more difficult extension of general comprehension abilities. (This misperception is most likely due to the ways in which reading comprehension and reading to learn are commonly tested in schools.)

Before defining fluent reading, we would like to comment on two terms commonly used to describe the activity of reading: **skills** and **strategies.** For us, *skills* represent linguistic processing abilities that are relatively automatic in their use and their combinations (e.g. word recognition, syntactic processing). In most educational psychology discussions of skills, they are seen as general learning outcomes of goal-driven tasks, acquired gradually and eventually automatised (Anderson, 1995; Proctor and Dutta, 1995; Schunk, 2000). *Strategies* are often defined as a set of abilities under conscious control of the reader, though this common definition is not likely to be true. In fact, many abilities that are commonly identified as strategies are relatively automatic in their use by fluent readers (e.g. skipping an unknown word while reading, rereading to reestablish text meaning). Thus, the distinction between skills and strategies is not entirely clear precisely because that is part of the nature of reading (and not a definitional problem).

Quote 1.3

During the 1970s, when it first dotted the reading landscape, the term *strategies* signified a form of mental processing that deviated from traditional skills-based reading. However, any distinctions between skills and strategies that seemed apparent then have begun to fade, leaving many to wonder where skills end and strategies begin. As a way to unearth those contrasts, we propose two differences between skillful and strategic processing, relevant to text-based learning: automaticity and intentionality. . . . Skills are, in essence, essential academic habits. They are the routinized, automatic procedures we employ when we engage in any nontrivial task. Thus, skilled readers, like skilled cooks or skilled accountants, have honed essential domain procedures to a level of automaticity. . . . The same procedures (e.g. finding main idea) can fit under both the skill and strategy categories. The appropriate label rests on whether the reader consciously evokes the procedure or is simply functioning in a typical, automatic way.

Alexander and Jetton (2000, pp. 295–6)

Quote 1.4

Skills refer to information-processing techniques that are automatic, whether at the level of recognizing grapheme–phoneme correspondence or summarizing a story. Skills are applied to a text unconsciously for many reasons including expertise, repeated practice, compliance with directions, luck, and naïve use. In contrast, strategies are actions selected deliberately to achieve particular goals. An emerging skill can become a strategy when it is used intentionally. Likewise, a strategy can 'go underground' [in the sense of Vygotsky, 1978] and become a skill. Indeed strategies are more efficient and developmentally advanced when they become generated and applied automatically as skills. Thus, strategies are skills under consideration.

Paris, Wasik and Turner (1991, p. 611)

Concept 1.2   **Sample reading strategies**

- Specifying a purpose for reading
- Planning what to do/what steps to take
- Previewing the text
- Predicting the contents of the text or section of text
- Checking predictions
- Posing questions about the text
- Finding answers to posed questions
- Connecting text to background knowledge
- Summarising information
- Making inferences
- Connecting one part of the text to another
- Paying attention to text structure
- Rereading
- Guessing the meaning of a new word from context
- Using discourse markers to see relationships
- Checking comprehension
- Identifying difficulties
- Taking steps to repair faulty comprehension
- Critiquing the author
- Critiquing the text
- Judging how well objectives were met
- Reflecting on what has been learned from the text

For example, in a number of cases, skills may have been learned as strategies but have become thoroughly automatised (e.g. mentally summarising a newspaper story to tell a friend). Strategies, for definitional purposes, are best defined as abilities that are potentially open to conscious reflection and use (see Concept 1.2 for some example strategies; see also Model Action Research Projects 8.1.1 to 8.1.5 in Chapter 8). We use the terms *abilities*, more generally, to refer to what readers do while reading and *processes* to refer to mental operations.

1.2   Defining fluent reading comprehension

Reading for general comprehension is, in its most obvious sense, the ability to understand information in a text and interpret it appropriately. However, comprehension abilities are much more complex than this definition suggests. To offer a more accurate picture of reading comprehension, we define it according to a set of necessary processes (see Concept 1.3). No one process defines reading comprehension by itself, but together they provide a fairly accurate account of the processes required for fluent reading. (See Alderson, 2000 and Grabe, 1999, 2000, for more detailed discussions.)

Concept 1.3   **The processes involved in fluent reading comprehension**

Fluent reading is:

1. a rapid process

2. an efficient process

3. an interactive process

4. a strategic process

5. a flexible process

6. an evaluating process

7. a purposeful process

8. a comprehending process

9. a learning process

10. a linguistic process

Fluent reading must occur *rapidly* in almost any purposeful context, and the more rapidly a text is (successfully) read, the better the various processing components are likely to operate. Thus, a good L1 reader will read almost all texts at rates between 200 to 300 words per minute. Related to rate is the notion that specific processes must be carried out *efficiently* in combination if comprehension is to take place. That is, the various processes involved in comprehension must be coordinated and certain processes need to be carried out automatically.

Reading is also an *interactive* process in at least two ways. First, the various processes involved in reading are carried out simultaneously. While we are recognising words very rapidly and keeping them active in our **working memories** (see Concept 1.4), we are also analysing the structure of sentences to assemble the most logical clause-level meanings, building a main-idea model of text comprehension in our heads, monitoring comprehension and so on. Combining these skills in an efficient manner makes general comprehension a time-consuming ability to master. Reading is also interactive in the sense that linguistic information from the text interacts with information activated by the reader from long-term memory, as background knowledge. These two knowledge sources (linguistic and background) are essential for building the reader's interpretation of the text.

Concept 1.4   **What is working memory?**

The term *working memory* is now generally preferred to *short-term memory*. Working memory refers to the information that is activated, or given mental stimulation, for immediate storage and processing. Working memory involves the active use of cognitive processes such as recognising and storing word information, using syntactic information, connecting pronoun references, building overall text structure, integrating and restructuring information, assessing inferences and adapting reader goals.

Balancing the many skills needed for comprehension also requires that the reader be *strategic*. The reader needs to recognise processing difficulties, address imbalances between text information and reader knowledge, and make decisions for monitoring comprehension and shifting goals for reading. Being a strategic reader means being able to read *flexibly* in line with changing purposes and the ongoing monitoring of comprehension. Similarly, reading is an *evaluating* process in that the reader must decide if the information being read is coherent and matches the purpose for reading. This evaluation also extends to the reader's motivations for reading, the reader's attitudes toward the text and topic, the reader's feelings of likely success or failure with text comprehension, and the reader's expectation that the information from the text will be useful (or interesting, or enjoyable).

Reading is always *purposeful* not only in the sense that readers read in different ways based on differing reading purposes, but also in the sense that any motivation to read a given text is triggered by some individual purpose or task, whether imposed internally or externally. Reading is also a *comprehending* process. The notion of comprehending is both obvious and subtle. It is obvious in that any person could say that understanding a text is the purpose for reading; it is less obvious with respect to the ways that such understanding might be carried out by the reader, as will be seen in the next section. One outcome of reading being a purposeful and comprehending process is that it is also a *learning* process. This aspect of reading should be evident to anyone who works in academic settings where the most common way for students to learn new information is through reading.

Lastly, reading is fundamentally a *linguistic* process (rather than a reasoning process), though this aspect of reading is often downplayed (as is the visual aspect). It makes little sense to discuss or interpret a text without engaging with it linguistically. For example, anyone who has tried to read a text on political policy written in Chinese – without knowing any Chinese characters – will quickly recognise the primacy of linguistic processes for reading comprehension. If we cannot understand any words, we are not going to comprehend the text.

1.3 Describing how reading works: Components of reading abilities

To this point, we hope to have persuaded readers that reading comprehension abilities are quite complex and that they vary in numerous ways depending on tasks, motivations, goals and language abilities. One might even get the impression that large differences exist among the various ways of reading. However, there is a set of common underlying processes that are activated as we read. In this section, we want to outline the way that reading comprehension processes are likely to work for skilled readers, assuming a purpose of general comprehension of a longer text (like when we read a book at night before going to bed). (See Grabe, 1999, 2000, for detailed descriptions and references.) For the sake of simplicity, we have divided this explanation into two parts: lower-level processes and higher-level processes (see Concept 1.5), common metaphorical designations that will be explained in the sections that follow. The lower-level processes represent the more automatic linguistic processes and are typically viewed as more skills orientated. The higher-level processes generally represent comprehension processes that make much more use of the reader's background knowledge and inferencing skills. It should be noted that we do not assume lower-level processes to be in any way easier than higher-level processes.

Concept 1.5   Reading processes that are activated when we read

Lower-level processes

- Lexical access

- Syntactic parsing

- Semantic proposition formation

- Working memory activation

Higher-level processes

- Text model of comprehension

- Situation model of reader interpretation

- Background knowledge use and inferencing

- Executive control processes

1.3.1   Lower-level processes

The most fundamental requirement for fluent reading comprehension is rapid and automatic word recognition (or **lexical access** – the calling up of the meaning of a word as it is recognised). Fluent L1 readers can recognise almost all of the words they encounter (98–100 per cent of all words in a text), at least at some basic meaning level. They also

---

Quote 1.5

[W]hen a reader is attempting to learn what is in text, reading is a word-by-word affair, with fixations on most individual words. For a skilled adult reader who is reading material carefully, each word is typically fixated for about a quarter of a second. That translates to about 200 words per minute when readers are reading to learn material.... Reading at a more relaxed pace occurs at a rate of between 250 and 300 words per minute.

Pressley (1998, p. 44)

recognise four to five words per second (about 230 milliseconds per word on average).

As amazing as it may seem, good readers can actually focus on a word and recognise it in less than a tenth of a second (less than 100 milliseconds). Thus, four to five words per second even allows good readers time for other processing operations. For good readers, lexical access is automatic. In addition to being very fast, it cannot be readily reflected on consciously, and it cannot be suppressed (a good definition of **automaticity**); that is, when the eye sees a word, the reader cannot stop him- or herself from accessing its meaning. Both rapid processing and automaticity in word recognition (for a large number of words) typically require thousands of hours of practice in reading.

> ## Quote 1.6
>
> Why does automaticity matter?... [D]ecoding and comprehension compete for the available short-term [memory] capacity. When a reader slowly analyzes a word into component sounds and blends them, a great deal of capacity is consumed, with relatively little left over for comprehension of the word, let alone understanding the overall meaning of the sentence containing the word and the paragraph containing the sentence. In contrast, automatic word recognition (i.e. recognizing a word as a sight word) consumes very little capacity, and thus, frees short-term capacity for the task of comprehending the word and integrating the meaning of the word with the overall meaning of the sentence, paragraph, and text.
>
> Pressley (1998, p. 61)

Many L1 researchers focus a lot of attention on word recognition abilities. They explore these issues not because they believe that word recognition *is* reading comprehension, but because reading comprehension cannot be carried out for an extended period of time without word recognition skills. However, these skills are difficult to develop without **exposure to print** (through many hours of reading practice). In L2 reading contexts, much less discussion is devoted to this topic. This avoidance is partly due to a limited understanding of the role of rapid and automatic word recognition processes in reading. It is also due to the tremendous difficulties involved in providing L2 students with the time, resources and practice needed to develop a very large recognition vocabulary. However, word recognition abilities cannot be ignored in L2 contexts if a goal is to help students become fluent L2 readers. A useful way to think of the relation between word recognition and reading comprehension is by analogy to a car. The car, as general reading comprehension, is the vehicle that gets you to your destination (in this case, understanding a text). But the car will not go anywhere without gasoline (much like word recognition), which is what we need to put into the car so that it will run.

In addition to word recognition, a fluent reader is able to take in and store words together so that basic grammatical information can be extracted (a process known as **syntactic parsing**) to support clause-level meaning. The ability to recognise phrasal groupings, word ordering information, and subordinate and superordinate relations among clauses quickly is what allows good readers to clarify how words are supposed to be understood. (For example, the word 'book', as in 'the book fell', will be recognised as a noun, rather than the verb 'to book', as in a police station. It will also be recognised as the subject that will be described, and as an inanimate object that will be followed by an 'event' description, 'fell'.) Syntactic parsing helps to disambiguate the meanings of words that have multiple meanings out of context (e.g. bank, cut, drop). Moreover, it helps a reader determine what pronouns and definite articles are referring to in prior text.

Quote 1.7

To claim . . . that syntactic processing [or syntactic parsing] is not necessary is frankly unbelievable. This is easily demonstrated. The following string represents an English sentence from which most (not all) function words and all inflectional morphemes have been deleted. Moreover, since ordering plays a major part in English syntax, the order of the remaining words has been jumbled.

begin several it recogniser module machine digital pass record speech

We challenge anyone, whether expert in the content area (artificial language) or not, to process this string. Things begin to be a bit better if we restore the original ordering:

Machine begin digital record speech pass it several recogniser module

However, it is only when we restore function words and inflections that the message becomes easy to extract:

The machine begins by digitally recording the speech and passing it to several recogniser modules.

Urquhart and Weir (1998, pp. 60–1)

Perhaps most importantly, **parsing** is done very rapidly without much effort or conscious attention (unless something does not work right; then the process becomes less automatic). So once again, rapid and automatic processing – at the level of initial syntactic parsing – is a necessary ability. The subconscious automaticity of syntactic parsing processes should be obvious to anyone who has taught high school or undergraduate university students in L1 settings; these L1 students can read fluently, but, in many cases, they have difficulty completing a grammar exercise at a conscious level (very prevalent in the US). In L2 settings, the need for rapid and automatic syntactic processing appears to be less obvious, because most L2 students develop an overt know-ledge of L2 grammatical structures before they become fluent L2 readers. With L2 students, what is often overlooked is not the fact that L2 students need grammar instruction to be readers but rather that, like developing L1 readers, they need countless hours of exposure to print (that they are capable of comprehending successfully) if they are to develop automaticity in using information from grammatical structures to assist them in reading.

A third basic process that starts up automatically as we begin any reading task is the process of combining word meanings and structural information into basic clause-level meaning units (**semantic proposition formation**). Words that are recognised and kept active for one to two seconds, along with grammatical cueing, give the fluent reader time to integrate information in a way that makes sense in relation to what has been read before. As meaning elements are introduced and then connected, they become more active in memory and become central ideas if they are repeated or reactivated.

This process is depicted in Concept 1.6 (where bolding signifies repetition or reactivation). As each sentence from a text is read (on the left-hand side of the diagram), a semantic proposition of that informa-tion is constructed (as shown on the right-hand side). Each semantic proposition reflects the key elements of the input (word and structure) and also highlights linkages across important units (in this case, verbs), where relevant. In the sentences in Concept 1.6, there are cause–effect relations between the first action and the second action, and between the third action and the fourth action. In the semantic proposition net-work that is generated, these relations are incorporated as well (as indicated by the brackets from the first verbal predicate to the second verbal predicate, and the third verbal predicate to the fourth verbal pre-dicate). The third sentence of the grammatical input actually has two propositions. One is signalled by 'however', and it indicates a larger

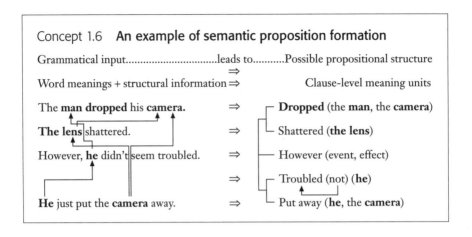

relation between sets of propositions; the other proposition reflects the new information presented in the sentence. Semantic propositions are formed in this way and a propositional network of text meaning is created. It is worth noting that this process of semantic network building anticipates the discussion in the next section (on building a text model of comprehension).

The process of ongoing semantic proposition formation, as described here, is not easily controllable in any conscious way (much like fluent word recognition and syntactic parsing). Only when some aspect of comprehension does not work right, or the meaning does not seem to fit, might a reader pause to consider how to extract the most appropriate meaning from the text being read. In such circumstances, we have time to become aware of the problem and address it more consciously.

The three processes discussed up to this point – lexical access or word recognition, syntactic parsing and semantic proposition formation – are typically seen as lower-level processes that occur relatively automatically for the fluent reader. When they are functioning well, they work together effortlessly in working memory (see Carpenter, Miyake and Just, 1994), which is best understood as the network of information and related processes that are being used at a given moment (**working memory activation**). The words that are accessed, the information that is cued grammatically and the emerging meaning are all active for a short period of time in working memory. If they are to be integrated so that an accurate sense of meaning is formed, the information must be combined rapidly. Working memory keeps information active for one to two seconds while it carries out the appropriate processes. Speed of processing is essential; it is not simply a nice additional aspect of comprehension abilities. If processing of active information is not done quickly enough, the information fades from memory and must be reactivated, taking more resources and making the reading process inefficient. (Working memory actually does more than support lower-level processing, as noted later in the chapter.)

Returning to the car analogy, working memory is somewhat like the engine of the car. The working parts fit together for efficient co-ordination and the fuel (word recognition) is converted to useful energy in the engine to drive the car. We would not, of course, want to suggest that a car is nothing more than the engine, since it is the car, and not just the engine, that gets us to our destinations. But a car, if it is going to get us to our destinations, must have an efficiently working engine. It is possible to envisage working memory as doing much the same for reading comprehension. In this way, the efficient coordination of information from rapid and automatic processes is a necessary component of fluent reading comprehension abilities.

1.3.2   Higher-level processes

Added to these lower-level processes is a set of higher-level comprehension processes that more closely represent what we typically think of as reading comprehension. As good readers, we form a summary model of what the text is likely to mean. We also construct a more elaborated interpretation of how we want to understand text meaning. Beyond understanding and interpreting the ideas represented by the text, we establish purposes for reading, combine reading strategies as needed, make inferences of many types, draw extensively on background knowledge, monitor comprehension, form attitudes about the text and author, and critically evaluate the information being read. Returning briefly to the car analogy, all of these higher-level processes, together, represent the car that will take readers to their destinations, assuming of course, that the car has an engine and gasoline.

The most fundamental higher-level comprehension process is the coordination of ideas from a text that represent the main points and supporting ideas to form a meaning representation of the text (a **text model of reading comprehension**, not to be confused with general models of reading, discussed later in the chapter). As clause-level meaning units are formed (drawing on information from syntactic parsing and semantic proposition formation), they are added to a growing network of ideas from the text. The new clauses may be hooked into the network in a number of ways: through the repetition of an idea,

> ### Quote 1.8
>
> What people remember is the gist.... For example, suppose you are beginning a paragraph-long text. The first sentence contains a number of ideas, with the reader coding the main idea of the sentence. This idea is held in active memory as the next sentence in the paragraph is read. Attempts are made to link the main idea from the first sentence to the ideas of the second sentence, with another main idea emerging from this synthesis, integrating the meanings expressed in the first two sentences of the paragraph.... Sometimes there will be a need for bridging inferences to reconcile the meaning of the previous sentences with the ideas in the new sentences.... Good readers do not make inferences willy-nilly, however.
>
>   In summary, during normal beginning-to-end reading of a text, such as a story, the reader processes the individual ideas but remembers the gist. In processing the text and constructing the gist, prior knowledge plays an important role, permitting the generation of inferences required to understand the text.
>
> Pressley (1998, pp. 46–7)

event, object or character; by reference to the same thing, but in different words; and through simple inferences that create a way to link a new meaning unit to the appropriate places in the network (e.g. part–whole, subordinate–superordinate; refer back to Concept 1.6). As the reader continues processing text information, and new meaning units are added, those ideas that are used repeatedly and that form usable linkages to other information begin to be seen as the main ideas of the text. More technically, they become, and remain, more active in the network. Ideas that do not play any further roles in connecting new information (i.e. ideas that are no longer named or referred to indirectly), or that do not support connecting inferences, lose their activity quickly and fade from the network. In this way, less important ideas tend to get pruned from the network, and only the more useful and important ideas remain active.

As the reader continues and builds an understanding of the text, the set of main ideas that the reader develops is the text model of comprehension. The text model amounts to an internal summary of main ideas (which is one reason why summary tasks for learning purposes are reasonable tasks to practise). The inferencing required of a reader to support this text model is typically not extensive unless the text information is so new that the reader has comprehension difficulties, or unless the reader's language-proficiency level is impeding comprehension. Background knowledge (whether understood as linked networks of knowledge, schema theory or mental models) plays a supporting role and helps the reader anticipate the **discourse organisation** of the text as well as disambiguate word-level and clausal meanings as new information is incorporated into the text model. (See Grabe, 1999, 2000, for more detailed descriptions and references.)

At the same time that the text model of comprehension is being built by the reader, the reader will begin to project a likely direction that the reading will take. This projection is influenced by background knowledge, inferences, reader goals, reader motivation, task and text difficulty, and reader attitudes toward the text, task and author. So almost immediately, the reader will begin to interpret the information from the text in terms of his or her own goals, feelings and background expectations. This reader interpretation (the **situation model of reader interpretation**) is built on and around the emerging text model. The reader is likely to interpret the text (and begin to create a situation model) differently if he/she knows that the text is the beginning of a good mystery novel, a biography of a well-known photographer or a social statement on waste in society.

Quote 1.9

What counts [as text comprehension] is how the reader comes to construct mental models of the text and the situations described in the text.

Two classes of mental models are needed, a model of what the text says (the text base) and a model of what the text is about (the situation model). . . . The text base is a mental representation of the propositions of the text, as extracted from the reading of successive sentences, supplemented only by inferences necessary to make the text coherent. The reader builds a situation model from the text base by combining knowledge sources through additional inference processes. Thus, a text base is essentially linguistic, consisting of propositions derived from sentences, whereas a situation model is essentially agnostic in its form of representation. . . .

[T]he main difference between a text base and a situation model is assumed to be one of inferences, with text bases inferentially poor and situation models inferentially rich.

Perfetti, van Dyke and Hart (2001, pp. 133–4)

For the fluent reader who has no great difficulties in understanding the text, the developing situation model of reader interpretation is the likely goal for reading comprehension. The situation model *integrates* text information with a well-developed network of ideas from the reader's background knowledge, and it *interprets* new information in the light of reader background knowledge, attitudes, motivations, goals and task purposes (Kintsch, 1998). The ability of fluent readers to integrate text and background information appropriately and efficiently is the hallmark of expert reading in a topical domain (e.g. history, biology, psychology).

The situation model of reader interpretation accounts for how a reader can understand both what an author is trying to say (as the text model) and how the reader interprets that information for his or her own purposes (the situation model). This duality of understanding explains how a reader can provide a summary of a text but also offer a critique of the text's position. It also explains how a reader can read a text (or a particular **genre**) to emphasise either what the author means or what the reader wants the text to mean. Thus, a poem is usually read with the goal of creating a reader interpretation, but a technical manual is usually read with the assumption that there is a preferred author interpretation of its contents. In this way, we can see how different genres both signal and lead to different ways of reading (in a sense, then, providing some of the justification for the existence of different genres).

This description of two higher-level processes reveals where background knowledge takes on the most importance and when inferencing abilities play a greater role in reading. As the reader transforms information from clause-level meaning units to the text model of comprehension, and then to the elaborated situation model of reader interpretation, both background knowledge and inferencing take on greater importance. Interestingly, it is at the point when the reader is interpreting the text (the situation model of reader interpretation) that wrong or incomplete background knowledge, or faulty inferences can lead a reader, even a fluent reader, astray.

Text-model and situation-model construction require the abilities to oversee, or monitor, comprehension, use strategies as needed, reassess and reestablish goals, and repair comprehension problems. How such a monitor (**executive control processing**) might operate cognitively is not entirely clear (see Gathercole and Pickering, 2000; Siegel, 1994). Despite the lack of details, we know that an executive control processor (or monitor) represents the way that we assess our understanding of a text and evaluate our success. Thus, our evaluation of the text information itself, or how we feel about the text, is typically part of our developing situation model (of reader interpretation). Our evaluation of how well we comprehend the text is dependent on an executive control processor.

In summary, the higher-level cognitive processes outlined here, in combination with the lower-level processes discussed earlier, form the cognitive processing resources that let us carry out reading for various purposes (Grabe, 1999, 2000). Usually, a specific reading purpose will lead to greater or lesser emphases on different reading processes. So, reading to find simple information will emphasise word recognition abilities and some background knowledge anticipation of what items (e.g. words, numbers) to look for. Reading for general comprehension will use a balanced combination of text model comprehension and situation model interpretation. Reading to learn will first emphasise the building of an accurate text model of comprehension, and then a strong interpretive situation model that integrates well with existing or revised background knowledge.

Reading comprehension processes, seen in this way, highlight the miraculous nature of reading comprehension. Reading comprehension is an extraordinary feat of balancing and coordinating many abilities in a very complex and rapid set of routines that makes comprehension a seemingly effortless and enjoyable activity for fluent readers. In fact, the many processes described here all occur in working memory, and they happen very quickly unless there are comprehension problems. So, roughly, in the space of any two seconds of reading time, fluent readers accomplish numerous operations (see Concept 1.7).

Three conclusions become clear when we consider the number of reading processes occurring each and every two seconds:

1. Reading comprehension processes work in parallel when some skills are relatively automatic.
2. Some processes need to be relatively automatic if reading is going to work efficiently.
3. Fast and efficient processing is the hallmark of fluent reading comprehension abilities.

It is important to emphasise, at this point, that these processes do not operate efficiently or effortlessly when readers encounter texts (and accompanying tasks) that are too difficult for them. Difficulties may arise when readers do not have adequate background information, do

---

Concept 1.7   **Reading processes occurring each and every two seconds we read**

Roughly, in each and every two seconds of reading, fluent readers:

1. focus on and access eight to ten word meanings

2. parse a clause for information and form a meaning unit

3. figure out how to connect a new meaning unit into the growing text model

4. check interpretation of the information according to their purposes, feelings, attitudes and background expectations, as needed

5. monitor their comprehension, make appropriate inferences as needed, shift strategies and repair misunderstanding, as needed

6. resolve ambiguities, address difficulties and critique text information, as needed

---

not have the necessary linguistic resources or have not read enough in the language to have developed efficiencies in reading. Readers, especially L2 readers, who encounter such difficulties can try to understand the text by using a slow mechanical translation process; alternatively, they can make an effort to form a situation model from past experiences and try to force the text to fit preconceived notions. In the first case, working memory efficiencies cannot operate well; in the latter case, a situation model unconnected to text information is imposed on reading comprehension, activating inappropriate background information and leading to poor comprehension. In either case, successful reading comprehension is not likely to occur.

In L2 reading contexts, where such problems commonly arise, readers resort to coping strategies by translating or by guessing to form a coherent account of the text, whether that account matches the text or not. If this experience is repeated on a continual basis, it is not hard to see why these learners would lose any motivation to become fluent readers. Yet, this problem also suggests a likely long-range solution. Students need to engage in reading for many hours at text- and task-levels appropriate to their abilities. It is only through extended exposure to meaningful print that texts can be processed efficiently and that students will develop as fluent readers.

1.4 Synthesising research perspectives: Models of reading

Many researchers and teachers attempt to create a general understanding of the reading comprehension process by means of a reasonable framework. So we often read about general **models of reading** (not to be confused with the text model and situation model concepts for comprehension processes that were discussed earlier). General models of reading serve useful purposes, most commonly by providing a metaphorical interpretation of the many processes involved in reading comprehension (cf. Grabe, 1999, 2000; Urquhart and Weir, 1998). Other models are more specific in nature, trying to account for, and interpret, the results of much research. In this section, we comment briefly on general metaphorical models and then discuss a few of the models of reading that are grounded in more specific research syntheses (see Concept 1.8).

1.4.1 Metaphorical models of reading

We typically hear about bottom–up, top–down and interactive models of reading, particularly in L2 discussions. These models represent metaphorical generalisations that stem from comprehension research conducted over the past three decades. As an initiation into thinking about reading comprehension, these models serve useful purposes; however, they do not clarify more recent research advances. Metaphorically,

---

Concept 1.8 **Models of reading**

Metaphorical models of reading	Specific models of reading
1. Bottom–up models	1. Psycholinguistic Guessing Game Model
2. Top–down models	2. Interactive Compensatory Model
3. Interactive models	3. Word recognition models
	4. Simple View of Reading Model

bottom–up models suggest that all reading follows a mechanical pattern in which the reader creates a piece-by-piece mental translation of the information in the text, with little interference from the reader's own background knowledge. In the extreme view, the reader processes each word letter-by-letter, each sentence word-by-word and each text sentence-by-sentence in a linear fashion. We know that such an extreme view is not entirely accurate. At the same time, there are aspects of this view (e.g. lower-level processes such as word recognition abilities and syntactic parsing) reflected in the overview of the reading process presented in this chapter.

Top–down models assume that reading is primarily directed by reader goals and expectations. Again, such a view is general and metaphorical. Top–down models characterise the reader as someone who has a set of expectations about text information and samples enough information from the text to confirm or reject these expectations. To accomplish this sampling efficiently, the reader directs the eyes to the most likely places in the text to find useful information. The mechanism by which a reader would generate expectations is not clear, but these expectations might be created by a general monitoring mechanism (i.e. an executive control processor). Inferencing is a prominent feature of top–down models, as is the importance of a reader's background knowledge. Top–down views highlight the potential interaction of all processes (lower- and higher-level processes) with each other under the general control of a central monitor. In extreme interpretations, there is a question about what a reader could learn from a text if the reader must first have expectations about all the information in the text. In fact, few reading researchers actually support strong top–down views.

Quote 1.10

Two decades of empirical research have largely resolved . . . debates in favour of the bottom–up models. A greater use of context cues to aid word recognition is not a characteristic of good readers; developing phonological sensitivity is critical for early success in reading acquisition; and instructional programmes that emphasize spelling-sound decoding skills result in better reading outcomes because alphabetic coding is the critical subprocess that supports fluent reading.

Stanovich and Stanovich (1999, p. 29)

The seeming compromise to satisfy everyone is to propose **inter-active models** of reading, again as a general metaphorical explanation. The simple idea behind this view is that one can take useful ideas from a bottom–up perspective and combine them with key ideas from a top–down view. So, word recognition needs to be fast and efficient, but background knowledge is a major contributor to text understand-ing, as is inferencing and predicting what will come next in the text. Unfortunately, using this logic leads to a self-contradictory model. As it turns out, the key processing aspects of bottom–up approaches – efficiently coordinated automatic processing in working memory such as automatic word recognition – are incompatible with strong top–down controls on reading comprehension. The automatic processing aspects of comprehension, by definition, need to be able to operate without a lot of interference from the moment-to-moment informa-tion gained from background knowledge or massive amounts of infer-encing. These top–down aspects of comprehension must be reserved primarily for higher-level processing.

More accurate ways to understand reading comprehension, even metaphorically, require 'modified interactive models' that highlight the number of processes, particularly automatic processes, being carried out primarily in a bottom–up manner with little interference from other processing levels or knowledge resources. So, word recognition may involve interactions of information from letters, letter-shapes, phono-logy and whole word orthography. But fluent word recognition does not usually involve information from context or background knowledge (because activating such supporting information, to be useful, would take too much time, greatly slowing down processing efficiency). Similarly, first efforts to activate grammatical knowledge seem to be carried out relatively automatically by fluent readers. For the most part, the flu-ent reader is not misled by the structural information that is quickly assembled (e.g. subject, verb, object = doer, action, recipient), and it would be inefficient to wait for confirming information from inferenc-ing or from context clues. On occasion, readers do use context to dis-ambiguate word meaning (e.g. bank, bug, dope). Sometimes readers find themselves being led down a wrong path with a complex sentence, and then the structure of the sentence emerges to a conscious level for a dose of problem solving (and much slower processing).

Asserting that a modified interactive model of reading may be useful does create complications when we consider the various purposes for reading noted at the outset of the chapter. If a reader is trying to under-stand a text as part of integrating information across multiple texts, then background knowledge and inferences play greater roles in developing text comprehension. Similarly, skimming a text for the main idea is likely to involve processing that appears to be much more top–down in nature. Keeping this caveat in mind, it is still possible to refer to a modified interactive model, or a hybrid bottom–up/top–down model, as a useful interpretation of general reading comprehension processes.

1.4.2   Specific models of reading as research syntheses

An alternative approach to generalised metaphorical models of reading is to consider recent accounts of reading comprehension, and determine which ones, at least for the present, provide good explanations for what we know about reading from research. In the past twenty years, a number of such models have been proposed. We will introduce, in turn, four (types of) models of reading that have achieved some prominence and that figure in many discussions of reading: the Psycholinguistic Guessing Game Model, the Interactive Compensatory Model, word recognition models and the Simple View of Reading Model.

The Psycholinguistic Guessing Game Model of Reading (Goodman, 1986, 1996) is well known among applied linguists; it is also recognised today among reading researchers as being fundamentally wrong (Gough and Wren, 1999; Pressley, 1998; Stanovich and Stanovich, 1999). This model portrays reading comprehension as a universally applicable iterative process of (a) hypothesising, (b) sampling and (c) confirming information based on background knowledge, expectations about the text, a sampling of surface features of the text and context information from the text. It is, despite protestations by Ken Goodman himself, a classic example of a top–down approach to reading comprehension. Proponents of this strongly top–down orientated model have used it to support suggestions for reading instruction that have not been particularly beneficial for students' reading development, despite the continuing popularity of the model. Good readers typically do not guess what words will appear next in the text and good readers make less use of context than poor readers while they are engaged in fluent reading. Moreover, reading development is not universally the same across languages, nor are all reading abilities easily transferred from one language to another (as we will see in the next chapter). Related views of reading, commonly referred to as **constructivist models** and **transactional models**, typically presume that readers are able to carry out basic reading comprehension processes rather than explaining how these processes can operate or how they develop (see Quote 1.11). In

Quote 1.11

Response-oriented curricula based on reader-response theories [e.g. con-structivist theories] were developed for high school and college literature classes.... Response-oriented classes, in which students are encouraged to discuss their individual reactions to what they have read, are [seen as] a bracing alternative [to traditional instruction].

[However], transporting a response-oriented approach to literature down to the early grades creates a new set of problems.... [First], excess-ive response to a pleasant, but not richly evocative, text may be as numbing as excessive questioning on minute details. Second, responding to a work presupposes that one can read the work....

Even if children read the text themselves, long discussions may take away time from more practice in reading. Harris and Serwer (1966) found that children in language-experience classes spent less time actu-ally reading and more time discussing what they read than children in tra-ditional classes. This discussion time was negatively correlated with achievement.

Stahl (1997, pp. 22–3)

some respects, the Guessing Game Model provides a useful interpreta-tion of an early stage of reading development, but representing just one stage of reading development has never been Goodman's intention.

A model of reading that is still relevant in the view of reading researchers is the Interactive Compensatory Model (Stanovich, 1980, 1986, 2000). This model argues that (a) readers develop efficient reading processes, (b) less-automatic processes interact regularly, (c) automatic processes operate relatively independently and (d) reading difficulties lead to increased interaction and compensation, even among processes that would otherwise be more automatic. For example, using context clues to understand a text better or to decide what a word means is a compensatory strategy when normally expected abilities break down, or have not yet been developed.

Basic word recognition models, as the major input for efficient reading comprehension, are also sources of model building, though without extending the analyses to higher-level comprehension pro-cesses (Plaut, McClelland, Seidenberg and Patterson, 1996; Seidenberg and McClelland, 1989). Most current versions of word recognition models are based on **connectionist theories** of how the mind organises information and learns from exposure to text. The key point is that these models are fundamentally bottom–up in orientation, and they account for a considerable amount of what we currently know about word recognition processes under time constraints.

A final recent account of reading comprehension abilities and reading development that has grown in popularity is known as the Simple View of Reading Model (Hoover and Gough, 1990). This model argues that reading comprehension is composed of a combination of word recognition abilities and general comprehension abilities (typically measured by listening comprehension). The basic idea is that when a decoding-skill measure and a (listening) comprehension-skill measure (both as percentage scores) are multiplied, the resulting score is an accurate measure of reading comprehension. This view, compatible with word recognition models and the Interactive Compensatory Model, has generated much discussion among reading researchers over the past decade (cf. Carver, 1997; Urquhart and Weir, 1998).

Quote 1.12

Skilled reading clearly requires skill in both decoding and comprehension.... A child who cannot decode cannot read; a child who cannot comprehend cannot read either. Literacy – reading ability – can be found only in the presence of both decoding and comprehension. Both skills are necessary; neither is sufficient.

Gough, Hoover and Peterson (1996, p. 3)

Quote 1.13

An increasingly common view in the research literature is that reading is essentially divided into two components: decoding (word recognition) and comprehension. The latter is often described as consisting of parsing sentences, understanding sentences in discourse, building a discourse structure, and then integrating this understanding with what one already knows. This comprehension process, however, is not seen as unique to reading, but also describes the process of listening.

Alderson (2000, p. 12)

1.5 Conclusion

In this chapter, we have outlined a view of reading that is well supported by current research in English L1 contexts and is compatible with L2 reading research of the past decade. Beginning from our discussion of purposes for reading and our extended definition of reading comprehension, we have sought to describe current research views on reading comprehension while also providing explanations that will have real implications for instructional contexts. We have also developed an account that focuses on individual reader processing. This emphasis on individual processes is not intended to deny the relevance of social factors on reading development (e.g. family literacy experiences, primary schooling, peer and sibling interaction around literacy events) or the relevance of social contexts on purpose and processes themselves (see Chapter 2). Rather, our intention is to highlight information that is not well known among reading teachers, and raise awareness of issues that curriculum planners and teachers should consider if reading instruction is to be appropriate for student needs and institutional expectations. Our view of reading, as summarised in Figure 1.1, reveals the complex nature of reading and the many factors that must be taken into account when assessing students' needs and planning meaningful reading instruction.

As we pointed out earlier, much of the research that supports the views presented in this chapter is drawn from L1 contexts. In the next chapter, we explore the differences between L1 and L2 reading. These differences should influence our interpretation of L2 reading comprehension abilities, the development of L2 abilities, and implications for reading instruction.

Further reading

For additional readings on a number of key issues in this chapter, refer to the following: For alternative views on *purposes for reading*, see Alderson (2000), Carver (1992), Enright *et al.* (2000), Urquhart and Weir (1998). For variations on the *reading to learn* concept, see Carver (1992), Enright *et al.* (2000), Goldman (1997). For comprehensive overviews of *general reading comprehension*, see Adams (1990), Pressley (1998), Snow, Burns and Griffin (1998), Thompson and Nicholson

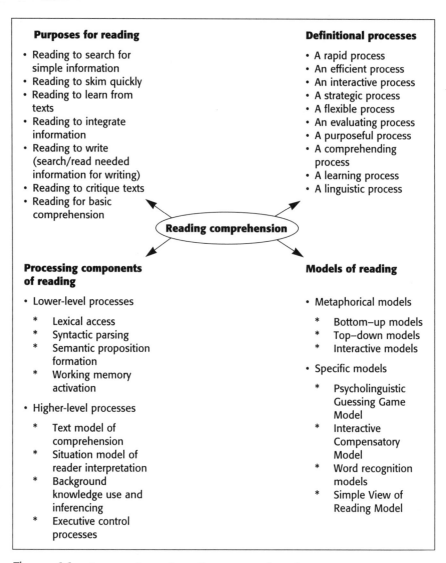

Figure 1.1   **An overview of reading comprehension**

(1999). For resources on *reading comprehension processes*, see Adams (1990), Perfetti (1985), Pressley (1998), Snow, Burns and Griffin (1998), Stanovich (2000), Stanovich and Stanovich (1999), Thompson and Nicholson (1999). For information on *working memory activation*, see Gathercole and Pickering (2000), Just and Carpenter (1992), Miyake and Friedman (1998). For specific models of reading that are similar in nature to the *Interactive Compensatory Model*, see Kintsch (1988, 1998),

Perfetti (1985, 1994). For readings that extend *basic word recognition models* to view working memory as the key resource for efficient reading comprehension abilities, see Carpenter, Miyake and Just (1994), Just and Carpenter (1992). For specifics on the *Simple View of Reading Model*, see Carver (1998), Chen and Vellutino (1997), Gough, Hoover and Peterson (1996).

Chapter 2

Comparing L1 and L2 reading

This chapter highlights differences that exist between L1 and L2 reading contexts and readers. In addition, it explores how those differences might influence classroom instruction. Three major types of differences form the core of the discussion:

- linguistic and processing differences
- individual and experiential differences
- socio-cultural and institutional differences

One of the more difficult tasks we face as reading teachers is deciding how to make use of reading research for our own purposes. The research on reading comprehension in first language (L1) contexts is extensive and complex. Research studies have looked at children and students ranging from three-year-olds to university level. Some studies have explored comprehension by varying the purposes for reading through a number of different tasks. Others have emphasised different skills that are usually seen as part of reading comprehension. For example, some studies focus on reading strategies, others study vocabulary development, others examine the role of discourse organisation and **text structure**, and yet others emphasise word recognition and reading **fluency**. Students participating in these studies have come from a range of social and ethnic backgrounds, with varying motivations and attitudes toward reading. As one might imagine, this range of emphases and reader variables makes it hard to generalise from the research literature to any one specific classroom context.

In second language (L2) contexts, the issues become even more complex. L2 students and research settings can vary as widely as those described for L1 contexts. In addition, L2 students have much wider ranges of language proficiencies, unlike most L1 readers who have considerable tacit grammar knowledge by the time they begin to read. Many L2 students have often already had experiences learning to read in an L1, more or less successfully (though others may have no L1 literacy experience). Moreover, they come with linguistic knowledge of their L1, even if most of it is tacit knowledge, and this knowledge can either support the transfer of reading skills or become a source of interference. Research efforts in L2 contexts also extend beyond the array of issues pertinent to L1 studies. For example, they explore the role of low-level language proficiency on reading and the impact of **transfer** at various ability levels, on various processes (e.g. word recognition, syntactic parsing, strategy use), and with different knowledge resources (e.g. general background knowledge, specific topical knowledge and cultural knowledge).

Aside from the additional complexities for research in L2 contexts, there are logistical difficulties with carrying out large-scale studies in many L2 settings because many sites for research cannot track L2 students for long periods of time. Moreover, the follow-up research that commonly occurs in L1 settings is less frequently done in L2 settings. There are also fewer L2 reading researchers to carry out such projects. These factors make it more difficult to assert wide generalisations from research in L2 contexts. Strong generalisations can only be developed after several near-replications of a research study across a number of L1 groups, across L2 proficiency levels and across socio-cultural and institutional learning contexts.

The differences between L1 and L2 reading contexts, however, go beyond numbers of studies and limitations of research methodology. L2 reading must account for issues that are qualitatively different from L1 issues. L2 learners, while learning to read, must broaden their linguistic knowledge, deal with transfer effects, and learn to use L2-specific resources (e.g. translation, glosses, bilingual dictionaries), among many other factors. All of these factors suggest that L2 reading can be quite different from L1 reading.

This chapter outlines 14 ways in which L2 reading comprehension processes and instruction may differ from L1 contexts. The 14 differences, explored in more detail in the remainder of this chapter, have been divided into three general areas: linguistic and processing differences, individual and experiential differences, and socio-cultural and institutional differences.

2.1   Linguistic and processing differences between L1 and L2 readers

This section presents seven major differences between L1 and L2 readers involving vocabulary, grammar, discourse, orthography and metalinguistic and metacognitive issues, as well as the amount of exposure that readers have to the L2 (see Figure 2.1). The linguistic and processing issues inherent in these differences are actually the most widely studied aspects of reading development and quite a bit of research can help us understand these differences and their possible impact on reading comprehension abilities. These differences highlight issues related to an L2 threshold, language transfer, differences across various student L1s and the simple fact that two languages are involved in comprehension processing in L2 settings.

2.1.1   Differing amounts of lexical, grammatical and discourse knowledge

As a first difference, most L1 students first learn to read after they have been learning their L1 orally for 4–5 years. In the US, students typically begin to read (formally) at the age of 6, in the first grade. By this time, they have learned most of the basic grammatical structures of their L1 as tacit knowledge. Further learning of the language structures

---

Linguistic and processing differences between L1 and L2 readers

1. Differing amounts of lexical, grammatical and discourse knowledge at initial stages of L1 and L2 reading
2. Greater metalinguistic and metacognitive awareness in L2 settings
3. Differing amounts of exposure to L2 reading
4. Varying linguistic differences across any two languages
5. Varying L2 proficiencies as a foundation for L2 reading
6. Varying language transfer influences
7. Interacting influence of working with two languages

Figure 2.1   Linguistic and processing differences between L1 and L2 readers

commonly used in written texts will continue regularly through the age of 12, but most of the basic structures are already well learned. Estimates of the vocabulary knowledge of a six-year-old vary considerably, but a commonly agreed upon range is 5,000 to 7,000 words. That is, a six-year-old in the first grade knows about 6,000 words when reading instruction begins. These linguistic resources provide a tremendous boost for young L1 students beginning to learn to read. It does not take much reflection to recognise how different this situation is from most L2 contexts (Grabe, 1999, 2000).

Unlike the L1 student's initial linguistic resource base, many L2 students begin to read simple sentences and passages almost at the same time that they learn the language orally. Other L2 students, primarily in academic reading courses, are not even expected to increase their oral L2 abilities to keep up with their reading development. It is true that curricula in certain L2 contexts (e.g. in ESL and bilingual settings in the US, the UK and Australia) encourage oral use of the L2 before a student begins to read, but this encouragement is extremely variable. In most cases, the vocabulary and grammar knowledge of the beginning L2 student marks a very different starting point from that of the beginning L1 reader. One obvious implication of these differences is that having L2 students sound out a word to 'discover' its meaning is likely to be less effective than it is in L1 settings (though not without value in L2 contexts). Beginning L2 students do not have a resource of several thousand words stored in their heads to be matched with the newly sounded out word. Thus, one benefit of developing accurate letter–sound correspondences as a support for reading is lost in most L2 settings; that is, L2 students cannot match a sounded out word to a word that they know orally since they do not yet know the word orally.

The lack of tacit L2 grammatical knowledge and **discourse knowledge** also suggests that L2 students need some foundation of structural knowledge and text organisation in the L2 for more effective reading comprehension. How much of a grammar and discourse foundation is needed is an open question, and one that is likely to vary considerably depending on the students being taught. Arguments that L2 readers do not need knowledge of grammar, occasionally voiced in the L2 literature, are clearly wrong (Alderson, 2000; Urquhart and Weir, 1998). Knowledge of discourse organisation may be very important for students who read L2 texts in more advanced academic settings, and patterns of discourse organisation may need explicit attention. Sometimes, students may know most of the vocabulary and understand the main concept(s) of a text, but they may not follow the specific development of the text, the new information being presented or the arguments being made. In some cases, L2 students may not be fully familiar with overall genre expectations of certain types of texts (e.g. newspaper stories, biographies, abstracts, reports, memos, editorials). Students recognise that something is not working the way they expect, but they do not know why.

Quote 2.1

Knowledge of structure is clearly important in efficient and strategic processing of text.

Goldman and Rakestraw (2000, p. 323)

Knowledge of text genres and structures allows readers to access information more readily and accurately, as they construct their personal interpretations of the text.

Alexander and Jetton (2000, p. 292)

Any sort of systematic attention to clues that reveal how authors attempt to relate ideas to one another or any sort of systematic attempt to impose structure upon a text, especially in some sort of visual representation of the relationships among key ideas, facilitates comprehension as well as both short term and long term memory of the text.

Pearson and Fielding (1991, p. 832)

2.1.2 Greater metalinguistic and metacognitive awareness in L2 settings

The general need to teach vocabulary, grammar and **discourse structure** in L2 settings from the very beginning acts as a support for early reading development and highlights our second L1–L2 difference: L2 readers often develop a greater awareness of the L2 itself as part of their reading resources, unlike L1 readers who typically have a more tacit knowledge of their native language (Garcia, 2000). In many L2 contexts (but not all), a good part of the students' knowledge of the L2 results from direct instruction in the classroom, or it comes about indirectly through instructional tasks, projects and outside reading. In these cases, students develop a greater **metalinguistic awareness** as a resource for reading. With the recent emphasis on awareness and reflection for language learning in L2 contexts, more L2 students now discuss, and reflect on, the linguistic resources (e.g. vocabulary,

> **Quote 2.2**
>
> Recently, much attention has been devoted to a particular kind of metalinguistic ability, phonemic awareness (i.e. the ability to reflect on and manipulate phonemes, the individual units of sound out of which spoken words are constructed). However, other types of metalinguistic awareness, such as morphological awareness and syntactic awareness, are also believed to play an important role in reading.
>
> Nagy and Scott (2000, p. 274)

morphology, grammar and discourse knowledge) that they use to assist them in comprehension. Unlike the tacit knowledge that is typical of L1 learners, many L2 students are often able to discuss and reflect on the linguistic resources available to them.

A natural extension of linguistic awareness is a more developed **metacognitive awareness** of the learning activities used while reading in the L2. Many students growing up bilingually or in ESL environments may approach L2 reading with many of the tacit resources of the L1 student; yet, a large percentage of L2 students approach L2 reading with quite different linguistic and learning backgrounds. In many L2 academic settings and foreign language settings, L2 students begin to read after they have been learning literacy skills and content knowledge for several years in their L1s. As a result, they develop a greater awareness of how they have learned to read, what learning strategies can work for them and how language knowledge can support literacy development. L2 students can more easily bring their **metalinguistic knowledge** to a conscious level to provide strategic support or understand comprehension failure. For example, while we do not believe that all L1

> **Quote 2.3**
>
> Cohen (1998:7) describes metacognition as dealing with: Pre-assessment and pre-planning, on-line planning and evaluation, and post-evaluation of language learning activities and of language use events. Such strategies allow learners to control their own cognition by coordinating the planning, organizing, and evaluating of the learning process.... He also acknowledges that the distinction between metacognitive and cognitive strategies may not always be clear-cut and there may on occasion be some overlap.
>
> Urquhart and Weir (1998, p. 180)

> **Quote 2.4**
>
> Greater involvement of [metalinguistic analysis and control processes] makes tasks more difficult, and this difficulty results in behavior appearing to be increasingly metalinguistic. However, no specific boundary in the development of either process signals a category shift into metalinguistic performance; it is a gradual transition into a continuously evolving domain.
>
> Bialystok (2001, p. 177)

Concept 2.1   **Metalinguistics and metacognitive knowledge**

Metalinguistic knowledge: Our knowledge of how language works. Metalinguistic knowledge includes knowledge of letters and sounds and how they relate, knowledge of words and word parts, knowledge of sentences and their parts, and knowledge of texts and genres and how they are organised.

Metacognitive knowledge: Our knowledge of what we know. Simply put, this knowledge permits us to reflect on our planning, goal setting, processing of tasks, monitoring of progress, recognition of problems and repair of problems. Metacognitive knowledge represents a basic way to understand learning strategies and, especially, our explicit and conscious use of reading strategies.

In both cases, our knowledge includes not only what we know (declarative knowledge) but also how we use this knowledge (procedural and conditional knowledge). In both cases, it is not straightforward to assert a separation between linguistic and metalinguistic knowledge, or between cognitive knowledge and metacognitive knowledge (see Quotes 2.3 and 2.4).

---

reading strategies transfer automatically to L2 reading contexts, it is still far easier to raise learner awareness of, and practice with, strategies that have been productive for them in L1 situations than would be the case with strategies that have never been used before by learners.

2.1.3   Differing amounts of exposure to L2 reading

A major difference for L2 reading, and one that strongly influences the linguistic knowledge differences mentioned above, is the total amount of exposure to L2 reading and to L2 print that a student experiences.

COMPARING L1 AND L2 READING   47

In many cases, the extent of reading practice in the L2 will mark the typical L2 reader as different from the L1 reader. As we emphasised in Chapter 1, the development of fluency and automaticity in word and syntactic processing is an essential foundation for reading. Most L2 readers are simply not exposed to enough L2 print (through reading) to build fluent processing (Koda, 1996; Lundberg, 1999). Nor do they have enough exposure to build a large recognition vocabulary. These differences between L1 and L2 reading situations are significant because L1 readers spend years building up the amount of exposure to print needed to develop fluency and automaticity. The extent of students' exposure to L2 print is an issue that we can (and should) explore with our students to understand better just how much L2 reading practice students have had, and what types of reading practice and L2 texts they have been exposed to.

2.1.4   Varying linguistic differences across any two languages

Linguistic differences across any two languages are likely to vary considerably, and these differences may influence L2 reading comprehension variably when students come from different L1s and are in the same L2 classroom. For example, students whose L1 is a Romance language (e.g. Spanish, French, Italian, Portuguese) tend to pay greater attention to the ends of words because there is much more grammatical information in the suffixes of their L1s than in English. As another example, words in languages such as Hebrew and Arabic, which have greater morphological complexity with embedded grammatical information, are read more slowly than words in a language such as English (Share and Levin, 1999; Shimron and Sivan, 1994). Another difference, which has been supported in multiple studies, reveals that readers of Chinese and Japanese make greater use of visual processing than do readers of English because of their L1 **orthography** (Hanley, Tzeng and Huang, 1999; Koda, 1997). There is also evidence that these differences lead to variation in reading rates and fluency in word processing, though these specific issues need much more research before any implications might be suggested for instruction (Liow, 1999; Muljani, Koda and Moates, 1998).

Two further differences across L1s with more general implications for L2 reading include orthographic differences and the extent of shared vocabulary or **cognates**. With regard to orthographic differences across languages, differing orthographies are more or less transparent with respect to **letter–sound relationships** (sometimes referred to

> **Quote 2.5**
>
> Italian children... learn to read very rapidly, and, only six months after the start of formal reading instruction, they are highly accurate at reading both words and non-words.... German... although less transparent than Italian, has very consistent grapheme–phoneme correspondences.... [T]he demands placed on working memory in successfully applying grapheme–phoneme correspondences to reading are much lower for a regular orthography than an irregular orthography like English.
>
> Harris and Hatano (1999a, pp. 2–3)
>
> [T]he heavy processing demands associated with morphemic [complexity] play a role even in the text-reading speed of highly literate bilingual Hebrew–English adults.... It is not only lack of L2 linguistic proficiency that slows down text reading for L2 beginners, but also the high morphemic density associated with inflected languages such as Hebrew.
>
> Geva, Wade-Woolley and Shany (1997, p. 140)

> **Quote 2.6**
>
> L1 processing experience has a lasting effect on the formation of L2 morphological awareness, thus accounting in part for performance variations in L2 lexical processing among ESL learners from typologically diverse L1 backgrounds.
>
> Koda (2000, p. 315)

as the Orthographic Depth Hypothesis, see Concept 2.2). That is, depending on the transparency of the orthography, a reader looking at a word will be able to sound out the word (or activate the word sounds in working memory) more or less easily. Some languages are seen as completely transparent (e.g. Serbo-Croatian, Finnish, Turkish); others are quite transparent (e.g. Greek, Italian, Spanish), and some a bit less so (e.g. German, Swedish); some are relatively more opaque (e.g. French, Danish), and some very opaque for an alphabetic language (e.g. English). Consonantal alphabetic languages are yet more opaque (e.g. unpointed Hebrew and Arabic), and some are very opaque (e.g. Japanese and Chinese are not alphabetic scripts) (Elley, 1992; Harris and Hatano, 1999b; Oney, Peter and Katz, 1997). The key issues here

---

Concept 2.2   **Orthographic Depth Hypothesis**

The Orthographic Depth Hypothesis (ODH) proposes that orthographic depth is directly related to the amount of lexical involvement in obtaining a word's phonology. According to the ODH, in shallow (i.e. phonologically regular) orthographies, such as Spanish, Serbo-Croatian, and Korean Hangul, a phonological code is assembled prior to lexical access through highly systematic analysis of intraword segmental information. By contrast, in deep (i.e. phonologically less regular) orthographies, phonological processing depends, in varying degrees, on lexical information. As a case in point, English orthography . . . is phonetically less regular than Spanish . . . as is evident in orthographically similar, but phonologically dissimilar, word-family members, such as 'anxious' and 'anxiety'.

Koda (1999, pp. 52–3)

---

revolve around what happens when a reader with a transparent L1 begins to read in a less transparent L2, or, what happens when a reader with a less transparent L1 begins to read in a transparent L2. In both cases, if both languages are fully alphabetic, there should be positive transfer to the L2 (Geva and Siegel, 2000; Harris and Hatano, 1999a).

At present, recognising that there are many other factors that influence reading, the research suggests that readers will process words differently in transparent and opaque orthographies. In general, L2 students will tend to use some L1 processing when they try to read the L2, although the tendency influences beginning L2 reading more than advanced L2 reading. For example, in beginning L2 adult reading, students must adapt from a lifetime of efficient word recognition processing in the L1 to accommodate word recognition processes in the L2. Whether or not the orthography of a student's L1 will influence L2 reading instruction (and when) is an issue that will not be easily resolved on general grounds (because there are endless L1s and L2s to compare). But it is an issue that is receiving increasing research attention. Understanding more about a student's L1 literacy skills and orthography may help explain possible difficulties in word recognition, fluency and reading rate (Harris and Hatano, 1999b; Muljani, Koda and Moates, 1998).

The final issue involving differences across L1s, and differences across any two languages (L1s and L2s), relates to the role of cognates. The development of L1 reading does not generally involve the use of cognates as support for reading comprehension. In L2 contexts, however, cognates may play a large role in supporting reading comprehension, depending on the particular L1 and L2. For example, for interesting historical reasons, French and English share thousands of cognates, and they are particularly useful at more advanced levels of reading. By extension, Spanish, Portuguese, and Italian all share thousands of useful cognates with English. In cases where a student has a Romance language as an L1, and is learning to read in English, cognates represent a significant resource if we help students to recognise and use them (Nagy, Garcia, Durgunoglu and Hancin-Bhatt, 1993). When students come from an L1 such as Chinese, there are very few cognates to assist them in L2 reading development.

2.1.5   Varying L2 proficiencies as a foundation for L2 reading

L2 proficiency plays a large role as a foundation for L2 reading (often discussed in the context of the Language Threshold Hypothesis). The **Language Threshold** Hypothesis argues that students must have a sufficient amount of L2 knowledge (i.e. vocabulary, grammar and discourse) to make effective use of skills and strategies that are part of their L1 reading comprehension abilities. The fundamental issue for L2 reading centres on the relative importance of L2 knowledge versus L1 reading abilities. The Language Threshold Hypothesis, as proposed by researchers, states that language knowledge is more important than L1 reading abilities up to some point at which the learner has enough L2 knowledge to read reasonably fluently. Although there are a number of qualifications, this hypothesis has been strongly supported by recent L2 reading research. A number of studies have demonstrated the greater importance of L2 linguistic knowledge (than L1 reading knowledge) for students in varying contexts.

Critics of this hypothesis have argued that there is no single set of linguistic knowledge that can be defined as presenting the necessary foundation (or the threshold). However, this objection does not represent a strong criticism because reading success varies with a number of factors. A given text may be too difficult to read because of its linguistic demands, but it also might be too hard to read fluently because of a new topic, poor organisation or insufficient time to read. The idea behind the linguistic threshold is not that there is a fixed set of language knowledge that students need. Rather, a variable amount of linguistic knowledge, combined with fluency of processing, is needed to read a specific text, on a specific topic, for a specific task. Students can be said to pass above the threshold (perhaps only temporarily for one

Concept 2.3   **Language threshold**

Language Threshold: This hypothesis states that L2 readers need to know enough L2 knowledge (vocabulary and structure) so that L1 reading strategies and skills can be used efficiently to help comprehend the L2 text. If the reader is devoting most of his cognitive resources to figuring out the language of the L2 text, there are few cognitive resources left over for the fluent comprehension processes that would normally support the L1 reader. Readers usually cross the threshold whenever they encounter L2 texts in which they know almost all of the words and can process the text fluently. Because L2 readers are all different in their L2 knowledge, topic knowledge and L2 reading experiences, there is no one level of general language proficiency that counts as the threshold for all readers or for all texts. The threshold will vary depending on the reader, the text and the topic.

specific text) when they have enough linguistic knowledge to read the text without great vocabulary and grammatical difficulty. As students are able to read more and more texts fluently, one can say that they are moving beyond the linguistic threshold, yet any new and difficult text might throw them back to a level of less fluent and inefficient reading.

One major consequence of passing through the linguistic threshold is that students free up cognitive resources, which were previously used to figure out language structures and vocabulary, to read more

Quote 2.7

Despite the common-sense assumptions of the importance of language knowledge, the belief has existed for some time that, if students cannot read well in their first language, they will be unable to read well in the second/foreign language. . . .

The clear conclusion of [L1 reading versus L2 language knowledge] studies is that second-language knowledge is more important than first-language reading abilities, and that a linguistic threshold exists which must be crossed before first-language reading ability can transfer to the second-language reading context. However, it is clear that this linguistic threshold is not absolute but must vary by task: the more demanding the task, the higher the linguistic threshold.

Alderson (2000, pp. 38–9)

strategically and transfer L1 strategic reading practices to the L2 setting. This hypothesis provides a strong argument for giving students a lot of exposure to reading, focusing on both fluency and texts that are not too difficult.

2.1.6 Varying language transfer influences

A natural extension of the Language Threshold Hypothesis is the larger issue of transfer, a uniquely L2 topic. An initial issue in discussing transfer, and one that is sometimes downplayed, is that transfer of L1 knowledge to L2 reading may support comprehension but it may also interfere with comprehension. A second major issue for transfer involves transfer of basic reading purposes (see Chapter 1) and (meta)cognitive knowledge, the latter including strategies, inferences, motivation, attitudes and background knowledge resources.

Transfer as interference is typically assumed to influence beginning and intermediate levels of L2 reading. When L2 students are asked to read material that is difficult for them, they will rely on any resources available to try to make sense of the text (refer to the discussion of the situation model in Chapter 1). At beginning L2 levels, students' strongest resources are their L1 language and reading abilities and their knowledge of the world. At times, these resources will provide enough support to carry out certain comprehension tasks; at other times, these same resources will mislead students or slow L2 processing routines. In

---

Concept 2.4 Transfer

Transfer refers to the idea that L2 readers will use their L1 knowledge and experiences to help them carry out L2 tasks. In the case of reading, transfer applies to a variety of language knowledge bases and cognitive abilities. Transfer can occur with phonological knowledge, topical knowledge, general background knowledge, problem-solving strategies and inferencing skills. We also tend to transfer our prior experiences to tasks of various sorts, including academic tasks that involve reading L2 texts. Sometimes transfer supports reading tasks; but sometimes it interferes with successful task completion. Transfer is also discussed more generally, in Educational Psychology, in terms of transfer of learning. Transfer in this broader context is usually seen as problematic in that skill learning in one context is difficult to transfer immediately to new contexts and situations (see Quote 2.8).

this latter situation, it is important to recognise that such interference is both natural and strategic on the part of students. The instructional goal at this level is for students to develop enough vocabulary, reading practice and processing fluency in the L2 so that they will rely less on L1 resources that might interfere. Of course, one of the best ways to move beyond heavy L1 interference in L2 reading is to be sure that students are not always reading texts that are too difficult for them; students should be given sufficient opportunities to read texts that are easy to read and enjoyable.

A different aspect of interference is likely to persist for much longer periods and may require consistent and direct teacher intervention, even at advanced reading levels. Students may not be aware of the varying purposes for reading called upon in L2 settings, particularly academic settings. They may still be making assumptions about the uses of reading that are appropriate to their L1 experiences but not as appropriate for some L2 reading purposes. These assumptions may also be influenced by different motivations for reading and different attitudes toward reading. To minimise these types of interference, it is important to explore goals for L2 reading, appropriate strategies for completing L2 reading tasks and inferences that connect background knowledge to text information with our students.

Positive transfer effects, on the other hand, represent valuable resources for L2 reading development. In the right circumstances, many aspects of L1 reading abilities support L2 comprehension, though this transfer typically assumes well-developed literacy abilities in the student's L1. Examples of positive transfer effects include the following: effective strategies for reading academic texts, appropriate purposes for reading, experiences with successful task completion, flexibility in monitoring comprehension and skills for analysing and learning new words. Positive transfer effects provide a means for accelerated development of L2 reading abilities when they are assisted by instruction and teacher guidance.

A very popular notion in language teaching is that skills transfer is uniformly good and an easily accessible resource for L2 students. There actually is very little evidence for these views, and there is now much evidence that such perspectives are simplistic and, at times, counterproductive (Anderson, 1995; Schunk, 2000). Aside from numerous studies documenting interference from L1 resources, there is growing evidence – from Language Threshold research and strategy research – that skills transfer is not uniformly automatic. One important consequence is the need to explore which L1 skills and strategies might be positive supports for L2 reading development and how such skills and strategies can be reinforced through direct instruction in, for example, word-recognition skills, vocabulary-learning strategies, cognate use and comprehension strategies.

> **Quote 2.8**
>
> [T]he literature on transfer tends to be pessimistic. [L.] Mikulecky (1990) claims that a major misconception in literacy studies is that 'mastering literacy in one context substantially transfers to other contexts', and adds 'Transfer of literacy abilities is severely limited by differences in format, social support networks, and required background information as one moves from context to context' (p. 25).
>
> Urquhart and Weir (1998, p. 3)

> **Quote 2.9**
>
> [I]t seems that the issue of transfer between literacies is not as straight-forward as we have tended to suppose.
>
> Bell (1995, p. 690)

2.1.7   Interacting influence of working with two languages

Closely related to transfer discussions is the very fact that two languages are involved in L2 comprehension processes. The inevitable interplay between two languages in L2 reading influences word recognition, reading rate, the organisation of the lexicon, the speed of syntactic processing, strategies for comprehension, experiences in task performance, expectations of success and failure, motivations for reading and a number of other possible points of interaction (Segalowitz, Poulson and Komoda, 1991). This factor is seldom discussed, perhaps because there is relatively little research that focuses specifically on this point, and also because there are no obvious implications for instruction beyond what has been noted above. However, this issue may become more important as more research is reported on cognitive processing in bilingual individuals and as research in discourse comprehension increases in the field of psychology. The issue of two languages working

---

Quote 2.10

Crosslinguistic interaction has attracted little attention among L2 reading researchers. Apparently, the lack of crosslinguistic focus is attributable, in part, to L2 researchers' heavy reliance on L1 theories without due regard for a significant difference: L2 processing, unlike L1 reading, involves more than one language.... [T]here has been little systematic exploration of the ways in which the interchange among linguistic systems affects L2 processing performance.

Muljani, Koda and Moates (1998, p. 100)

---

at the same time also reveals a range of non-linguistic factors that distinguish L1 and L2 reading comprehension; these factors are discussed in the next section of the chapter.

2.2 Individual and experiential differences for L1 and L2 readers

In addition to the seven linguistic and processing differences noted above, there are further distinctions between L1 and L2 reading. A number of these differences centre around other resources and experiences that influence L2 reading comprehension, including students' proficiency levels in L1 literacy skills, their differing personal experiences with and motivations for L1 and L2 reading, their attitudes toward authentic texts and their training in the use of various supporting resources (see Figure 2.2). Each of these differences will be discussed, in turn, in the following sections.

Individual and experiential differences between L1 and L2 readers

1. Differing levels of L1 reading abilities
2. Differing motivations for reading in the L2
3. Differing kinds of texts in L2 contexts
4. Differing language resources for L2 readers

Figure 2.2   Individual and experiential differences between L1 and L2 readers

2.2.1   Differing levels of L1 reading abilities

An important L1–L2 difference is that L2 readers are influenced by their levels of L1 reading abilities. In one respect, this point could have been made in the discussions of transfer above; students who are weak in L1 literacy abilities cannot be expected to transfer many supporting resources to L2 reading contexts. The types of abilities that students use in their L1 reading represent the upper limit of what can be expected for linguistic transfer, strategic practices, problem-solving experiences, task-completion skills and metacognitive awareness of reading processes. All too often, teachers and researchers do not carefully examine the L1 reading skills of their students. Without such knowledge, we are more limited in deciding what skills and strategies to focus on and promote for transfer.

2.2.2   Differing motivations for reading in the L2

When comparing L1 and L2 reading contexts, it is likely that we will find different individual motivations for reading, as well as differing senses of self-esteem, interest, involvement with reading and emotional responses to reading. As students progress through different levels of education, and as academic-task demands increase, L2 students tend to have differing (and perhaps more conflicting) combinations of motivations for reading L2 texts. Some of these differences in motivation will be based on varying academic goals, socialisation practices from home and community, prior educational instruction or broad cultural frameworks for literacy uses (see below). These possible differences should be explored in classroom settings (e.g. through discussions, student-interest surveys, simple surveys of parents and community members, parent–teacher conferences and family literacy projects). This information may help us understand student strengths and weaknesses beyond any language assessment measure and may lead to more effective instruction (see Dörnyei, 2001b).

Aside from specific motivations for reading and task performance, students bring with them varying underlying attitudes toward L2 reading, which are often linked to perspectives on past educational experiences in both L1 and L2 contexts and to socio-political differences between L1 and L2 societies. These experiences shape perceptions of how well they can perform tasks, and lead to student self-perceptions of how successful they are as students (and readers). These perceptions, in turn, influence the students' self-esteem, emotional responses to reading, interest in reading and willingness to persist. No one disputes the fact that students' self-perceptions, emotional attitudes toward reading, interest in specific topics, and willingness to read texts and learn from them are important issues for the classroom learning environment. Unfortunately, these issues are often ignored in discussions of reading comprehension instruction, but in L1 reading research, they are now seen as important predictors of academic success (Guthrie, Wigfield and Von Secker, 2000). L2 teachers are not likely to be given much guidance on these issues, so it is an important topic for teacher research and classroom exploration (see Model Action Research Projects 9.1.7, 9.1.8, 9.1.9 in Chapter 9).

2.2.3   Differing kinds of texts in L2 contexts

The experiences that individual students have with differing kinds of texts in L1 and L2 contexts are additional potential sources of reading comprehension differences. Because L1 and L2 readers are likely to have different experiences with various text genres, they develop diverse approaches to the range of texts that they encounter. In many L2 contexts, students read quite simple texts, yet in other L2 contexts, students read texts far more difficult than they should be encountering. In the cases of the simpler texts (as in certain L2 reading textbooks and graded readers), these reading experiences may not match the reading experiences of L1 readers at comparable cognitive-ability levels. In settings where L2 students are asked to read difficult, often authentic, texts, reading experiences at first glance appear to be similar to L1 students, but closer examination reveals that the texts are often much shorter in length, a recognition on the part of materials developers of the difficulties students are likely to have with authentic texts. L2 students, over a period of time, are also less likely to be exposed to the full range of text genres that are commonly read by L1 students, partly because a number of these genres are read outside of class or even outside of educational task requirements. It is not obvious what impact these differences have on L2 students, except that the range of texts that they could be reading is generally restricted (and new vocabulary exposure may be more limited).

2.2.4   Differing language resources for L2 readers

Important L1–L2 differences centre on the use of bilingual dictionaries, glosses, translation and cultural background resources in L2 contexts, but not in L1 contexts. Bilingual dictionaries are, by definition, unique to L2 reading. L2 students often use learner dictionaries that carefully attend to the ways in which words are defined. Neither of these resources is typical of L1 literacy learning. L2 students often read materials with glosses for more difficult terms. It is true that glosses are also found in L1 textbooks (e.g. in science-learning textbooks that often require extensive technical vocabulary development), but they most often assist readers with unusual vocabulary, technical terms or archaic words. In L2 contexts, glosses commonly provide synonyms for vocabulary that is above learners' levels but well within the range of vocabulary knowledge expected of L1 readers. L2 students write out translations of texts and do their own mental translations as ways to assist comprehension. Such translation resources are unique to L2 settings. Finally, L2 students can reference specific L1 cultural knowledge and text resources for L2 reading tasks (e.g. proverbs, special and sacred texts, and cultural narratives). How these resources influence L2 reading comprehension for different groups of readers is not well known, but they indicate a clear difference between L1 and L2 readers, and they should be investigated in the classroom for insights that a teacher might gain (see Hartmann, 2001).

Pointing out unique and distinct resources for L2 students is only part of the issue. We need to evaluate the effectiveness of these resources, and students need to be taught to use these resources efficiently. For example, effective teachers do not take an absolute stand on bilingual dictionary use because students are likely to use bilingual dictionaries no matter what is said. Rather, the issue becomes which bilingual dictionaries to use, when to use them and how to use them effectively. If we 'ban' bilingual dictionaries, we only guarantee that students will not receive the guidance needed to use them efficiently – since we can be sure they will use them on their own (see Model Action Research Projects 7.1.3, on the use of dictionaries, and 7.1.4, on the effectiveness of glosses, in Chapter 7).

2.3 Socio-cultural and institutional differences influencing L1 and L2 reading development

Aside from specific individual differences, linguistic and otherwise, there are a number of larger cultural and social issues that operate outside of the specific classroom context (see Figure 2.3). Reading development and reading instruction are strongly influenced by parental and

> **Socio-cultural and institutional differences influencing L1 and L2 reading development**
>
> 1. Differing socio-cultural backgrounds of L2 readers
> 2. Differing ways of organising discourse and texts
> 3. Differing expectations of L2 educational institutions

Figure 2.3 Socio-cultural and institutional differences influencing L1 and L2 reading development

community attitudes toward reading and uses of literacy. This is true for both L1 and L2 contexts, but, as will become apparent in the sections that follow, these factors do not always operate in the same way, either between L1 and L2 contexts, or across various L2 contexts.

2.3.1 Differing socio-cultural backgrounds of L2 readers

A key difference between L1 and L2 reading settings, but one often overlooked, relates to the L1 socialisation to literacy practices that L2 students bring from their L1 cultural backgrounds. In some cultures, literacy is relatively uncommon, and written communication often involves scribes and letter writers. Other cultures use literacy extensively, but emphasise certain uses over others, often placing greater value on sacred texts or other highly valued traditional texts. Yet other societies use literacy extensively, despite the fact that individual limitations in literacy skills are common and socially accepted. Finally, societies like the US, the UK and Australia socialise citizens to believe that everyone should be literate. In such settings, the literacy environment is intense and pervasive (i.e. signage, labels and texts of all types are found everywhere).

Quote 2.11

[W]hat it means to be literate, how this literacy is valued, used and displayed, will vary from culture to culture. Some cultures have enormous respect for the printed word, such that it is implicitly accepted as authority, and cannot be questioned. Others fear the implications of putting any opinions in print, since the greater permanence accorded to opinions thereby makes the owner of the opinion more 'accountable'.

Alderson (2000, p. 25)

In each cultural context, assumptions about how to use text resources also tend to differ. Some social groups see texts as sacred and unchanging; others consider texts as serving utilitarian purposes but not to be highly valued; others view texts as sources of truth to be studied; yet others value texts as alternative interpretations of realities and facts that can be disputed. In each setting, individuals are socialised in their L1 education to engage with texts in specified ways (Lundberg, 1999). L2 readers moving from one orientation to another are likely to encounter some difficulties in reading texts for purposes that do not complement cultural assumptions; these students may need teacher assistance in making these shifts. In almost all cases, L2 students will have some difficulties with framing assumptions presented in L2 texts when these texts make use of cultural assumptions that the L2 students do not share. These mismatches in assumptions may cause serious problems when L2 students read literary and contemporary-culture texts.

2.3.2   Differing ways of organising discourse and texts

Another major distinction between L1 and L2 reading contexts is the differing cultural and social preferences given to particular ways of organising discourse and texts. In literate societies around the world, people develop preferred ways of organising information in written texts (and also in oral texts for that matter). For example, people make arguments in writing by presenting observational and numerical evidence, by emphasising a culturally accepted logic, by pointing to a persuasive example or by referring to traditional wisdom or religious doctrines. Certain socio-cultural preferences for making an argument or taking a position then tend to become conventionalised in writing so that the structures and organisational plans for writing tend to reflect an expected way to write an argument. Thus, purposes for writing, beliefs about the preferred way to make an argument and the ways in which information is used in writing all influence how texts may be organised and how linguistic resources are employed. The study of this phenomenon is sometimes referred to as contrastive rhetoric (Connor, 1996; Grabe and Kaplan, 1996). The essential point for the purposes of reading is that L2 text resources may not always be organised in ways that match students' L1 reading experiences.

Additional factors related to text organisation that may influence L2 reading comprehension include differences in (a) the ways in which texts express interpersonal relations with the reader (e.g. the use of 'I' and 'you' as pronouns), (b) expectations about the amount of new information that is embedded in a text (e.g. the use of many nomin-alisations), and (c) assumptions about how explicitly reader interpre-tation should be guided (e.g. with supporting details, descriptions and explanations). These issues suggest the benefits of exploring the discourse organisation of texts as part of instruction and raising stu-dent awareness of the ways in which information is presented (or not presented), all the while being cautious with certain over-generalised claims about discourse differences across languages (see Model Action Research Projects 8.1.6, focusing on patterns of rhetorical organisa-tion, and 8.1.9, focusing on the identification of signal words indicat-ing sequence and contrast, in Chapter 8).

2.3.3 Differing expectations of L2 educational institutions

Our fourteenth, and last, distinction between L1 and L2 reading is shaped by the different attitudes, resources and expectations of L1 and L2 educational structures. L2 students are shaped in their assumptions and their performances by their previous L1 institutional experiences (with, for example, national exams, national curricula, teacher beha-viour, classroom management, teacher inspectors and district and regional mandates), which could be in sharp contrast with the L2 insti-tutional settings in which they find themselves (Hanley, Tzeng and Huang, 1999; Leki, 1992; Lundberg, 1999). Additional differences include the amounts of funding for teacher training, level of teacher experience, amount of money devoted to educational resources, level of support for educational infrastructure, teacher–student relationships and size of classes. Of course, these differences can be found within L1 contexts, with ethnic minority groups often experiencing lower levels of institutional support. However, these differences may be magnified considerably with L2 students from many different socio-cultural and language backgrounds, and these differences can lead to reading difficulties that might otherwise be unexpected (McKay, 1993).

In line with this issue are the differences that stem from group social-isation to the usefulness (or non-usefulness) of institutional structures generally and, on many occasions, the potential oppressiveness of these institutional structures more specifically. In L1 contexts, ethnic minor-ities often see school institutions as representing interests at odds with their own, and they tend to develop resistant attitudes toward educa-tional efforts (Ogbu, 1987). In L2 contexts, students may bring strong attitudes from the L1 to the L2, with little room to accept the L2 as a relatively utilitarian tool for further learning. At the same time, many

L2 students do adopt a strongly utilitarian attitude toward the L2, an attitude that may be quite different from their attitudes toward their L1s. A utilitarian attitude may, in turn, limit students' willingness to engage in a long-term consistent effort to learn to read fluently.

2.4 Conclusion

The many differences that exist between L1 and L2 reading contexts point out the complexities of L2 reading comprehension (see Figure 2.4 for a summary of differences). Not only are L2 students and student groups as diverse as L1 student groups, but they are involved in learning goals that are even more complicated than those in most L1 literacy environments. Many of the assumptions associated with L1 reading instruction should be rethought and modified in the light of these differences. On the basis of this chapter, it should also be apparent that there is no straightforward blueprint for how a teacher should adapt instruction for all L2 contexts. It is also clear that no one-size-fits-all approach or set of procedures can be offered.

Becoming informed about the many possible differences between L1 and L2 students can assist all of us in (a) interpreting reading research and the many assertions made about effective reading instruction, (b) recognising the particular demands of L2 reading and (c) investigating pertinent concerns in our own classrooms. We should not wait for sweeping assertions from research, nor should we be swayed by claims of 'perfect' classroom solutions. Rather we should use our own classrooms, and our own students, as a forum for meaningful classroom-based research. Real classroom environments often provide the best context for exploring L2 learning issues important for effective learning. The differences showcased in this chapter represent useful starting points for meaningful and purposeful teacher-initiated enquiry, as shall be illustrated in Section III of this volume.

Because of the many differences that exist between L1 and L2 reading, we can anticipate certain problems that L2 students are likely to encounter in a majority of L2 reading settings. In the next chapter, we highlight a number of these easily anticipated problems, describing them as dilemmas for L2 reading instruction. An examination of these dilemmas not only highlights the complexities of L2 reading and reading instruction, but also reveals areas where more formal and classroom-based research is needed.

Linguistic and processing differences

1. Differing amounts of lexical, grammatical and discourse knowledge at initial stages of L1 and L2 reading
2. Greater metalinguistic and metacognitive awareness in L2 settings
3. Differing amounts of exposure to L2 reading
4. Varying linguistic differences across any two languages
5. Varying L2 proficiencies as a foundation for L2 reading
6. Varying language transfer influences
7. Interacting influence of working with two languages

Individual and experiential differences

8. Differing levels of L1 reading abilities
9. Differing motivations for reading in the L2
10. Differing kinds of texts in L2 contexts
11. Differing language resources for L2 readers

Socio-cultural and institutional differences

12. Differing socio-cultural backgrounds of L2 readers
13. Differing ways of organising discourse and texts
14. Differing expectations of L2 educational institutions

Figure 2.4   Differences between L1 and L2 reading

Further reading

For additional readings on a number of key issues in this chapter, refer to the following: On *language threshold*, see Alderson (2000), Bernhardt and Kamil (1995), Bossers (1992), Carrell (1991), Lee and Schallert (1997), Schoonen, Hulstijn and Bossers (1998). On *transfer*, see Durgunoglu (1997, 1998), Geva and Wade-Woolley (1998), Liow (1999), MacWhinney (1997), Verhoeven (1994), Verhoeven and Aarts (1998). On *the interplay between two (or more) languages in reading*, see Kroll and deGroot (1997), Liow (1999), Segalowitz (1986), Shimron and Sivan (1994). On *motivation as a predicator of academic success*, see Guthrie *et al.* (1998), Guthrie, Wigfield, Metsala and Cox (1999). On *the use of different L2-specific resources to facilitate reading*, see Jacobs (1994), Kern (1994), Luppescu and Day (1993), Treville (1996). On *cultural and social issues related to reading*, see Lundberg (1999), Snow, Burns and Griffin (1998).

Chapter 3

Dilemmas for L2 reading research and instruction

This chapter explores 13 dilemmas that emerge when students learn to read in a second language and the implications of the dilemmas for L2 reading instruction. The chapter focuses on the following:

- implications for curriculum development and instructional practice that emerge from recent L1 and L2 reading research

- dilemmas that have important ramifications for L2 reading instruction, even though they are one step removed from teaching because of their linkages to research and theory

- dilemmas that are practical in nature, suggesting direct implications for L2 instruction

In this chapter, we explore challenges that arise for reading instruction in light of current theoretical ideas about reading and the differences that exist between first language (L1) and second language (L2) reading. The views from reading research introduced in Chapter 1 highlight the importance of numerous factors that influence reading comprehension abilities, including efficiency, automaticity, linguistic knowledge, content and background knowledge, and strategic responses to texts. Much of this persuasive research has been carried out on L1 learners. In Chapter 2, we examined the many differences that exist between reading in L1 and L2 contexts. The issues raised in Chapters 1 and 2 help us understand the strengths and weaknesses that L2 readers bring to reading tasks and reveal many of the challenges that we face when teaching L2 reading. Yet, rather than view these challenges in a negative light, we see them as providing us with insights that can be used while we consider research findings, look at our own classrooms more critically and experiment with innovations to enhance teaching and learning. The complexities of L2 reading also stimulate thought-provoking questions such as these: Should we simply assume that L1 reading theory and research fit L2 contexts? Should we assume that L1–L2 differences are unimportant? We think that the answer in both cases is 'no' because L2 teaching contexts are simply too complex to make such assumptions.

To highlight the complexities that exist for L2 reading teachers, we propose 13 dilemmas as a way to explore issues raised by research and L1–L2 differences. In some cases, the issues are practical in nature, suggesting direct implications for instruction. In other cases, they have important ramifications for L2 reading instruction even though they are one step removed from teaching because of their direct linkages to research and theory. In all cases, we need to remember that research studies can be directly relevant to teaching goals. At the same time, awareness of the possible limitations of research gives us the power to interpret assertions made about 'implications for instruction' (most often found in concluding sections of research reports).

3.1 Reading research and instruction: A source of dilemmas

We first want to highlight some of the advances made by recent research and theory construction. Significant progress has been made in reading research, and reading instruction is better for these advances, even if the practical implications sometimes complicate our lives. Advances in L1 contexts have led to many improvements in reading instruction, especially in terms of instructional techniques that build strategic processes and linguistic knowledge bases. The corresponding research in L2 contexts has not made as much headway. This is partially due to the fact that in many L2 contexts (but not all), there is less research funding, less political support for minority-student or foreign-language needs, less stable student populations on which to carry out large long-term research studies and fewer L2 reading researchers. Nevertheless, several key findings have emerged from L2 research, at times supporting L1 research findings, and at other times highlighting L2-specific issues.

The relationship between research findings and their implications for L2 instruction requires careful interpretation. Even in cases where

1. The need to develop reading fluency and word recognition automaticity
2. The existence of a second language proficiency threshold in reading
3. The varying influences of L1 reading skills, strategies, and background knowledge on L2 reading
4. The importance of a large recognition vocabulary for reading
5. The importance of discourse structure and the instructional benefits of graphic representations
6. The need for language awareness and attention to language and genre form
7. The importance of metacognitive awareness and strategic reading
8. The need for extensive reading for reading development
9. The importance of student interest, motivation and positive attitudes for learning
10. The importance of content-based instruction and the benefits of integrating reading and writing
11. The varying but powerful influences of social-context factors on reading success
12. The varying but powerful cultural influences on reading success

Figure 3.1   **Research findings with implications for L2 instruction and curricular planning**

insights from L1 and L2 reading research appear to be the same, they tend to emphasise issues in different ways. For example, vocabulary learning and a large recognition vocabulary are now seen as important for both L1 and L2 readers, although the notion of 'large' tends to be discussed differently. L1 and L2 students start reading with very different levels of pre-existing vocabulary knowledge. So, for L2 contexts, 10,000 words would be 'large'. In contrast, for L1 contexts, 40,000 words is considered 'sufficiently large'.

Despite 'hidden' differences such as these, research points out similarities in reading comprehension abilities across L1 and L2 settings and suggests major implications for L2 curricular planning. Figure 3.1 lists twelve important research findings, based on sound research efforts in both L1 and L2 settings over the past two decades, with important implications for reading instruction.

The research findings highlighted here, coupled with the subtle differences in implications for instruction when applied to L1 and L2 contexts, suggest challenges for translating research into specific and usable instructional practices. One way to explore these challenges is by noting the dilemmas that these research findings create. As we do so, it will become apparent that research does pose dilemmas, because there are no easy or simple solutions to them. The remainder of this chapter, therefore, highlights the dilemmas involved in translating research findings and theoretical issues, from both L1 and L2 contexts, into specific actions that we, as teachers and curriculum designers, can use in L2 settings.

We have divided our discussion of dilemmas into two parts. The first part addresses general dilemmas for L2 reading (see Figure 3.2 in the next section), that is, dilemmas that stem from different conceptualisations of reading and over-generalised implications for instruction. In the second part, we highlight dilemmas that have more obvious implications for instruction (see Figure 3.3 later in the chapter). When discussing each dilemma, we identify the dilemma and its possible origins and then propose possible steps for resolution. In many cases, we suggest that teachers engage in action research – in their own classrooms and with their own students – as a way to understand the issue better and to generate realistic solutions in relation to their own teaching environments. On numerous occasions, we refer to sample action research projects that are developed more fully in Section III (Chapters 6–9) as a way to illustrate more specific steps that can be taken.

3.2   General dilemmas for L2 reading

This section introduces five general dilemmas for L2 reading (see Figure 3.2). Each dilemma highlights issues that underlie the relationship between research and instruction and that stem from different views of reading and over-generalised implications for instruction. They do not address specific instructional issues.

- There are so many differing contexts for L2 reading instruction that no set of research findings can be presumed to apply equally to all of them.
- Social contexts influence reading development in various ways, but the range of possible social contexts to consider, and the many different ways that they can affect learners, make any predictions about the impact of combined social-context factors almost impossible to specify.
- Learning to read does not fit well with a notion of learning rules and practising them, or learning separate strategies and practising them outside of the reading context.
- A problematic but commonly held view is that learning to read involves the same abilities for all students from any L1, and that these abilities develop naturally, much like speaking and listening abilities.
- L2 research often discusses the importance of learning from context for reading comprehension, yet we do not share a well-defined interpretation of what the term 'context' might mean, or how its multiple meanings might be a source of misunderstanding.

Figure 3.2   General dilemmas for L2 reading

3.2.1   Dilemma 1: Contexts for L2 reading instruction

One of the most obvious and far-reaching dilemmas is the fact that *there are so many differing contexts for L2 reading instruction that no set of research findings can be presumed to apply equally to them all*. The endless combinations of student groups, proficiency levels, instructional and institutional backgrounds, amounts of exposure to print, levels of L1 reading abilities, settings (including ESL, EFL, FL and bilingual) and more, all indicate that no small set of research studies can possibly inform teachers, materials writers and curriculum developers equally in all settings.

A possible resolution to this dilemma rests with teachers themselves. Rather than expecting researchers to inform us about the most appropriate practices and implications for instruction, we can take it upon ourselves to interpret research findings in light of the specific contexts in which we work and our students learn. In some circumstances, especially those in which researchers make strong efforts to link their research to actual practice or in which research evidence makes persuasive cases for curricular and instructional innovations, we can see immediate relevance and applications to our own classrooms. In other cases, we can consider suggested implications and, knowing our classroom contexts as we do, determine their likely impact on student learning or explore them through action research.

3.2.2   Dilemma 2: Social-context influences on L2 reading

A second general dilemma centres on the ways that varying social contexts (aside from immediate instructional contexts) influence students' reading comprehension abilities. A 'social-contexts' view of L2 reading has been recognised as important for the past decade, but it has not been well articulated. A broad framework has yet to be established that can relate these influences to the development of L2 reading abilities in a range of educational situations. Most reading researchers recognise that *social contexts influence reading development in various ways, but the range of possible social contexts to consider, and the many different ways that they can affect learners, make any predictions about the impact of combined social-context factors almost impossible to specify*.

Two responses are useful in this regard. First, we can develop lists of the social-context factors that, in general, seem to influence learning in our instructional contexts the most (e.g. parental and community support, money for books, socio-economic status of parents, educational level of parents), and the conditions under which they influence reading development (e.g. positive student attitudes, student access to books, educational institution promotion of literacy, positive attitudes of siblings and peers to reading, number of visits to the library). An effort to categorise these factors could reveal a useful list of concerns to explore in the classroom, focusing on those factors (e.g. student attitudes toward reading) that can be altered (see Model Action Research Project 9.1.9 in Chapter 9).

Second, we benefit from becoming aware of the range of social-context issues that can have an impact on learning to read, more specifically, and which of these factors may be prominent among learners in our immediate classroom contexts. For example, we ought to find out which of our students might have (a) unusual educational experiences, (b) home circumstances that may impact on their abilities to carry out expected academic tasks or (c) L2 learning limitations (or L1 literacy limitations) that could impact on their abilities to develop L2 reading skills or their motivations for learning. In some cases, records that document this information may be accessible. In other cases, we may gain the most by exploring these issues over time through action research.

Quote 3.1

The ... 1992 International Association for the Evaluation of Educational Achievement (IEA) Study of Reading Literacy ... identified home environments as 'the single most critical factor in the development of literacy'. The study also showed that amount of voluntary reading and number of reading materials in the home were positively correlated with reading achievement.

Greaney (1996, p. 13)

Quote 3.2

Environments that support emergent literacy include (1) rich interpersonal experiences with parents, brothers, and sisters, and others; (2) physical environments that include literacy materials, from plastic refrigerator letters to storybooks to writing materials; and (3) high positive regard by parents and others for literacy and its development in children.... There are strong positive correlations between amount of storybook reading during preschool years and subsequent vocabulary and language development, children's interest in reading, and early success in reading.

Pressley (1998, p. 91)

3.2.3   Dilemma 3: Reading development versus rule learning

A third dilemma follows from recent research in cognitive psychology on the nature of learning in general. This research is only now having an impact in applied linguistics and will, in the future, have a greater influence on instruction. Briefly put, *learning to read does not fit well with a notion of learning rules and practising them, or learning separate strategies and practising them outside of the reading context; yet rule-based assumptions about language learning predominate much ESL/EFL/FL instruction.* Rather, students learn complex skills, such as reading, through extensive exposure and practice (Ellis, 1996, 1998).

The assumption that learning progresses from readily stateable rules is a common perspective for L2 instruction. Reading, however, requires continual practice at all of the following: (a) pattern matching, (b) over-learning basic processing skills while reading, (c) noticing and attending to language but not in any fixed sequence, (d) extensive feedback and (e) extensive practice with reading. Students need to develop an ability to recognise most words automatically to become fluent readers. This perspective may also be true for awareness of discourse structure and reading strategy learning. Reading, as a complex skill, requires the development of expertise in an ill-defined learning domain (unlike problems that can be solved straightforwardly), and research on expertise in complex domains needs to be incorporated into views of L2 reading development (Ericsson, 1996).

This dilemma suggests the need to rethink the learning (and teaching) of complex skills and the importance of being more open to learning processes that are not easily seen as rules-to-be-learned. In fact, research in the field of expertise and performance training reinforces the old but too readily discarded notion that learning requires considerable practice, time on task, and the over-learning of basic processes so that they can be used automatically for more complex cognitive tasks. The complexity of reading does not mean that rules, generalisations and specific strategies should not be introduced in instruction; they should be. But such instruction should only be viewed as a starting point for reading development. In a basic sense, reading is a performance skill and practice is essential; it does not commonly involve readily stateable rule systems to be learned. How we provide this extensive practice, of course, leads to other dilemmas (some of which are discussed in the upcoming section on instructional dilemmas).

> **Quote 3.3**
>
> What we need to bear in mind is that skilled readers don't get that way overnight. They learn how to do this complex thing we call reading by doing it repeatedly, over long periods of time, with lots of different texts, and with lots of opportunities for practice applying strategies, and monitoring their processes and evaluating the effectiveness of different strategies for themselves in different reading situations.
>
> Carrell (1998, p.17)

3.2.4   Dilemma 4: Reading as a cultural socialisation practice

A fourth dilemma involves *the commonly held, but likely erroneous, set of views that learning to read involves the same abilities in all situations, and that these abilities develop naturally, much like our speaking and listening abilities.* However, based on persuasive research over the past fifteen years, neither common assumption is true. Until recently, many L2 researchers and teachers have assumed that reading in different languages is very much the same, calling on the same processing requirements. As a result, they also assumed that all L1 reading skills should transfer automatically from the L1 to the L2. Yet it is now evident that L1 reading skills do not automatically transfer to the L2 context, nor do reading processes in different languages appear to be exactly the same (as noted in Chapter 2), particularly among beginning L2 readers.

The direct consequences of these assumptions have been twofold: previously, it was believed that reading (as a universal process) was a language skill that developed naturally, much like speaking and listening (see discussions in Byrne, 1996; Juel, 1999). However, we know that this view cannot be right, simply because a billion people around the world – who can speak and listen with ease – cannot read or write. One would be hard pressed to claim that almost a fifth of the world's population is somehow not natural. Second, many reading curricula and instructional practices were designed with the idea that students would learn to read naturally, and that students did not require teacher 'intervention' to become readers. The teacher's role was seen less as an instructor and more as a facilitator of the students' natural growth. Because of this orientation toward reading, there are many students who would have become better readers if they had been introduced to and taught reading abilities more explicitly (Snow, Burns and Griffin,

> ### Quote 3.4
>
> Arguments that reading and writing develop analogously to oral language are not supportable based on what is now known about reading and writing, and such arguments should be dropped. No one with an informed understanding about the development of reading and writing believes that they develop as oral language does. Whereas learning to read and write are conscious, intentional processes, oral language development is for the most part anything but intentional. Oral language typically is acquired from immersion in a speaking community, while reading and writing simply do not develop that way.
>
> Pressley (1998, p.184)

1998). We now know that reading requires the cultural transmission of this ability from generation to generation.

This dilemma, although theoretical in its claims, has had a profound effect on teaching and learning practices in L2 reading contexts. One response to this dilemma requires us to be more informed about (a) central issues in reading theory and research, (b) unsupportable claims, which are too often made about reading and (c) instructional practices that are based on wrong assumptions about reading abilities and their development. For example, students are sometimes taught to read by recognising the first one or two letters of a word and guessing the word. This practice retards automaticity in word recognition because students are not encouraged to look at and process the full string of letters in the word (see McGuinness, 1997). As another example, students are taught to use context cues to guess word meanings. However, guessing word meanings from context represents both a poor way to learn vocabulary and a somewhat unreliable way to achieve good comprehension of a text (Gough and Wren, 1999). Good readers guess much less than poor readers precisely because they are efficient word recognisers and they know so many words.

On a more practical level, we can respond to this dilemma by knowing (a) *how* to teach skills that are essential for the development of reading comprehension, (b) *why* we are teaching certain skills (e.g. fluency and word recognition) and knowledge bases (e.g. strategic awareness) and (c) *when* to provide direct instruction, guide students' efforts, or permit students to work on their own. We can learn how to engage students in meaningful reading-related tasks that directly support

Quote 3.5

There is now a large body of studies indicating that poor readers primarily differ from good readers in context-free word recognition, and not in deficiencies in ability to use context to form predictions. In fact, poor readers often rely *more* on context to try to derive meaning than do good readers, because poor readers lack efficient word recognition.

Juel (1999, p. 202)

Quote 3.6

In short, children who are having trouble identifying the individual words of a text quickly and accurately will also encounter difficulty in comprehending what they read.

Children who rely mostly on visual cues at the expense of phonological information will experience progressive deterioration in the rate of reading development as they grow older.... Despite this evidence...' whole-language educators continue to argue that explicit and systematic instruction in letter-sound correspondence is unnecessary.

Tunmer and Chapman (1999, p. 83)

students' learning by taking advantage of in-service training opportunities, conference workshops, resource books and extended courses. In addition, we can engage in action research. For example, we can systematically examine findings from research (such as those listed in Figures 3.1) in the light of our own classroom practices to determine which aspects of reading are already being addressed in our classes and which might be added to the curriculum to provide more effective reading instruction. We can carry out brief and informative action research projects that focus on specific instructional practices (e.g. word recognition exercises, use of graphic organisers, strategy training, teacher modelling of reading strategies) or new curricular components (e.g. sustained silent reading as a form of **extensive reading**, content-based instruction). In this way, we will be better able to evaluate what is suggested from research and determine which instructional practices work (as examples, see Model Action Research Projects 8.1.1, 8.1.3, 8.1.8 in Section III).

3.2.5   Dilemma 5: Understanding context effects in reading

A fifth general dilemma for L2 reading involves the role of context use in reading instruction and student learning. *L2 research often discusses the importance of learning from context for reading comprehension, yet we do not share a well-defined interpretation of what the term 'context' might mean, or how its multiple meanings might be a source of misunderstanding.* The notion of context use can be understood and discussed in at least the following five ways:

1. It can refer to the more rapid activation of words during word recognition simply because semantically associated words tend to help activate each other automatically.
2. It can refer to an ability to disambiguate information already in working memory as more text is read and processed.
3. It can refer to a reader's anticipation of what a reading will be about as a pre-reading anticipation ability.
4. It can mean predicting where a text will go and how it will be organised, as a more general discourse expectation ability.
5. More commonly in L2 settings, context refers to guessing (and learning) the meanings of new words as they are encountered in a text by association with surrounding text.

The first two interpretations of 'context' characterise well-documented automatic context effects that occur during reading. The third and fourth interpretations are also commonly referenced context effects that are important for reading but, in these cases, the effects are attributable as much if not more to background knowledge as they are to surrounding text. Due to the influence of background knowledge, there is also the possibility that students may activate the wrong background information as contextual support. Teachers need to check student expectations to be sure whether context effects are actually beneficial or not. The final interpretation of context effects, though popular, is not well supported in the research literature. Good readers do not generally use context to guess the meanings of upcoming words as they read. Instead, this is a trait of a weak reader who is not yet able to read fluently (Pressley, 1998; Stanovich, 2000). Moreover, guessing the meanings of words from context, *as a way to learn new vocabulary*, has proven to be a less effective means of vocabulary learning than most other approaches. Nevertheless, using context for guessing word meanings, *as an independent reading strategy*, is useful for trying to understand the text as a

Quote 3.7

It is often incorrectly assumed that predicting upcoming words in sentences is a relatively easy and highly accurate activity. Actually many different empirical studies have indicated that naturalistic text is not that predictable.... Across a variety of subject populations and texts, a reader's probability of predicting the next word in a passage is usually between 0.20 and 0.35.... Indeed ... this figure is highest for function words, and is often quite low for the very words in the passage that carry the most informational content.

Stanovich and Stanovich (1999, p. 16)

whole when no better resource is available and when the purpose is to help the reader continue reading with minimal disruption.

One response to this context dilemma requires that we become better informed about the many roles of context in reading comprehension. This response requires some awareness of the research on the various roles of context to decide how to bring in context as an instructional support. Moreover, we should treat strong claims for guessing-from-context exercises cautiously. We can also engage in action research to find out good ways to help students use context to anticipate information in a text, predict the upcoming discourse organisation in a text, and guess the meaning of unknown key words that are disrupting comprehension when they are reading on their own.

Quote 3.8

One problem with relying heavily on semantic context cues is that many words will be read incorrectly.... Relying heavily on semantic context cues is a weak strategy, the preferred strategy of weak readers only.

Pressley (1998, p. 44)

3.3 Instructional dilemmas for L2 reading

In addition to dilemmas that emerge from theorising and differing conceptualisations of the reading process, there are dilemmas that arise

- A large vocabulary is critical not only for reading but also for all L2 skills, for academic performance and for related background knowledge. Yet the means for developing a large vocabulary are not consistently developed in L2 reading instruction, nor is the issue typically given a high priority in L2 instructional contexts.
- Reading fluency probably requires that a reader know 95 per cent or more of the words encountered in most texts, but this is a difficult criterion to meet in many L2 contexts.
- Discourse knowledge is important for reading but few teachers are prepared to teach students how to make use of discourse information to build comprehension. Moreover, few reading curricula focus on text structure and discourse organisation as consistent components of instruction.
- Reading strategies and strategy instruction are often discussed and presented in textbooks as independent entities. Yet, the goal of reading instruction is not to teach individual reading strategies but rather to develop strategic readers.
- There is little exploration in L2 reading research of the transition from learning-to-read to reading-to-learn, yet this transition is expected to occur in many L2 contexts.
- The integration of language abilities is essential for advanced L2 reading in academic settings, yet it is commonly downplayed in favour of administratively more manageable reading classes and separate writing classes.
- Motivation is now generally viewed as important for learning but we lack a keen understanding of the relationships between motivation, attitudes, interest and attributions and their effects on L2 reading abilities.
- Students learn to read by reading a lot, yet reading a lot is not the emphasis of most reading curricula.

Figure 3.3   Instructional dilemmas for L2 reading

more specifically from the linguistic knowledge bases and processing resources central to reading instruction (see Figure 3.3). Our understanding of these knowledge bases and resources, and how they develop to support reading, is based in good part on findings from L1 reading research. However, we know that the L2 reading situation creates different contexts for learning to read. These differences create dilemmas for instruction that need to be recognised and addressed in some way.

3.3.1   Dilemma 6: Building a large recognition vocabulary

As a first instructional dilemma, we know that *a large vocabulary is critical not only for reading but also for all L2 skills, for academic performance and for related background knowledge. Yet the means for developing a large vocabulary are not consistently developed in L2 reading instruction, nor is the issue typically given a high priority in L2 instructional contexts.* Moreover, we are not sure just how large the recognition vocabulary base needs to be for fluency, though it is likely to represent a major dilemma for developing L2 readers. In L1 contexts, estimates of vocabulary size for students finishing secondary school are most commonly cited at about 40,000 words. Some estimates are much smaller, as little as 17,000 (word families), and other estimates are as high as 100,000 words. Assuming that L1 readers entering higher-education institutions can recognise 40,000 words, how does an L2 reader cope with L2 vocabulary demands if they are going to study at a university in their L2? How can L2 students learn so many words to read fluently in university courses? In K-12 contexts, how can L2 students catch up with L1 students if L1 students are learning 3,000 new words each year?

> ## Quote 3.9
>
> We ... estimate that L2 learners familiar with the 11,123 most frequent base words ... would actually know one or two per cent more than 88.9 per cent of the word tokens of an average written text. Should they also be familiar with most of the proper names occurring in a text, then they might come very close to knowing 95 per cent, a percentage generally held desirable for a reasonable level of text comprehension.
>
> Hazenburg and Hulstijn (1996, p. 150)

Three research responses have been offered to these questions. One response argues that the number of words known by L1 students at the completion of secondary school is not 40,000, but 17,000, from which an important sub-set (e.g. the most frequent 3,000 word families) can be taught. However, the reasoning behind this argument might be overly optimistic. It assumes that word meanings can be easily understood as word families; that is, if a reader knows the basic meaning of a word family, then all derived forms can be understood as well. However, this logic only works up to a point. Take, for example, the word 'state'. As a verb, it could lead to 'stated', or 'states'. But as a plural noun, 'states', we move into different meanings entirely (as in mental states, political states, metaphorical states). Further, can either meaning of the basic form lead easily to an understanding of 'stately woman', or 'stateroom', or 'stateside', or 'statehouse'? Moreover, the words 'status', 'statue', 'stage', 'state', 'station', 'stand', 'statute', and 'stable' all can be traced back to the Latin *stare* (to stand). But are they all from the same word family and, if not, where do we draw the boundaries? Or, we can say that 'runner' comes from 'run', but one meaning of 'walker' is certainly hard to infer from 'walk', (as in, 'his walker broke'), and the same is true for 'tell' and (bank) 'teller'. Moreover, this perspective makes no effort to count idiomatic expressions (e.g. to break a leg), word compounds (e.g. sweatshirt, briefcase), and multiple meanings of words (e.g. 'spring' as in the season between winter and summer, the coil in a mattress, a place where water comes up naturally from the ground, to move quickly).

A second response follows from research that investigated how many words L2 students need in order to minimally comprehend university-level L2 texts. Hazenburg and Hulstijn (1996) argued that about 10,000 word families at minimum were needed. (Once again there is a question of how to understand the usefulness of 'word families'.) Despite concerns about word families, these researchers argued persuasively that L2 students do not need to know as many words as L1 readers do to read advanced L2 texts. However, if their notion of word families is translated into a one to two ratio for actual words, probably a conservative adjustment, L2 students still need at least 20,000 words. So the dilemma may be modified a bit by their research, but vocabulary size is still a serious dilemma.

Quote 3.10

[I]ndividuals with a vocabulary of fewer than ten thousand base words run a serious risk of not attaining the reading comprehension level required for entering university studies.

Hazenburg and Hulstijn (1996, p. 158)

A third response, partially extending the first response, is to recognise that L2 students will not develop a very large recognition vocabulary until they have had thousands of hours of practice reading L2 texts. Unfortunately, we cannot teach students all the words that they need to know in a reasonable amount of time. Instead, we can focus on the 2,000 to 3,000 most common words as an essential foundation for word-recognition automaticity, and then focus on vocabulary that is appropriate to specific topics and fields of study. This third response requires a strong commitment to vocabulary instruction as an important component of reading development, and it is a view that many L2 reading researchers now accept. The dilemma for teachers, then, is how to teach vocabulary consistently and effectively, and how to get students to become collectors of words. Aside from in-service training and resource texts, we can conduct action research to identify which vocabulary teaching techniques lead to productive learning. (As related examples, see Model Action Research Projects 7.1.2, 7.1.3, 7.1.4, 7.1.5, 7.1.6 in Chapter 7.)

3.3.2 Dilemma 7: Promoting fluency in L2 reading

A related instructional dilemma involves reading fluency and automaticity. In L2 contexts, *reading fluency probably requires that a reader know 95 per cent or more of the words encountered in most texts, but most L2 students cannot reach this criterion level.* And these words need to be recognised automatically with minimal conscious effort. Because fluency and automaticity are now seen as essential foundations for reading comprehension, how can they be developed and how can they be incorporated into larger curricular planning?

> **Quote 3.11**
>
> One's performance fluency – that is, the observable speed, accuracy, and fluidity of skill execution which indicate that the skill is fluent – arises from a less easily observed underlying cognitive fluency.... One important aspect of cognitive fluency is the degree to which underlying processes are executed in an automatic, as opposed to a controlled, fashion.
>
> Segalowitz, Segalowitz and Wood (1998, pp. 53–4)

One response to this dilemma is to integrate a range of instructional activities into L2 reading lessons to promote fluency and automaticity. The most common ways to promote fluency through instruction are through **timed-** and **paced-reading** activities, extensive reading (both in and out of class), word recognition exercises of various types, **read alouds** in groups and pairs, and a range of **rereading** activities (common in low-level L1 instruction, but seldom even discussed in L2 reading instruction). Of course, there are many complicating issues involved in using these types of fluency approaches effectively in the reading curriculum, and exploring these issues through action research could be productive for teachers responsible for L2 reading development. (As examples, see Model Action Research Projects 7.1.1, 7.1.6, 7.1.7, 7.1.8, 7.1.9 in Chapter 7.)

> **Quote 3.12**
>
> One possible reason for the [L1] fourth-grade slump may stem from lack of fluency and automaticity (that is, quick and accurate recognition of words and phrases).... Lack of fluency tends to result, ultimately, in children's reading less and avoiding more difficult materials.
>
> Chall and Jacobs (1996, p. 38)

3.3.3   Dilemma 8: Raising awareness of text structure and discourse organisation

As a third instructional dilemma, *few teachers are prepared to teach students how to make use of discourse information to build comprehension, even though it is a widely accepted fact that discourse knowledge is important for reading. Moreover, few reading curricula focus on text structure and discourse organisation as consistent components of instruction.* Yet, L2 readers need to learn to recognise and use text structure signalling devices and discourse organisation as ways to comprehend texts better. Text structure signalling involves the uses of text signals that connect sentences and parts of sentences together. These signals include pronouns, definite articles, repetitions of words and synonyms, words that highlight informational organisation (e.g. first, second, third, however, on the other hand, in contrast), and transition words, phrases, and sentences. (Refer to Figure 8.10 in Chapter 8 for a more extensive list of signal words.) Discourse organisation more broadly refers to larger units of text, how they are organised and how they can be recognised. Good readers are able to recognise problem–solution and cause–effect sequences in texts; they can recognise comparisons and contrasts as well as strong classification systems that are being explained. More generally, good readers recognise the obvious signalling of narrative organisation (such as story structures, see Chapter 4) as well as argumentative for-and-against organisation. Good readers also pick up cues for discourse organisation from the use of basic verbs and nouns. (See Figure 8.8 in Chapter 8 for a more complete listing of discourse patterns.) Signalling information and discourse organisation both regulate the amount of information presented in a text as well as the ways in which this new information is introduced. All of these textual features of discourse contribute to comprehension, particularly with more difficult texts.

Quote 3.13

Interventions that focus on genre structure indicate that instruction that improves readers' awareness of how to identify different genre structures can be effective in improving memory and learning of text content.

Goldman and Rakestraw (2000, p. 325)

Quote 3.14

Some readers intuitively acquire text structure knowledge through continual exposure to different text structures. However, many readers are not so lucky. It is up to the classroom teacher to inform not-so-lucky students about different text structures and how to look for these structures as they read.

Dymock (1999, p. 175)

One way to respond to this dilemma is for teachers to learn to exploit the discourse aspects of a text in ways that will help students understand better. Support can be provided through formal training, regular practice in exploiting texts and action research projects that promote teacher learning by experimenting with new teaching techniques. Such techniques can, for example, (a) encourage students to explore signalling cues in texts by examining features of texts that are prominent and that help guide the reader, (b) involve teachers in analysing texts with students to show how larger units of information are presented and signalled and (c) encourage teachers to use **graphic representations** to highlight the organisation of text information and raise student awareness of the **rhetorical organisation** of the text (see Model Action Research Projects 8.1.6, 8.1.7, 8.1.8, 8.1.9 in Chapter 8 for more details).

3.3.4   Dilemma 9: Developing the strategic reader

A fourth instructional dilemma centres on the role of strategies in reading comprehension, abilities that everyone agrees are important. *Reading strategies and strategy instruction are often discussed and presented in textbooks as independent entities and relatively easy to teach. Yet, the goal of reading instruction is not to teach individual reading strategies but rather to develop strategic readers, a development process that requires intensive instructional efforts over a considerable period of time.* This goal is much more difficult to accomplish than teaching a set of individual strategies. (For more detailed coverage of Learning Strategies, see Cohen and Oxford, forthcoming.)

Quote 3.15

An unfortunate finding of many research studies is that students can learn strategies and apply them effectively, but fail to maintain their use over time or generalize them beyond the instructional setting. Many factors impede strategy transfer, including not understanding that the strategy is appropriate for different settings, not understanding how to modify its use with different content, believing that the strategy is not as useful for performance as other factors (e.g. time available), thinking that the strategy takes too much effort, or not having the opportunity to apply the strategy with new material.

Schunk (2000, p. 211)

Helping students to develop efficient reading strategies that are relevant to varying needs has proven to be extremely challenging for various reasons. First, being a strategic reader requires sets of strategies (see Concept 3.1) that work well in combination to carry out tasks or solve commonly occurring problems. These combinations shift with new task variations, new texts, new topics and new goals. Second, becoming a strategic reader takes a considerable amount of time, and most curricula and teaching materials do not recognise this requirement. Some L1 strategic reading programmes estimate a long extended period of continuous effort and attention to develop strategic reading responses in students (Pressley, 1995, 1998). Third, using strategies effectively does not typically involve conscious decisions on the part of the fluent reader. Strategic readers are able to verbalise consciously the strategies that they use when asked to reflect, but they usually do not think consciously of these strategic choices because they have used them effectively so often. In effect, strategic readers automatise common, or default, strategic responses to typical situations. They focus more conscious attention when common strategic responses prove to be ineffective.

As an example, readers often think of summarising as a strategy, one that is useful for learning from academic texts. But a less conscious

Concept 3.1   **Common strategies used by skilled readers**

Specifying a purpose for reading

Planning what to do/what steps to take

Previewing the text

Predicting the contents of the text or section of text

Checking predictions

Posing questions about the text

Finding answers to posed questions

Connecting text to background knowledge

Summarising information

Making inferences

Connecting one part of the text to another

Paying attention to text structure

Rereading

Guessing the meaning of a new word from context

Using discourse markers to see relationships

Checking comprehension

Identifying difficulties

Taking steps to repair faulty comprehension

Critiquing the author

Critiquing the text

Judging how well objectives were met

Reflecting on what has been learned from the text

Quote 3.16

The teachers were aware that students did not learn strategies quickly: facile use of strategies across a wide range of tasks and materials occurred only after extensive practice, which included struggling to adapt strategies to a wide range of academic problems.

Pressley (1998, p. 211)

application of this strategy likely occurs every time a reader picks up a novel at night to read for pleasure. We probably ask ourselves, 'Now, where am I? What was going on in the story when I stopped reading last night?' But we do not sit and consciously ponder these questions; we just seem to open the book and start reading. Sometimes we look back a paragraph or two, close to where we had left off, as a way to recharge our memories, but we do not consciously think, 'Tonight, I'm going to reread or skim the last page from last night to get myself on track.' Instead, what likely happens is that we open the book and, in the process, enough gets activated that we can move ahead. If, by the time we start to look at the page, the story line has not activated itself from memory, we just skim back a page without thinking about it consciously because this has been an effective default strategy thousands of times. Yet, in a basic way, these start-up processes while reading for pleasure are another way to engage in summarising. Many strategies become routine responses when the task is common and the text is not too difficult.

The dilemma for teaching is that strategic reading abilities require a lot of practice over an extended period of time and a lot of exposure to reading. There are no shortcuts. Initially, readers need to work out, at a more conscious problem-solving level, strategy responses that seem to work in a given setting. Often these strategies are introduced one by one, with the help of a teacher or someone else. After several encounters with similar problems, the effective response (i.e. strategy) becomes routine, yet flexible. Over time, readers build up a repertoire of effective strategic responses to sets of similar problems that might arise (Brown, Pressley, Van Meter and Schuder, 1996). And even good readers, when they encounter a totally new type of problem (like the first time they read a computer manual), will slow down to develop new strategic responses. The L2 reading teacher has at least three options to address this dilemma:

- One response is to assist students to transfer L1 reading strategies in situations in which (a) students have sufficient L2 proficiency, (b) the relevant strategies can be discussed and reflected upon or (c) the reading tasks have been encountered in L1 settings. (It should be noted here that there are likely to be fewer useful L1 strategies to transfer when the L2 task is one that has not already been encountered in L1 contexts.)

- As a second response, we, as teachers, can integrate strategy use and discussions about strategy use into every lesson; strategy instruction, then, basically becomes an ongoing discussion about understanding texts, making use of text information for comprehension and using strategies to enhance reading comprehension. This approach involves introducing strategy uses, modelling them overtly through verbalising, raising student awareness of different strategies, encouraging students to use strategies, guiding students in reflecting on strategy uses, discussing difficult text meaning through the use of strategies and providing students with opportunities for reading a lot and engaging in tasks that require strategic reading.

- As a third response, we can carry out action research projects to improve our effectiveness as teachers of strategic reading. These projects can involve learning about strategy uses in reading, understanding metacognitive awareness in reading and exploring a range of instructional practices that seem to be effective (see Model Action Research Projects 8.1.1, 8.1.2, 8.1.3, 8.1.4, 8.1.5 in Chapter 8 for more detailed examples).

Quote 3.17

We know that in order to develop active learners who have a repertoire of strategies, a substantial amount of time must be committed to instruction. Such instruction should not only be intensive, but should also be of significant duration.

Nist and Simpson (2000, p. 654)

3.3.5 Dilemma 10: Promoting reading to learn

As a related dilemma, *there is little exploration in L2 reading research of the transition from learning-to-read to academic reading-to-learn, yet this transition is expected to occur in many L2 contexts.* Actually, the transition to reading-to-learn is a strategic response to texts and tasks in academic settings where students are asked to read primarily informational texts with large amounts of new information that they are expected to understand and use. Too often, L2 students are asked to read texts that may be very difficult, and either the texts are too short to represent the advanced reading that is expected in more academic settings or the students are not held accountable for demonstrating that they have learned the information as expected in academic settings. In other contexts, students are asked to read material that is much easier than the

---

Instructional practices that can help students' transition from learning-to-read to reading-to-learn

- Practising effective summarising strategies
- Using graphic representations for organising text information
- Identifying key vocabulary and learning these words
- Combining information from multiple sources
- Recognising types of evidence in texts
- Recognising levels of informational importance signalled in texts

---

Figure 3.4   **Sample instructional practices that can help students' transition from learning-to-read to reading-to-learn**

texts that they will encounter in later academic classes. In either case, the transition from learning-to-read to reading-to-learn is often not addressed explicitly in L2 reading classrooms.

There are three possible responses to this dilemma. A first response is that students not be asked to engage heavily in academic work with L2 texts until they are capable of performing reading-to-learn tasks that reflect appropriate academic demands. The goal is not that academic literacy activities should be put off, but rather that teachers address students' reading-to-learn needs gradually as part of a larger reading-to-learn curriculum. This recommendation, one that is too often ignored in L2 programmes, would work best as part of school-wide curriculum planning. As a second response, we can work with longer and more difficult informational texts and teach students the strategies and skills to cope with the learning demands and academic learning tasks associated with these texts. These tasks could then be incorporated into a reading curriculum and practised on a regular basis. Students could be taught how to (a) analyse the expectations of anticipated tasks with advanced-planning strategies, (b) organise and relate information from the texts in coherent ways and (c) use these informational resources to complete meaningful tasks. Finally, we can carry out action research projects, exploring, for example, the types of texts that L2 students will read in later courses, the match or mismatch between texts read in class and texts used for assessment purposes, the types of tasks assigned in higher-level courses, the experiences of students who are now in more advanced courses or the effectiveness of one or two instructional practices that should help students with reading-to-learn (see Figure 3.4). (See Model Action Research Project 9.1.5 in Chapter 9 as a detailed example of one related project.)

3.3.6   Dilemma 11: Integrating language skills for reading development

A sixth instructional dilemma applies at both classroom and curricular levels. *Much reading instruction, and most L2 instruction, involves lessons in specific (and separate) language skills (e.g. reading, writing, speaking, listening, grammar, pronunciation), or simply the use of generic textbooks that minimise the integration of language abilities. But the integration of language abilities is essential for advanced L2 reading in academic settings* (though perhaps less critical for a number of foreign language settings). In many advanced academic settings, reading needs to be integrated with other language skills as part of the expectations of reading-to-learn, reading-to-integrate and reading-to-evaluate. The commitment to integrate other language skills with reading is not widely made at more advanced levels of L2 instruction. In particular, we should ask why so many advanced L2 curricula still separate reading and writing instruction when there is now strong evidence that an integrated reading–writing instructional approach has a number of learning benefits (Tsang, 1996).

> **Quote 3.18**
>
> A good case can be made for the fruitful interaction between reading and writing in the language classroom, both activities being seen as potentially complementary to each other. Zamel (1992) argues that reading and writing instruction benefit each other in an integrated approach and argues for 'writing one's way into reading'. Silberstein (1994: 70–1) argues that by integrating instruction students come to understand the way in which both readers and writers compose text.
>
> Urquhart and Weir (1998, p. 211)

The integration of language skills, and particularly reading and writing, forms natural connections in academic contexts. Reading is commonly combined with writing to summarise information, take notes, integrate information in reports, prepare for tests, write short responses to reading assignments, evaluate evidence and write critiques, and write longer research papers. Reading and listening combine naturally as well when students listen to lectures related to something previously read or to be read, and take notes on the topic. Reading and listening also combine in many group activities and projects that often lead to written output or an oral presentation. Such tasks are fairly common in academic settings and they tie in with the goals of reading-to-learn, reading-to-integrate and reading-to-critique, as discussed in Chapter 1. Advanced reading instruction needs to provide students with practice in these tasks (as do, in principle, advanced writing and listening classes). (See Rost, 2001.)

Quote 3.19

Coherent instruction links reading, writing, and rich knowledge domains. In coherent instruction, student engagement is increased . . . conceptual learning from text is facilitated . . . reading achievement is fostered . . . and reading within content areas can be sustained.

Guthrie and Wigfield (2000, p. 416)

There are two possible ways to respond to this dilemma. First, we can initiate a version of content-based instruction that is responsive to the teaching of integrated language skills, with an emphasis on academic reading abilities. Such a syllabus or curriculum would organise reading and writing tasks around texts and visual resources on a coherent theme. Students would explore the theme, and more specific topics within the theme, while practising the many tasks that integrate skills and require advanced reading abilities (see Guthrie *et al.*, 1998; Guthrie, Wigfield, Metsala and Cox, 1999). A second response to the need for integrated-skills practice involves action research on the place of integrated-skills tasks in our classes. More specifically, we can focus on the integrated-skills tasks that would be most appropriate for our students (assessed in terms of text and task difficulty, student needs, student motivation, teacher resources and so forth) as well as the instruction needed to support student learning from these tasks.

Quote 3.20

Nothing motivates like successful accomplishment of interesting and appropriately challenging tasks.

Pressley (1998, p. 257)

3.3.7 Dilemma 12: Building motivation

The next instructional dilemma centres on motivation. We lack a keen understanding of the relationships between motivation, attitudes, interest and attributions (expectations for success or failure based on past experiences) and their effects on L2 reading abilities. There is little research concerning the role of affective factors on the development of L2 reading abilities (cf. Day and Bamford, 1998). On a more practical level, motivating students to read in their L2 (or even in their L1) is a serious dilemma. *Much of the battle in getting students to develop reading skills rests with their attitudes toward reading. These days, however, most students read little in either the L1 or the L2, and they do not enjoy reading. The lack of motivation is also reflected in L2 curricula where reading itself is not given a high priority in terms of class time.* Both teachers and students come to feel that there are 'more important things to do'. Students too often are uninterested (as are some teachers), and curriculum developers and administrators have unrealistic expectations about how quickly fluent reading abilities can be developed (without a lot of practice in reading) (see also Dörnyei, 2001b).

Teachers who understand the importance of motivation, interest, and self-esteem – as important factors in reading development – can work with students to determine what motivates them and how to cultivate better attitudes toward reading. These goals can be carried out through surveys of student interest, evaluations of students' past experiences with reading (in both L1 and L2 contexts), interviews with students about the importance of reading and discussions about what interests and motivates teachers and other successful L2 readers. Action research projects provide ideal ways to explore these issues with students (see Model Action Research Projects 9.1.7, 9.1.8, 9.1.9 in Chapter 9 for more detailed examples).

Quote 3.21

Students with high intrinsic motivation, a learning goal orientation, and high self-efficacy are relatively active readers and high achievers.... Why should this be? It is likely that motivational processes are the foundation for coordinating cognitive goals and strategies in reading.... [B]ecoming an excellent, active reader involves attunement of motivational processes with cognitive and language processes in reading.

Guthrie and Wigfield (2000, p. 408)

3.3.8 Dilemma 13: Encouraging students to read extensively

The final instructional dilemma involves extensive reading (i.e. exposure to print). As we have stated on a number of occasions, *students learn to read by reading a lot, yet reading a lot is not the emphasis of most reading curricula*. Typically students are assigned to read at home and not in classes or school libraries. Teachers (and administrators) commonly feel that if students are reading silently in classes, then they (the teachers) are not doing their jobs (teaching). But the primary way to develop fluent reading comprehension, based on a wide range of research, is extended practice in reading. Although extensive reading, by itself, is not sufficient for the development of fluent reading comprehension abilities, such abilities cannot be developed without extensive reading (Day and Bamford, 1998; Gough and Wren, 1999).

There are a number of responses to this dilemma. Certainly reading at home needs to be encouraged, and interesting texts need to be available for that purpose. In classroom contexts, there should be free reading time, sustained silent reading opportunities, reading lab periods, library reading and time for reading extended texts together (see Stoller, 1994a). To build extensive reading in class, we need to have good text resources, enough time and school and curricular support. Action research projects related to this issue could focus on (a) discovering different ways to bring more silent reading into the curriculum, (b) developing effective ways to implement extended reading practice, (c) finding text materials that students will want to read in class (and at home), (d) measuring outcomes of extended reading activities over time and (e) establishing ways for students to recommend interesting materials to their classmates (refer to Action Research Project 6.1.2, in Chapter 6, for a more extended example).

Quote 3.22

In summary, there is a rather strong case, a case based on hard facts, that increasing the amount of children's playful, stimulating experience with good books leads to accelerated growth in reading competence. This conclusion appears to be a universal of written language development, true not only of English-speaking children learning to read English, but also true of children from various language groups learning their home language, a second language from their own country, or a foreign language.

Anderson (1996, p. 74)

> ### Quote 3.23
>
> The frequent admonition for children to 'Read, read, read' makes sense in that extensive reading promotes fluency, vocabulary, and background knowledge.... Immersion in reading alone, however, is unlikely to lead to maximally skilled comprehension.
>
> Pressley (2000, p. 556)

3.4 Conclusion

Additional dilemmas could easily be noted, such as those related to the importance of varying instruction for students with increasing proficiency levels, the problems unique to adult literacy instruction and the benefits of developing appropriate grammar knowledge for reading. Despite these dilemmas, as well as numerous others, it is remarkable that so many L2 students become fluent readers. This simple fact raises yet another dilemma: *How do so many L2 students become successful readers in spite of all the dilemmas noted in this chapter?* One possible answer is that many students become successful L2 readers because they adapt the instruction that they receive to their needs, become deeply involved with classroom topics and issues, and then are motivated to read further. These students very often perceive the importance of reading as well as the 'escape' provided by reading. So they develop personal approaches to reading development, combining useful instruction, personal persistence for learning and extended practice. In a sense, they develop their own content-based language instruction.

We would like to close the chapter with a final thought. We are encouraged by the fact that so many L2 students learn to read well. Despite the dilemmas that teachers encounter, the obstacles that learners face and the many unanswered questions that emerge from research findings, many L2 learners become proficient readers. Thus, the main message emerging from this chapter is not to say that L2 reading cannot be taught or cannot be learned; rather, it is to explore how learning and teaching can be carried out more effectively. This exploration can be accomplished best through a careful and critical understanding of the many dilemmas facing students and teachers, the consideration of reading-related concepts emerging from these dilemmas that have implications for instruction (see Figure 3.5) and an exploration of ways to make instruction work better for more students.

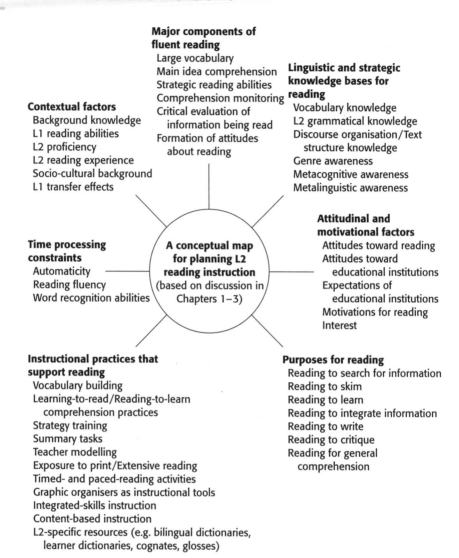

Major components of fluent reading
Large vocabulary
Main idea comprehension
Strategic reading abilities
Comprehension monitoring
Critical evaluation of
    information being read
Formation of attitudes
    about reading

Linguistic and strategic knowledge bases for reading
Vocabulary knowledge
L2 grammatical knowledge
Discourse organisation/Text
    structure knowledge
Genre awareness
Metacognitive awareness
Metalinguistic awareness

Contextual factors
Background knowledge
L1 reading abilities
L2 proficiency
L2 reading experience
Socio-cultural background
L1 transfer effects

Time processing constraints
Automaticity
Reading fluency
Word recognition abilities

A conceptual map for planning L2 reading instruction
(based on discussion in Chapters 1–3)

Attitudinal and motivational factors
Attitudes toward reading
Attitudes toward
    educational institutions
Expectations of
    educational institutions
Motivations for reading
Interest

Instructional practices that support reading
Vocabulary building
Learning-to-read/Reading-to-learn
    comprehension practices
Strategy training
Summary tasks
Teacher modelling
Exposure to print/Extensive reading
Timed- and paced-reading activities
Graphic organisers as instructional tools
Integrated-skills instruction
Content-based instruction
L2-specific resources (e.g. bilingual dictionaries,
    learner dictionaries, cognates, glosses)

Purposes for reading
Reading to search for information
Reading to skim
Reading to learn
Reading to integrate information
Reading to write
Reading to critique
Reading for general
    comprehension

Figure 3.5 **A conceptual map for planning L2 reading instruction (based on discussion in Chapters 1–3)**

Further reading

For additional readings on a number of key issues in this chapter, refer to the following: On the *role of exposure and practice in reading*, see Anderson (1996). On the *role* of *complex skill development*, see Anderson (1995), Proctor and Dutta (1995), Wagner and Stanovich (1996). On *why the notion of reading as a natural process is not a good way to think about how reading is learned,* see Pressley (1998), Stanovich and Stanovich (1999), Tunmer and Chapman (1999). On *why guessing word meanings from context is not an efficient way to learn vocabulary,* see Laufer (1997), Parry (1991). On the *limitations of context effects on reading performance,* see Gough and Wren (1999), Juel (1999), Stanovich (1986), Stanovich and Stanovich (1999). On *dilemmas related to reading,* see Grabe (1995, 1996, 1999, 2000). On the *integration of skills in content-based curricula,* see Carson (1993, 2000), Carson and Leki (1993), Nelson and Burns (2000), Stoller (1997, 1999), Stoller and Grabe (1997). On *sound instructional practices for the reading classroom,* see Grabe and Stoller (2001). On the *benefits of explicit instruction over implicit instruction,* see McGuinness (1997), Snow, Burns and Griffin (1998), Tunmer and Chapman (1999).

II Exploring research in reading

Chapter 4

Key studies in L1 reading

This chapter focuses on ten L1 reading research studies that have made major contributions to our understanding of reading and learning. The studies are explained in easy-to-understand terms to show how researchers get started, how research is conducted and how results are interpreted. A review of these studies will help practitioners understand important aspects of reading, including the following:

- the relationship between exposure to print and reading abilities
- the influence of incidental exposure to words on vocabulary development and reading
- the impact of fluency training and strategy instruction on reading
- the role of student attitudes, interests and motivation on reading development

The first three chapters of this book outline a theory of fluent reading, the differences between first language (L1) and second language (L2) reading, and the dilemmas created for L2 reading instruction by over-generalisations from L1 reading research as well as noted differences between L1 and L2 contexts. These introductory chapters highlight the fact that we know a lot about reading in general, but much less about L2 reading and how best to teach L2 reading more specifically. Chapters 1–3 also illustrate the benefits that we, as reading teachers, gain from (a) understanding reading research and theory building, (b) developing abilities to interpret and evaluate research studies and corresponding implications for instruction and (c) carrying out small-scale action research projects in our own local contexts. What we can learn from each of these sets of activities has the potential to help us improve reading instruction. In this chapter and the next, we consider how research can be understood, how it can be interpreted better, and how good research studies on reading have been carried out. Chapter 4 will focus on understanding key L1 reading research studies. Particularly important in this chapter is the link between specific research efforts and the types of implications from research that lead to theory building and recommendations for instruction (from Chapters 1–3).

4.1   Research studies as stories: An extended example

Every research study, in essence, represents a story. We read stories almost every day and do not see them as difficult; in fact, we often think of reading stories as pleasurable. So why don't most of us think of reading a research study as pleasurable? Certainly, the story structure of a research article is different from what we are used to in more standard story telling. A lack of familiarity with the many conventions of a research 'story' sometimes makes it hard for us to follow the story line. Nevertheless, research studies are stories and they contain features of story structures. Only the format and the formal reporting features are truly different, reflecting a different target audience that has a set of well-defined expectations. In this section, we translate the story experience of an extended research study, one that has had a major influence on L1 reading research for the past 10 years.

This story – which could be thought of as a mystery that unfolds over a period of eight years – begins with two researchers (Byrne and Fielding-Barnsley) who wanted to understand what makes children into better readers at early stages of reading development. They wanted to find out if practice in relating letters and sounds (**letter–sound knowledge**), along with practice in identifying phonemic sounds in words (**phonemic awareness**), would make children better readers or not. One conflict that they encountered early on was that another teaching method was being promoted by school officials as the only way to teach reading, even though there was little evidence of better reading development among children with this method. The researchers wanted to see if their ideas about beginning reading would give students an advantage.

The researchers anticipated a number of challenges early on. First, they recognised the need to measure the long-term effects of their ideas for teaching and learning. Fundamentally, they wanted to know if their ideas would make a difference in student performance 3 or 4 years after the study. Second, they wanted to make strong arguments from their work, so their work had to be controlled and balanced. They needed to be sure that their results, if in their favour, would not be due to luck, but rather would be because their ideas actually made a difference in student performance. A third problem that they planned for was related to the fact that students come and students go. Consequently, they needed to look at enough students to be able to make general statements even when some students moved away or could not be located years later.

The researchers realised that they needed three tools to accomplish their mission: (a) an instrument for checking students' abilities before training, (b) procedures for the training itself and (c) procedures to determine what changes in student performance had occurred after the training. Because the researchers knew that their study would provoke criticisms, they wanted to be careful. They took three precautionary steps. First, they looked for measurement instruments that were appropriate for their study and that other researchers had used successfully. Then they adapted some of these instruments to fit their own research setting and gather the most appropriate information to answer their questions. Finally, they had to make sure that all students in the study were receiving similar instruction. After taking this final precautionary step, they could say that differences between groups of students were more likely to be because of specific training differences (rather than differences in regular instruction).

In a first study (1989), Byrne and Fielding-Barnsley wanted to demonstrate the importance of their ideas. They worked with 13 kindergarten children to see if the children could be trained to match consistent symbols (i.e. colour-coded geometric symbols like a blue circle and red triangle) with words used in compound forms (i.e. 'little boy', represented by a red triangle followed by a green square; 'big boy', represented by a blue circle followed by a green square). When confronted by new compound forms like 'little fish' (red triangle followed by yellow diamond), they were to associate the red triangle with 'little'. Ten of the 13 children could do this well. These 10 children, however, could not transfer this ability (to match words with symbols) to the ability to relate sounds in words to consistent symbols (with symbols representing sounds, rather than words, so that words like 'fat' and 'bat' were made up of three symbols each, the first ones different, the last two identical). Children could not detect and identify repeated sounds in new spoken words. The conclusion reached by the researchers was that identifying individual sounds in words will not be easily learned by automatic transfer from more general symbolic learning skills. This difficulty showed a likely need for explicit instruction in beginning literacy, and particularly in letter–sound correspondences.

After demonstrating the importance of their ideas, the researchers needed to develop an appropriate direct-instruction programme. They trained children through a series of seven stages to accomplish the following three goals: identify sounds in words, divide words into separate sounds and explicitly learn the sound–symbol correspondence. After testing students at the completion of each stage, they found that students could not develop the **alphabetic principle** (transferring letter–sound relations to new words) until they had been directly taught *both* symbol–letter correspondences and sound-identification skills. The researchers found that direct training in both abilities helped young children learn the alphabetic principle.

With this set of results in hand, Byrne and Fielding-Barnsley (1991) carried out their major **training study** that they designed for teaching sound-identification skills and letter–sound correspondences. They recruited 126 children (average age 4 years, 7 months) from four pre-schools and divided them into two groups: 64 in the experimental **treatment group** and 62 in the **control group** that followed the standard curriculum. At the beginning, they tested the two groups to be sure that they were equal in verbal abilities, **concepts about print**, rhyme recognition and **phoneme-identification abilities**. The experimental children then received a total of 6 hours of explicit training in phoneme identification, sound segmentation and letter–sound correspondences over a period of 12 weeks (30 minutes per week). At the end of the training, the experimental children could identify phonemes in words significantly better than control children; these results were not really surprising because the children in the experimental group had been practising the identification of phonemes as part of their training.

As a second phase to their study, all children were reorganised into three new groups: those who were successful in (a) phoneme identification, (b) letter–sound knowledge or (c) both abilities. (Eighty per cent of the children who were successful in both abilities came from the original experimental group, whereas 20 per cent were from the control group.) The researchers found that 75 per cent of the children who were good in both abilities could 'read' a set of new simple words

> ### Quote 4.1
>
> The purpose of this study was to evaluate a new program.... The program emphasizes recognition of phoneme identity across words.... Comparison of pretraining and posttraining measures of phonemic awareness showed greater gains by the experimental group in comparison with controls. The increased levels of phonemic awareness occurred with untrained as well as trained sounds.
>
> Byrne and Fielding-Barnsley (1991, p. 451)
>
> The data clearly show that recognition of phoneme identity can be trained with the program used in this study.... This result indicates that phoneme identity is a stable construct once it is achieved.
>
> Byrne and Fielding-Barnsley (1991, p. 454)

when, seeing a written word, they were asked to choose between two spoken words. Only 4 per cent of the other children (those without *both* abilities) could 'read' the words. Once again, the researchers demonstrated that young children need both phoneme-identification abilities and knowledge of letter–sound correspondences and that they benefit from direct instruction in these abilities.

The researchers did not stop with this study because they wanted to build a more persuasive argument. Anyone looking at their results could have said that the experimental children did better simply because they had been trained on the very skills that were measured. What the researchers really wanted to determine was if the 6 hours of direct instruction would have any long-lasting benefits for the experimental children. So Byrne and Fielding-Barnsley (1993) did a one-year follow-up study of the children to find out. Even though the children were now spread across a number of schools, they found 63 of the experimental children and 56 of the control children (for a total of 119 children, average age 6 years, 0 months) and gave them a set of follow-up tests. They tested for six basic skills: (a) phoneme-identification skills (e.g. children match two pictures of objects, from among four, that begin with the same sound), (b) phoneme-elision skills (e.g. children look at a word such as 'small' and identify a new word without the first sound), (c) alphabet knowledge, (d) word identification, (e) **pseudoword identification** (e.g. children hear a made-up word such as 'sut' and point out the right written form after looking at 'sut' or 'ig') and (f) spelling of simple pseudowords. The pseudoword tests were important to the study because they prevented children from using prior knowledge of real words; the pseudowords led to a purer measure of applying the alphabetic principle. The experimental children, one year after the initial training, were significantly better in phoneme-identification skills, phoneme elision skills, and pseudoword recognition (requiring strong knowledge of the alphabetic principle). (Remember that these groups were matched in verbal-ability tests and phonemic-awareness skills at the outset of the first study in 1991.) The researchers noted, however, that the differences were no longer as great as a year earlier, a natural expectation from another year and a half of school exposure.

Quote 4.2

In the original study, preschoolers were trained with the program for 12 weeks and gained in phonemic awareness and knowledge of the alphabetic principle as compared with a control group. The children were retested at the end of kindergarten on phonemic awareness, word identification, decoding, and spelling. Children who enter school with advanced levels of phonemic awareness scored significantly higher on each of the measures.

Byrne and Fielding-Barnsley (1993, p. 104)

As a second part of their 1993 study, they again regrouped the children into those who had demonstrated successful phoneme-identification skills at the end of the earlier pre-school study (across both experimental [80 per cent] and control [20 per cent] groups) and those who had not. They found that the successful group was significantly better on all follow-up study measures (phoneme identification, phoneme elision, spelling, word identification, pseudoword identification). So although the modest original instructional **treatment** still showed a benefit, the principle that children need early phoneme-identification skills was a powerful predictor of early literacy skills measured one year later.

The researchers, still not entirely satisfied, asked themselves another question: Will these differences continue into later years? So in 1995, Byrne and Fielding-Barnsley published another study based on 2- and 3-year follow-ups of the initial pre-school training groups. At the end of Grade 1 (Australian system), they found 64 of the experimental children and 54 of the control children (for a total of 118 children, average

> **Quote 4.3**
>
> Children in our samples who entered elementary school understanding that words can share individual sounds performed at higher levels in reading real words and pseudowords and in spelling than children who did not understand this concept.
>
> Byrne and Fielding-Barnsley (1993, p. 109)

age 7 years, 2 months). They tested these children once again with some similar tests and some new tests to reflect emerging reading abilities. After more than 2 years since the original 6-hour training programme, the experimental children were still scoring significantly higher than control children on pseudoword reading abilities (but no longer significantly better on real word reading abilities). Additional testing was conducted at the end of Grade 2 with 62 experimental children and 53 control children (for a total of 115 children, average age 8 years, 2 months). By this time, some of the earlier tests no longer measured differences, and new tests were used for measuring grade-appropriate abilities in speed of processing, word recognition, pseudoword recognition, listening comprehension, reading comprehension and exposure to print. Experimental children still scored higher in word recognition, pseudoword recognition, listening comprehension, and reading comprehension, but only pseudoword recognition remained significantly better.

> **Quote 4.4**
>
> This article reports a follow-up study of children in grades 1 and 2 who had been instructed in phonemic awareness in preschool. Compared to a control condition, the trained children were superior in nonword reading 2 and 3 years later and in reading comprehension at 3 years.
>
> Byrne and Fielding-Barnsley (1995, p. 488)

As a final step in their long and persistent search, the researchers again regrouped the children based on their success in phoneme identification while in pre-school (rather than on whether they received the 6 hours of training in pre-school). The students who were initially successful in phoneme identification remained significantly better in all word recognition and pseudoword recognition measures more than 3 years later. (They also had higher scores in listening comprehension and reading comprehension, but differences were not all significant.) Byrne and Fielding-Barnsley concluded from this work that children benefit from phoneme-identification skills (as well as knowledge of letter–sound correspondences) with regard to reading abilities. Moreover, they showed that a six-hour instructional programme taught in pre-school has a lasting benefit on abilities needed for fluent reading.

Quote 4.5

The persistent effects of the preschool training on decoding should be considered in context. [R]ecall that training was conducted more than three years prior to the most recent testing round, and then only for 6 hours in total.... Thus, it might be expected that any advantage accruing from the preschool exposure to an element of the alphabetic principle, phonemic structure, would wash out in several years in a school system that uses code-based teaching. Apparently it does not.

Byrne and Fielding-Barnsley (1995, p. 497)

This long story is a significant one. At a time when so many people are debating the strengths of holistic and natural approaches to reading versus direct instruction in skills that support reading, the long-term efforts of Byrne and Fielding-Barnsley add strong evidence that certain types of direct instruction can benefit children who are learning to read. As one might imagine, the original story – in its various segments – was reported in a very different manner – in a condensed scientific way, as expected by other professional researchers. Together, the various studies tell a very interesting story that lasted more than 7 years in all. The researchers' story started with an idea. Then they posed a question; they developed materials; they tested students before teaching them (to have fair groupings and establish baselines); they taught the children; and then they tested the children to see if the instruction added anything to the children's abilities. One, two and three years later, they found the children and tested them again to see if their research ideas held up over time. This sequence can certainly be seen as a 'quest' narrative or possibly an epic narrative.

4.2 Nine key research studies

Most research studies share similarities with the Byrne and Fielding-Barnsley studies. At the core, there is a simple and straightforward format for telling these stories: a real concern; a good question; a way to collect information – often by means of teaching or testing with materials that are created or used from other studies; and means for reviewing and then interpreting results. What is not plainly visible in this simple sequence is the human side of the story. In the story just told, the researchers had to find schools, teachers and children to work with; they made sure that all materials would work well; they talked to teachers, parents, administrators and the children themselves to make sure that the testing would be appropriate; and they tried to anticipate the problems that they would encounter. Throughout the entire process, there were always concerns to be fair, reliable and accurate, and there was the need to come up with unique and clever ways to observe and measure student abilities.

The 'moral of the story' is that research is an understandable process, even if certain details related to controls and statistics can seem overwhelming at times. In this section of the chapter, we briefly highlight nine interesting research stories (see Figure 4.1). They were chosen for their contributions to the L1 reading field and because they

1. address central questions about reading in L1 contexts
2. focus on distinct issues in reading
3. reveal different ways to do research about reading

In every case, the researchers have made major contributions to our understanding of reading and learning. (The particular research discussed typically represents only one aspect of their contributions to the field.) Each study contributes real 'food for thought' to practitioners interested in improving reading instruction in their classrooms.

4.2.1 A study on amount of exposure to print

For the past decade, Keith Stanovich and his colleagues have been exploring the impact that exposure to print (i.e. amount of reading) has on reading abilities and on the types of knowledge that are useful for reading. One of the primary goals of their research has been to demonstrate ways in which reading a lot influences individual cognitive abilities. They have consistently asked two basic questions: What impact

Topics of select L1 research studies	Researchers
1. Relationship between exposure to print and reading abilities	Cipielewski and Stanovich (1992)
2. Role of incidental exposure to words in vocabulary development and reading	Nagy, Herman and Anderson (1985)
3. Impact of fluency training on reading	Stahl, Heubach and Cramond (1997)
4. Influence of discourse organisation on reading comprehension	Beck, McKeown, Sinatra and Loxterman (1991)
5. Impact of strategy instruction on students' reading comprehension	Brown, Pressley, Van Meter and Schuder (1996)
6. Process of reading-to-learn	Perfetti, Britt and Georgi (1995)
7. Reading development in relation to different instructional techniques	Tan and Nicholson (1997)
8. Role of student attitudes, interests and motivation on reading development	Guthrie, Wigfield, Metsala and Cox (1999)
9. Development of a theory of reading	Carver (1997)

Figure 4.1 **Topics of L1 research studies summarised in the next sections of chapter**

will amount of reading have on reading abilities? What impact will amount of reading have on individual cognitive differences related to literacy?

Most studies that explore how much people read have used **self-reporting surveys** in which, for example, students themselves say how much they read each week. Instead, Stanovich has developed a way to carry out these studies by creating checklists of common authors, magazine titles, book titles and so forth, and then matching what people check off as known with other measures taken of these people's abilities. In one important study, for example, Cipielewski and Stanovich (1992) gave 82 fifth-grade students a **title-recognition checklist test**. These students had also taken the Stanford reading test that year and all had taken the Iowa Test of Basic Reading Skills in the third grade. The researchers showed that amount of exposure to print significantly predicted reading ability differences on the fifth-grade reading test even after removing the influence of their reading ability scores from the third grade.

Over the past decade, in more than a dozen empirical studies, Stanovich and his colleagues have shown that there are strong relations between amount of exposure to print (determined by checklist scores) and cultural knowledge, general knowledge, vocabulary knowledge,

> ### Quote 4.6
>
> [I]ndividual differences in third- and fifth-grade growth in reading were significantly related to indicators of print exposure.... [T]he extent to which individuals engage in literacy activities is a significant contributor to developing reading ability....
>
> [T]he print exposure measure was able to account for variance in fifth-grade reading ability after third-grade reading ability had been partialled out.... These results strengthen the case for advocating a more prominent role for reading activity in models of reading development.
>
> Cipielewski and Stanovich (1992, pp. 74, 85)

reading skills, spelling, orthographic knowledge of words and verbal fluency. (Amount of reading is only minimally related to phonological processing in word recognition, which is why reading a lot will not solve all needs, even with beginning readers.) These studies have been replicated in multiple settings, and have been used with students from the first grade to university and adult-education levels (Cunningham and Stanovich, 1998; Stanovich, 2000; Stanovich *et al.*, 1996; Wagner and Stanovich, 1996).

What makes Stanovich's approach particularly interesting is his ability to show that the amount one reads has a strong relationship with reading ability even after some other likely influences on reading abilities have been eliminated (using **regression methodology**). His research does not predict that amount of reading must be a *cause* of later reading abilities, because the cause and the effect could go in the reverse direction (i.e. good reading abilities can lead to a greater amount of reading, though most likely the two support each other; cf. Cunningham and Stanovich, 1998; Stanovich, 2000). What he has done is examine a major issue in reading with innovative checklist measures and with minimal self-reporting biases. He has been able to quantify the strength of the relationship between reading exposure and reading abilities with a fairly simple process. He has also been able to demonstrate the amount of influence that literacy practices (i.e. amount of reading) have on a whole range of language-based cognitive processing. Stanovich's story is a sound one: His question is good, he has taken some measures and compared them to other measures, he has controlled the possible interpretations of his findings and he has made strong arguments for the importance of reading a lot. This decade-long enterprise makes for a very good 'quest' story.

4.2.2   A study on reading and vocabulary learning

For the past fifteen years, William Nagy and his colleagues have been exploring how students learn so many words in their school-age years when very few of these words are actually taught to them. At the heart of this issue is the importance of vocabulary knowledge for reading and how vocabulary is learned in support of reading (issues also raised in Chapters 2 and 3 of this book). Nagy, Herman and Anderson (1985) and Nagy, Anderson, and Herman (1987) have argued that students who read a lot will be exposed to many new words. Although students do not learn most of these new words while reading to understand the texts, they learn quite a few of them through **incidental learning**. So, the question that Nagy and his colleagues asked is straightforward: How many words will be learned through incidental exposure to new words while reading? It is important to note that incidental learning is not a claim about subconscious learning – rather, it means that the goal of the reading task is not to learn the words in the text, but to understand the text. Students, however, still notice and attend to words as they move through texts, even if only for very short periods of time.

To test their ideas, Nagy, Herman and Anderson (1985) first collected two texts and made a list of the words that students might not know from them. Then they gave the list to two groups of students and asked them to put check marks next to the words that they knew. Each

---

Quote 4.7

We hypothesize . . . that incidental learning from context proceeds in terms of small increments so that any one encounter with a word in text will be likely to produce only a partial increase in knowledge of that word. On the other hand, we also hypothesize that learning from context is more effective than many have assumed. . . . If coupled with a sufficiently large volume of exposure to written language, incidental learning from context should be able to account for a substantial amount of vocabulary growth.

Nagy, Herman and Anderson (1985, p. 237)

Our results strongly suggest that a most effective way to produce large-scale vocabulary growth is through an activity that is all too often interrupted in the process of reading instruction: Reading.

Nagy, Herman and Anderson (1985, p. 252)

group of students was then asked to read one of the two texts and take a vocabulary test covering many of the words that the students indicated they did *not* know. (The words on the test came from both texts, the text that the students had read and the one they had not read.) The researchers wanted to see if students would score better on words that were in the text they had read than on the words from the text they had not read. The students performed somewhat better on the vocabulary from the text that they had just read, even though they did not know these words before reading. The results of these studies showed that students who read stories with new words can learn one to three new words out of every 20 new words that they are exposed to while reading; this is equal to learning 5–15 per cent of the new words encountered in the reading.

This small percentage may not seem important. However, it offers a good explanation for the role of reading in vocabulary learning. Nagy, Herman and Anderson made the following argument. If fifth-grade students read about a million words in the course of a year (30 minutes per day, @ 100 wpm), they are likely to encounter about 21,000 unknown words (approximately 2 per cent of total words read). If they learn 5–15 per cent of these new words, they should learn 1,000 to 3,000 words by incidental exposure through reading over the year. Over 10 years of schooling, students could learn 10,000 to 30,000 new words simply from reading-to-understand. The relationship between vocabulary learning and reading is actually very complex, but this set of studies offers important insights into how L1 students could learn the large recognition vocabulary that they need as fluent readers. These studies, and the extending studies since then, make a very interesting 'quest' story about how a large vocabulary can be learned.

4.2.3   A study on the impact of fluency training on reading

The importance of reading fluency has been argued for some time, but relatively few research studies have demonstrated a strong effect for fluency training. However, a recent study by Stahl, Heubach and Cramond (1997) has demonstrated that fluency training – combining **story previews** and rereading, **paired readings**, extensive reading in class (i.e. **Sustained Silent Reading**), reading at home and questions and discussions around readings – can lead to major gains in reading abilities. The questions asked by Stahl, Heubach and Cramond were important ones: Would a training programme that combined direct

---

Concept 4.1 **Fluency**

Fluency itself is as complex a notion for reading as it is for speaking and writing. In the case of reading, fluency involves a combination of speed, accuracy and fluidity of processing (Segalowitz, 2000). These features of fluent reading reflect cognitive abilities to process visual and semantic information efficiently, combining automatic and attentional skills most appropriately for the reading task involved. Fluency also needs to be understood in relation to other important factors, such as age, difficulty of task, familiarity of topic and amount of total exposure to the L2.

---

instruction in reading fluency skills with reading a lot be beneficial to students? Could such a curriculum sustain student interest over an entire school year?

In the Stahl, Heubach and Cramond study, experimental training during the first year of a 2-year project was carried out with low-achieving second-grade students in two schools. Four classes of students were recruited for the study. All four classes used the same revised grade-level basic reader, were given time in class for reading additional materials and were encouraged to focus on understanding the texts through group discussion and post-reading exercises. They also engaged in rereading and paired reading activities – somewhat common in elementary L1 reading curricula, but rare in L2 reading curricula.

Most students in this study were reading below grade level at the start of the year but, as a result of the training, the average reading comprehension gain at the end of the training year was almost two grade levels. Students showed consistent progress throughout the school year (in a setting where many students fall below grade-level expectations). Student reading rates and accuracy of oral reading (both fluency measures) also improved equally strongly across all classes. The results were so uniformly positive that a plan for a formal **comparison study** was abandoned and the 'fluency curriculum' was continued for a second year, with an additional six classes from other schools, for a total of ten second-grade classes. Again, with students who were initially below grade-level going into second grade, comprehension improved by almost two grade-levels by the end of their year in the curriculum.

A separate study involved interviewing three classes of students on their attitudes toward the fluency curriculum. Almost all the students were enthusiastic about all aspects of the curriculum. All students felt that they learned to read better. Almost every student answered

> ## Quote 4.8
>
> This paper reports the results of a two-year project designed to reorganize basal reading instruction so as to stress fluent reading and automatic word recognition. The reorganized reading program had three components: A redesigned basal reading lesson, stressing repeated reading and partner reading; a choice reading period during the day; and a home reading program. Over the two years of the program, students made significantly greater than expected growth in reading ability in all 14 classes.
>
> Stahl, Heubach and Cramond (1997, p. 1)

> ## Quote 4.9
>
> The program was sustainable over two years, teachers and children perceived it and its various components positively, and it led to overall gains in achievement.... We also learned about the reciprocal nature of instruction and text difficulty.... With the greater support given to readers through repeated readings of the instructional text in various venues and with various procedures, children were able to learn from material that they initially read with greater difficulty than expected.
>
> Stahl, Heubach and Cramond (1997, p. 35)

positively about sustained silent reading, reading at home and reading with partners. None of the students appeared to become bored with the repeated-reading activities.

The questions that Stahl, Heubach and Cramond asked were important. The researchers had some ideas about the potential importance of extensive reading, rereading, and paired reading and they developed a way to teach these activities to students. Then they measured improvement in comparison with expected grade-level progress. Their study is an ideal story about a successful training programme with major implications for school curricula.

4.2.4   A study of discourse organisation and reading comprehension

Over the past twenty years, Isabel Beck and her colleagues have been examining how text structures influence reading comprehension. In one set of studies, she and her colleagues revised texts to follow certain principles of discourse organisation to see if these revisions would influence student reading (e.g. using clear reference overlap across clauses, providing definitions for terms to minimise ambiguous inferences, making **given and new information** more transparent, and adding explanations to simplify multi-stage inferences). In particular, they asked the following question: Would revised history texts lead to improved student understanding of the texts? Because understanding difficult texts, and learning from texts, is such a common concern in education, this question reflects a fundamental issue in literacy development.

Beck, McKeown, Sinatra and Loxterman (1991) explored these issues by examining fourth- and fifth-grade history texts covering the American pre-Revolutionary War era (1756–75). They revised a text on the causes of the war using select discourse-organisation principles: adding explanations, making connections obvious, linking events and people more directly, and making sure that given information generally preceded new information in each sentence. They then gave the original version and the revised version to two groups of students. They asked students to answer comprehension questions and do a **free-recall measure** of the events.

Quote 4.10

[T]he goals of the present study were (a) to make revisions in the sequence of textual materials from a fifth-grade social studies textbook based on a cognitive processing perspective, (b) to describe the theoretical motivations for those revisions and (c) to demonstrate the effects of the revisions empirically by examining students' comprehension of the original and revised materials.... The general operations used in making revisions were clarifying, elaborating, explaining and providing motivation for important information, and making connections explicit.

Beck *et al.* (1991, pp. 254, 256)

The effects of the revisions we made demonstrate that a text-processing approach is effective for creating comprehensible text. The proportion of questions correctly answered was reliably higher for the students who read the revised version than for the students who read the original text.

Beck *et al.* (1991, p. 272)

The results of this study showed that students understood the revised text significantly better than the original version, recalling significantly more information and scoring significantly higher on comprehension questions. Beck *et al.* concluded that revising a text on the basis of assumed discourse organisational features can help students understand the text and learn from it. They also carried out careful **qualitative analyses** of student responses in the **recall task** and showed that students were also able to understand the reasons for the war. This study demonstrated that texts can be made more comprehensible in principled ways following major concepts from discourse analysis (as opposed to formulaic simplification rules).

Being realistic, Beck and her colleagues realised that their revision principles, although they could be offered to textbook writers, would probably not become consistent features of future student textbooks; thus, students would still experience difficulties with textbook comprehension. Other ways to improve student comprehension had to be explored if students were required to read **inconsiderate texts** on a regular basis. How they pursued this latter question is another story that has a successful outcome (Beck *et al.*, 1996, 1997; Kucan and Beck, 1997). Through an instructional approach called 'Questioning the Author', they taught students to interact with texts and question text information and writer purpose critically. In this way, students learned to deal with difficulties that they encountered while trying to understand informational texts.

4.2.5 A study of strategic reading development

Over the past fifteen years, Michael Pressley and his colleagues have explored how strategy instruction could be used to help students' reading comprehension. In early studies, they asked which strategies would be useful for instruction, proving beneficial for students. In later studies, they asked how students learn to become strategic readers. For the past ten years, Pressley has promoted an approach called **Transactional Strategy Instruction** (TSI) that leads students to become strategic readers, rather than learners of individual strategies (Pressley, 1998; Pressley and Woloshyn, 1995; Pressley *et al.*, 1992). Based on existing strategy-training research, Pressley has consistently argued that students need an instructional approach (such as TSI) with the following features (from Brown, Pressley, Van Meter and Schuder, 1996):

1. Instruction must be long term because becoming a strategic reader takes years.

2. Teachers explain and model effective comprehension strategies through think-aloud demonstrations and discussion. Typically only a few strategies are emphasised over a period of time.

3. Teachers coach students to use strategies as needed. Many mini-lessons are given about when and why it is appropriate to use particular strategies.

4. Both teachers and students model the uses of strategies for one another on a continual basis. Conversations about text meaning include discussion of strategies to improve comprehension.

5. The usefulness of strategies is emphasised and students are reminded frequently about the benefits of strategy use. Issues of when and where to use strategies are discussed often. Students explain how they use strategies to process texts.

6. Strategy instruction is viewed as a vehicle to generate discussion and dialogue about student comprehension of texts.

The larger goal of such approaches is the gradual development and flexible use of strategies to comprehend new and challenging texts. In a specific study pursuing this goal, Brown, Pressley, Van Meter and Schuder (1996) posed a simple question: Would students increase their reading comprehension as a result of Transactional Strategy Instruction? They tested this idea in five experimental and five control second-grade classrooms with low-performing students. Six students from each class were selected and matched on a reading comprehension measure. The experimental students were taught reading using TSI during a year-long programme. At the end of the year, all students were tested with standardised measures for word study skills and reading comprehension. The experimental students performed significantly better than the control students. This finding of significant differences is remarkable because relatively few students were involved in the experiment, and very few earlier studies had ever shown that strategy instruction leads to significant performance differences on standardised reading comprehension tests.

The researchers also interviewed students on their strategy use in fall and spring semesters. In the fall, experimental and control students mentioned the same number of comprehension strategies. In the spring, the experimental students described significantly more comprehension strategies. Finally, in a series of other analyses of discussions and **think alouds** during lessons, the researchers showed that experimental students provided more elaborate interpretations of text information and

> ### Quote 4.11
>
> Second-grade low-achieving students experienced a year of either trans-
> actional strategies instruction or highly regarded, more conventional second-
> grade reading instruction. By the end of the academic year, there was
> clear evidence of greater strategy awareness and strategy use, greater
> acquisition of information from material read in reading groups, and
> superior performance on standardized reading tests by the transactional
> strategies instruction students.
>
> Brown, Pressley, Van Meter and Schuder (1996, p. 18)

discussed strategy use more frequently. Overall, Pressley and his colleagues demonstrated the effectiveness of Transactional Strategy Instruction for low-performing second-grade students. The study offers
a strong 'quest' narrative based on an important question about the
effectiveness of strategy instruction.

4.2.6   A study of reading-to-learn from multiple texts

In the past decade, Charles Perfetti and his colleagues have been exploring the cognitive processing involved in reading multiple texts
on a topic, and the process of reading-to-learn (Perfetti, 1997; Perfetti,
Rouet and Britt, 1999). Being able to learn from reading is a common
expectation in academic settings, though it was not explored extensively
in research studies until the 1990s. Perfetti, Britt and Georgi (1995)
conducted an important study to examine the reading-to-learn issue.
They asked a simple question: What will students learn, and how will
they learn, from reading multiple texts on the Panama Canal? They
studied six university students who agreed to enrol in a special 6-week
course on the Panama Canal. Using a **multiple case-study approach**,
the researchers taught a course that examined the politics of the Panama
Canal during three time periods: (a) at the time of its construction, (b)
in 1977 during negotiations for the return of the canal to Panama and
(c) in a future time with a hypothetical scenario. Each time period represented a different segment of the course. The researchers wanted to
find out what ideas were learned, how quickly ideas were learned, how
well ideas were learned and how students reasoned through conflicting
information when reading multiple texts representing each of these
time periods.

Students met individually with researchers nine times in all: five times for the first segment of the course, three times for the second segment and once for the third segment. Students were asked to read a text for each meeting (after the first one). For each meeting, they answered questions about the text and revised a summary of core events about the Panama Canal (not a separate summary of each individual reading). Student work was collected and analysed, as were background tests on reading comprehension, general history and the Panama Canal. Perfetti, Britt and Georgi scored summaries and question sets to create numerical data, but they also conducted a careful qualitative analysis of each student's learning progress across all the readings and tasks with notes and observations of each session.

Quote 4.12

Students learned most of what there was to learn about core events from the first text, and about all there was to learn by the second text.... [W]e emphasize that the course of learning [from texts] cannot be described as 'events-first, facts-second'. Every student learned important supporting facts from the very first opportunity. Details are clearly important, neither ignored nor delayed in their learning.... The heart of the story is the events and their most important details together.

Perfetti, Britt and Georgi (1995, pp. 45–6)

[A]n important factor to both the quality of learning and the quality of reasoning was the use of multiple texts. Although the study was not designed to establish this conclusion, it appears that both learning and reasoning were affected by the requirement of learning from more than one text. More clearly, reasoning was directly affected by what students had read, with many instances of altered views and modified arguments as a result of the most recently read text.

Perfetti, Britt and Georgi (1995, p. 174)

Perfetti, Britt and Georgi found that students could write summaries of core events after the first reading, and that the basic summary of main events did not involve major restructuring after the second reading and summary task. As students read additional texts with conflicting historical accounts, their written interpretations of the core events varied, showing that they had learned and adjusted their understanding with each new reading. Through a variety of questions and reasoning tasks, researchers showed that the students learned both a set of basic events and differing text interpretations of the events following each reading. In effect, the researchers showed how readers could develop a stable situation model of text interpretation (refer back to Chapter 1) that did not depend on any one text. At the same time, students could comprehend and reason about each text in ways that suggested specific text-model understanding of each text.

> **Quote 4.13**
>
> Our conclusion ... is simply that there is value in multiple text learning. It allows students a richer representation of the situation to be learned. It forces an awareness of texts, as opposed to situations, and it can be structured so as to focus on thinking and problem solving.
>
> Perfetti, Britt and Georgi (1995, p. 189)

With this extended study, the researchers provided evidence of the combination of text-model understanding of a text and situation-model interpretation that goes beyond individual texts (for more information, refer back to Chapter 1). They also showed how the careful study of tasks and multiple readings on a topic led students to learn and reason anew with each text, even though the event summaries remained relatively constant. Moreover, students who read these texts developed more sophisticated reasoning processes about the politics of the Panama Canal than did a group of three control students, suggesting that reading from multiple text sources leads to more in-depth knowledge and aids reasoning about the topic. This study, which evolved from several years of preparatory studies, offers a story of how students can learn from multiple texts, but it also shows how researchers can study student learning from texts through **case studies**, summaries, questions about texts and careful observations of students. These researchers used many complementary research approaches to search for a good answer to an important question.

4.2.7 A study of flashcard training and reading development

For the past decade, Tom Nicholson has been exploring issues in reading development and examining techniques and procedures for reading instruction that may or may not be helpful to students. Nicholson and his colleagues have explored the role of **phonological awareness** in reading, the role of context in reading, social factors that influence reading development and the importance of word recognition abilities, vocabulary learning and comprehension processes on reading development (Nicholson, 1991, 1993; Thompson and Nicholson, 1999). In a recent study, Tan and Nicholson (1997) re-examined the role of flashcards and asked a simple question: Would flashcards be effective in building word recognition fluency, oral reading accuracy and reading comprehension? Because recent common wisdom suggests that flashcard training may not be an effective instructional technique, the results of this study offer an important lesson on 'received wisdom'.

Tan and Nicholson taught 42 below-average-reading children (ages 7–10) word fluency skills and word recognition in three **matched groups**: two groups used flashcard training techniques and one group acted as a control, hearing the words and learning them aurally. All groups received five 20-minute training sessions, one per week, based on texts the students were reading that week (a total of five texts over 5 weeks). Words selected for training represented approximately 10 per cent of the words in the text being read that week. All groups were provided with meanings of words. In one experimental group, students were simply shown a word on a flashcard and a simple two-word phrase on the back side to reinforce its meaning. In the second group with flashcards, students were shown words highlighted in longer phrases and sentences on the front side of the flashcards. In both flashcard groups, students practised saying the words quickly. They then read a random list of the same words until they could say the words correctly at a rate of less than one per second. The control group was not trained to say

---

Quote 4.14

Forty-two below-average readers, between 7 and 10 years of age, were given single-word training, phrase training, or no training. Trained children learned to decode target words quickly and accurately using flashcards; untrained children only discussed the target words and read them once. Trained and untrained children read aloud passages containing target words and were tested on their comprehension. Trained children had better comprehension than did the untrained children when questioned about passages and asked to retell them.

Tan and Nicholson (1997, p. 276)

the words to an expected rate of better than one word per second. For each of the five stories read, all groups of students were also given 12 comprehension questions and were asked to recall the stories through standard prompting techniques.

The results, after training, showed that the flashcard groups performed significantly better than the control group in speed and accuracy of naming. Even more important, the flashcard groups performed significantly better on reading comprehension and story **recall measures**. This study demonstrates that fluency in word recognition, through flashcard practice, improves reading comprehension with below-average readers. The results are even more remarkable because there were only five training sessions, and only 10 per cent of the words in the story were practised. At the same time, the researchers do not suggest that flashcard training is the only way to develop fluency, or that flashcards are the only type of training needed for improved word recognition. However, the study points out the importance of keeping an open mind about traditional techniques when there are good rationales for their use. The study also makes a good story: The quest is to see if flashcard training might have some place in the classroom. The conclusion is that it probably does for readers who need to build word recognition fluency.

Quote 4.15

For many years now, the use of flashcards for instructional purposes has been seen as an ineffective technique for improving reading skill.... [T]he use of flashcards alone will not provide the basic skills required to become a good reader, although it is possible to improve speed and accuracy of specific word recognition.... What flashcards can do, once decoding skills are developed, is provide opportunities for practice and overlearning, which is necessary to make progress in reading. Other procedures, such as repeated reading, can also provide pupils with necessary practice in word-recognition fluency and speed.

Tan and Nicholson (1997, p. 286)

4.2.8 A study of student motivation and reading

For many years, John Guthrie has been interested in a wide range of issues central to reading instruction, the development of reading abilities and reading theory. Among the many questions that he has asked and then explored are the roles of student attitudes, interests and motivations to read and their relations to reading development. Although many studies have argued that motivation, interest, self-esteem and attitudes toward reading are central to reading development, relatively few research studies have demonstrated this relation conclusively (Guthrie *et al.*, 1998; Guthrie, Wigfield, Metsala and Cox, 1999; Guthrie, Wigfield and Von Secker, 2000). Pursuing this issue in a recent study, Guthrie, Wigfield, Metsala and Cox (1999) asked the following three questions about reading amount and motivation: How well does amount of reading predict reading comprehension? How well does motivation to read predict amount of reading? How well does motivation predict reading comprehension?

Quote 4.16

We report the results of 2 studies.... Study 1 included 3rd and 5th graders. We measured their motivation and reading amount with questionnaires and their reading comprehension with 2 performance tests. Results revealed that reading amount significantly predicted text comprehension.... Study 1 also showed that reading motivation significantly predicted reading amount.... In study 2, we investigated the same variables in Grades 8 and 10.... The results showed that reading amount significantly predicted text comprehension with other variables controlled. Further, motivation predicted reading amount with other variables controlled and directly predicted text comprehension.

Guthrie *et al.* (1999, p. 231)

Guthrie and his colleagues carried out two studies to explore these questions. In the first of two studies reported, 154 third-grade students and 117 fifth-grade students participated. They read passages, answered comprehension questions and were tested on amount of learning from texts. Students also filled out questionnaires on (a) amount of prior knowledge about the topics of the readings, (b) amount of reading done in school and out of school and (c) reading motivation. The researchers wanted to control their results so that the amount of prior knowledge and prior comprehension abilities would not be hidden causes of their results (otherwise, these knowledge and ability resources could be possible causes of connections between amount of reading and reading abilities, or between reading motivation and reading abilities). The results of the study showed that amount of reading had a small but significant effect on reading comprehension after controlling for prior reading comprehension scores and prior knowledge of the topics (for all 271 children). Their results also showed that motivation did not directly influence reading comprehension scores with these elementary level students, but motivation was a major cause of amount of reading completed.

Their second study was conducted to confirm these results and to allow for more general claims. For the second study, data were collected from a large nationwide survey of reading abilities. They used the data to measure reading comprehension and recombined data to measure amount of reading and reading motivation with more than 11,700 tenth-grade students. They found that reading amount again had a small but significant effect on reading comprehension. In addition, motivation had a major impact on reading comprehension, providing the best single explanation for reading performance. Motivation was also the strongest single factor predicting the amount of reading done by students.

Quote 4.17

Reading motivation was a direct predictor of reading amount in both Study 1 and 2.... [I]f reading amount predicts achievement in text comprehension as highly as the literature indicates, accounting for reading amount becomes an important theoretical and practical issue for researchers. Our results and those of previous studies suggest that motivation is a preeminent predictor of reading amount.... In our view, one of the major contributions of motivation to text comprehension is that motivation increases reading amount, which then increases text comprehension.

Guthrie *et al.* (1999, p. 250)

These results provide a strong argument for the importance of motivation. Motivation directly impacts the amount of reading done by students in both elementary and secondary levels. Amount of reading, in turn, influences reading comprehension abilities. Perhaps more importantly, motivation also strongly predicted reading-comprehension abilities as students became more fluent readers. This study is another strong quest story (with multiple event episodes) that has important implications for teaching reading (see Dörnyei, 2001a).

4.2.9   A study of reading theory and reading efficiency

This last study is somewhat different from all of the others in this chapter. As a research study it is conceptually difficult; it is included here because it addresses some of the most fundamental questions about reading and reading development (and it does represent a distinct way of carrying out reading research). For the past twenty-five years, Ron Carver has been exploring key issues in reading development, reading rate and **reading efficiency** (Carver 1990, 1992, 1993, 1994, 1998). In a recent study, Carver (1997) synthesised much of his previous research to develop a theory of reading efficiency based on data collected from many of his past studies. So although the study reported here does not involve students being trained or tested at one specific time, it does ask fundamental questions: What are the components of general reading ability and how well do they explain reading abilities? To answer these questions, Carver assembled test data from a number of prior studies and then analysed these data to demonstrate that reading abilities are essentially a combination of **comprehension accuracy** and reading rate. This is a very big claim so his method and his procedures deserve some recognition.

Carver first hypothesised a set of relations among reading abilities (many of which had been the topic of previous research studies). He proposed a hierarchy of skills assumed to support reading. At the highest level, he said that general reading abilities can be explained by measures of comprehension accuracy (equal to the Simple View of Reading, see Chapter 1) and reading rate. In turn, comprehension accuracy can be explained by a combination of listening comprehension (verbal processing) and word-decoding skills. Reading rate can be explained by decoding abilities and simple speed of naming words and numbers.

To test these ideas, he developed a unique approach. He compiled measures of each ability for several groups of students. Then he showed

---

Quote 4.18

The idea that verbal knowledge aptitude, decoding aptitude, and naming speed aptitude are very important factors in reading is very similar to the conclusions drawn by Stanovich, Cunningham and Feeman (1984), who advanced verbal comprehension, decoding accuracy, and decoding rate as three relatively independent abilities that are important in predicting early reading progress.

Carver (1997, p. 27)

that the reliable score of one measure, for example, reading comprehension accuracy, was almost fully accounted for statistically by the combined reliable scores of other abilities, specifically, in this example, listening comprehension and word-decoding measures. In this way, he showed that (a) reading rate is a product of word-decoding abilities and cognitive processing speed; (b) comprehension accuracy is a product of word-decoding skill and listening comprehension abilities; and (c) overall reading abilities are a product of comprehension accuracy and reading rate abilities.

The study by Carver is a major contribution to theorising about reading abilities, with important implications for the teaching and testing of reading. It suggests that reading instruction and assessment should focus on both comprehension abilities and reading rate (and fluency) abilities. Another interpretation could be to say that reading abilities involve comprehension of extended text under some time pressure to read fluently. So rate and fluency (and, by extension, amount of reading) play important roles in reading comprehension abilities. A further implication is that word-decoding skills represent fundamental abilities underlying both comprehension and rate (fluency), a finding argued in many experimental studies. Of course, there are many further issues and questions to be examined in light of the results of Carver's study. He has made a strong initial case for his view of reading abilities, but confirmatory studies will have to follow. The claims of his theory are large (and exciting for their potential), so much converging evidence will be needed. The importance of the Carver study for the present chapter is that it shows how carefully collected data from a set of prior studies can be synthesised to provide new insights. It certainly qualifies as an extended quest (over more than a decade) based on a fundamental question about reading.

4.3   Seeing the story structure of research studies

The studies described in this chapter have highlighted a number of central issues and questions about reading abilities and reading development. Moreover, the studies reflect a variety of ways to explore questions, collect information, and conduct **quantitative** and **qualitative** **analyses**. These studies also introduce major research personalities in English L1 reading research, though there are many other major contributors to L1 reading research knowledge.

Beyond the importance of the research described here, these studies also represent ways to tell stories. The researchers (the storytellers) all propose good questions, demonstrate the importance of their questions, provide background information and explain the impetus for the study (setting the scene). The researchers prepare for their studies and plan ways to answer the questions raised. They all go through a series of steps to collect the information needed (like episodes of a story). After collecting information, they analyse it in ways that should help them find answers (much like the final confrontation in stories). The results are reported and the implications are discussed (akin to the story climax, conclusion and implied moral). In short, research studies are interpretable as stories. The difficulties that many people face in understanding these stories are due to the compressed and specialised way in which the stories are told, but the stories are important to everyone who wants to know more about reading and how to teach it well.

4.4 Conclusion

This chapter has focused on L1 reading research and its connection to the discussion of reading in Chapters 1–3. In the next chapter, we introduce an additional set of research studies, though with a different emphasis. The studies just reported cover student groups that may be several steps removed from many L2 settings, and this difference cannot be ignored. The studies introduced in Chapter 5 bring us closer to the L2 teaching situation, focusing on research interests in L2 contexts. Moreover, they introduce us to researchers, applied linguists for the most part, who tend to have closer connections to L2 instructional practices. The implications of their work argue much more directly for teachers to adjust the ways in which they teach and modify the materials that they use.

Further reading

All of the researchers referred to in this chapter contribute regularly to reading research journals (see Chapter 10, section 10.1). Any search through these journal data bases will reveal more work by these researchers. We have also provided a more complete set of references to the work of these researchers on the ALIA web site for this volume.

Chapter 5

Key studies in L2 reading

This chapter reviews 10 research studies conducted in L2 contexts. The studies illustrate useful methods for conducting research and showcase topics pertinent to L2 settings, including the following:

- the importance of word-level issues in L2 reading development
- the influence of discourse organisation on comprehension
- the use of select instructional techniques for reading classes
- the benefits of extensive reading
- the role of social and cultural influences on reading

Conducting research in second language (L2) classrooms has much in common with the research done in first language (L1) settings. The topics are often the same, methods and procedures are typically the same and ways of analysing the information collected are also mostly the same. There are differences, however. Among these differences in L1 and L2 research are the issues discussed in Chapters 2 and 3. For example, L2 research, unlike L1 research, often looks at the roles of language proficiency and language knowledge as important factors in reading development. L2 research often explores transfer issues of L1 linguistic, strategic and content knowledge on L2 performance, and whether this transfer might be positive or negative. Moreover, L2 research often examines the issue of a second language threshold, a unique L2 issue. Finally, L2 research explores cultural factors and unique instructional resources that might influence reading development.

In the previous chapter, we examined a number of studies that have strongly influenced the field of L1 reading research. These research efforts have, to some extent, influenced instruction as well, although the gap between research and relevant implications for instructional practices is real. Many major research studies have a strong impact on instruction only years later, and often not quite in ways initially proposed by the researchers. One goal of this chapter and the previous one (and of the book overall) is to show that the connection between research and instruction needs to be strengthened. Although it is true that some research should not be translated hastily into teaching techniques, it is also true that important ideas stemming from reading research – that would benefit students' learning – are often lost for years. We cannot predict ahead of time which research ideas and results ought to influence teaching relatively quickly, but we can explore research ideas, claims and interpretations within our own classrooms. The goal is not so much to refute research claims, but rather to see if the claims make sense in specific teaching contexts and if they can lead to improved teaching practices and better student learning.

This chapter has two major goals along the lines of the comments above. First, it outlines major topics that are commonly explored in L2 reading contexts. Second, the chapter presents a number of key L2 reading research studies. These studies, like those presented in Chapter 4, are introduced as interesting stories. They can be compared with the research studies from the previous chapter to identify the different issues raised, often variations on a common theme, and the range of research methods used.

5.1   Topics to explore in L2 reading research

The previous chapters of this book have revealed many topics that are worthy of exploration in L2 reading research. To organise our discussion of L2 reading research, and represent the range of issues that can be addressed, we have divided our discussion into seven distinct, though sometimes overlapping, areas. These areas, listed in Figure 5.1, provide us with a way to talk about major issues and key research studies within a manageable framework. We make no claim to any special insights into reading by using this framework, but we feel that it provides a useful guide for our discussions to follow.

The first set of topics, word-level issues in reading development, includes word-recognition skills, automaticity, fluency and vocabulary knowledge of various types. In the case of vocabulary, word frequency and size of vocabulary represent only two issues in a much larger set of

1. Word-level issues in reading development
2. Discourse organisation and text comprehension
3. Main idea comprehension and instructional routines
4. Extensive reading and motivation
5. Topics unique to L2 reading settings
6. Social and cultural context influences on reading
7. Assessment of reading

Figure 5.1   **Areas typical of L2 reading research**

interesting issues associated with knowledge of words: (a) multiple meanings of a word, (b) parts-of-speech forms, (c) common collocations, (d) derivational forms and (e) the general semantic fields in which a word commonly appears. Other topics, related to word learning and fluency, focus on the role of cognates, translation, definitions, glosses and dictionary use.

The second set of research topics focuses more specifically on extended units of text and the comprehension of information that they contain. Included in this group is the importance of grammatical knowledge, the awareness of grammar as a discourse organising system, discourse organisation knowledge, text structuring principles and strategies for text comprehension (including comprehension and main idea strategies, metacognitive monitoring and repair strategies). For the purposes of this discussion, word-comprehension and word-learning strategies are part of the word-level grouping, above.

The third grouping of research topics centres on main idea comprehension practices as well as specific instructional routines, including the uses of specific techniques to promote comprehension such as post-reading questions, fill-in exercises and writing and speaking tasks based on text information. Instructional routines cover a wide range of ways to organise classrooms and instruction. These issues include, as a partial list, the following: organising classroom layout; structuring class activities; responding to student questions; determining appropriate amounts of practice, skill building and homework; deciding how to correct student answers; selecting reading texts and deciding on the most effective ways to read in class; engaging in discussions that promote text comprehension; planning effective interactional patterns with students; organising group work; assigning and correcting homework; using curriculum projects; and pacing lessons effectively. Other topics within this group centre on the use and development of materials and resources for instruction, for example, when and how to place activities in relation to reading texts, how to create appropriate exercises, how to adapt exercises and activities, how to select and build a class library and how to build project resources.

The fourth major grouping of reading research topics examines the uses of extensive reading and ways to build student motivation. Extensive reading can be incorporated into a curriculum through both in-class and out-of-class practices. Both options require considerable planning if activities are to be successful. One major factor that determines success with extensive reading is motivation. Research to determine what does and does not motivate students often examines student interests, prior experiences, levels of self-esteem, and attitudes toward reading, the L2 and school.

The fifth set of L2 reading research topics focuses primarily on questions that arise almost solely in L2 settings. These topics, by their very nature, do not directly impact any specific set of instructional practices. These L2 issues include (a) the role of transfer, (b) the impact of a language threshold, (c) the influence of L1 cultural preferences and expectations for literacy uses and literacy tasks in school settings and (d) the influence of prior L1 training and educational experiences. Generally, these issues refer to the individual learner, though cultural preference issues overlap with our sixth grouping of research topics (see below).

The sixth set of research topics involves issues that are related to instruction but not necessarily components of instruction, more specifically social and cultural context factors that influence reading. Social and cultural factors extend across a wide array of concerns: (a) social and family influences on reading abilities, (b) the role of parents and communities in promoting literacy, (c) the influences of peers on reading habits and reading motivation and (d) the impact of social groups on valuing literacy practices or even resisting school socialisation expectations.

The seventh set of research topics relates to reading assessment, which often brings up images of standardised tests, multiple-choice questions or summary writing. In fact, researchers can explore a much broader range of topics including so-called alternative methods of assessment such as reading portfolios, checklists, individual student observations, student interviews, group performances, charts of progress over time, extensive reading booklists, oral presentations and performances, and several other options. We should note, at this time, that we will not be addressing issues related to reading assessment directly in the immediate discussion, or elsewhere in the volume, because we feel that the topic merits a separate volume or a much larger book

General L2 research areas	Studies associated with research areas
Word-level issues in reading development	1. A study on learning new words (Parry, 1991)
	2. A study on L2 word-recognition abilities (Muljani, Koda and Moates, 1998)
	3. A study on knowing enough words for academic success (Hazenburg and Hulstijn, 1996)
Discourse organisation and text comprehension	4. A study on the benefits of recognising discourse organisation (Carrell, 1992)
	5. A study of strategy uses by L2 readers (Anderson, 1991)
	6. A study of mental translation as a reading strategy (Kern, 1994)
Main idea comprehension and instructional routines	7. A study on using previews and preview discussions before reading (Chen and Graves, 1995)
Extensive reading and motivation	8. A study on the benefits of extensive reading (Elley, 1991)
Topics unique to L2 reading settings	9. A study on metacognition and the language threshold (Schoonen, Hulstijn and Bossers, 1998)
Social and cultural context influences on reading	10. A study on becoming literate in a second language (Bell, 1995)

Figure 5.2   **Research studies associated with different L2 reading research areas**

from us (see Alderson, 2000; Chalhoub-deVille, 1999; Read, 2000; Urquhart and Weir, 1998; Weir, forthcoming).

In our presentation of key L2 research studies in the next section of this chapter, we use the organising framework presented here as a way to be sure that we cover a variety of topics, and also offer a reasonable representation of issues pertinent to L2 reading. Each of the 10 L2 research studies (see Figure 5.2) presented in the next section represents at least one of the first six main groupings of L2 research topics.

5.2   Ten good stories from L2 reading research

Research conducted in L2 settings contains the same storytelling elements as studies conducted in L1 settings. The 10 studies to follow cover issues that are commonly addressed by L2 reading research and introduce a range of ways of doing research. We need to emphasise that the studies discussed here are not necessarily 'better' than the many other studies that could have been selected, and we do not mean to slight other outstanding researchers by this set of studies. As anyone who has devoted time to L2 reading will understand, certain studies resonate strongly for individual readers. The following studies are simply those that have resonated with us and have influenced our thinking on L2 reading.

5.2.1   A study on learning new words

In this study of word-level issues in L2 reading development, Kate Parry (1991) asked how L2 students learn new vocabulary that is encountered in university-level academic courses. She posed the following questions: How do L2 students in academic courses cope with the heavy demands of so many new words and terms, and what strategies do they adopt to be successful in their studies? These questions are actually quite difficult to answer because students must be examined closely over a period of time to account for what students actually do in such situations. Over a number of years, Parry worked with four university L2 students and collected data documenting their efforts to learn the new words needed for an introductory anthropology course.

As part of this multiple case study, four students were asked to keep a list of all words that they found difficult as they read their anthropology texts and what they guessed these words to mean. Two of the students were asked to record think-aloud comments as they added words to their lists; those same students were given a translation task based on

---

Quote 5.1

We who teach English as a second or foreign language must acknowledge that little vocabulary building gets done through our own direct agency, for we do not cover a wide range of words in class, and many of us spend no time at all on discussing collocations and semantic relationships. We seem, rather, to act on the assumption that if we teach our students grammar, and reading and writing skills, they will build their vocabularies on their own as they engage in other activities; and that this will happen particularly in the context of academic reading.

Parry (1991, p. 630)

an anthropology text. Three of the students were given a post-test on the words that they noted as difficult. All four students took the vocabulary portion of the Michigan Test of English Language Proficiency to determine their language abilities for later interpretation purposes. As a result of these data-collection procedures, Parry had an enormous amount of information to analyse.

In her 1991 published account of this **longitudinal study**, Parry chose to focus on three issues: which words were seen as difficult, the degree of effectiveness of guessing meanings for difficult words and problems encountered with guessing. Parry reported descriptive numbers that clarify the learning situation. Three of the students listed relatively few words as difficult, the fourth, with a lower reading ability, listed a higher percentage. The students did not have the most difficulty with technical anthropology words; rather, more general, but not very frequent, sub-technical words appeared to cause the most difficulties. None of the students appeared to be very successful with guessing word meanings, being successful about 50 per cent of the time. In many cases, words were not learned well, as revealed in post-course testing. In the students' comments on guessing meanings, there are strong indications that students guess plausible meanings from context, but those meanings often turn out to be wrong. Thus, Parry's study raises important concerns about the limitations of guessing new word meanings from context.

In her conclusion, Parry notes that the one student who spent the least time worrying about inferring word meanings from context read the most (and possibly had the best reading skills). He appeared to be the most successful ultimately in learning new words, most likely

---

Quote 5.2

What we need to think about, as language teachers, therefore, is how students can learn to recognize those words whose meaning they must know accurately in order to understand a particular text.

Parry (1991, p. 650)

To establish a firm foundation for the vocabulary building to be done in academic courses, we should encourage our students to read as much as they can before they leave our classes.

Parry (1991, p. 649)

because he read much more overall and was exposed to many more words in meaningful contexts. Although Parry's results do not indicate what students in other contexts should do to learn vocabulary, her study offers important insights into the limitations that certain strategies had for these students, thereby raising important questions about word-learning assumptions that need to be investigated in additional contexts with more students. The study represents another good story, this time with four students learning, or not learning, the words that they need to be successful readers.

5.2.2   A study of L2 word-recognition abilities

In recent years, L2 reading researchers have become much more aware of the importance of rapid and automatic word-recognition skills for fluent reading, which has prompted explorations of differences among L2 students in their word-recognition abilities. As might be expected, there is strong evidence that low-proficiency L2 students are much slower in word recognition than are more proficient L2 students. However, a number of other factors can influence L2 word-recognition abilities, and these need to be explored to understand better how L2 reading processing might differ from L1 reading processes, and at what stages such differences might be most influential. In a 1998 study by D. Muljani, Keiko Koda and Danny Moates, the researchers asked three fundamental questions along these lines: First, will word frequency lead to different speeds of word recognition across different L2 student groups with differing L1 orthographic backgrounds: Indonesian (Bahasa) and Chinese (Mandarin)? Second, will L1 familiarity with an alphabetic orthography (Bahasa) lead to more rapid word-recognition abilities? And third, will L2 words that match L1 orthographic letter sequences be recognised more rapidly?

To explore answers to these questions, Muljani, Koda and Moates recruited three groups of students: 16 native English speakers, as a control group; 16 Indonesian ESL students, whose L1 has an alphabetic orthography; and 16 Chinese ESL students, whose L1 does not have an alphabetic orthography. The Indonesian and Chinese students were matched on English reading abilities, length of residence in the US and educational backgrounds before carrying out the experimental tasks. All students were asked to look at a computer screen and, when a word appeared, they were to press a button as quickly as possible to indicate if the letter string on the screen was a real word or not a real word (a **lexical decision task**). The computer recorded response times for

> **Quote 5.3**
>
> Reading is a complex task involving a number of subcomponent processes. In order to gain fluency, therefore, many subcomponent processing skills – those at lower levels in particular – must become automated. In addition, a majority of L2 readers must cope with the change from one orthographic system to another.
>
> Muljani, Koda and Moates (1998, p. 99)
>
> [W]ord recognition efficiency improves with increased experiential exposure to printed information in the target language.
>
> Muljani, Koda and Moates (1998, p. 101)

each word in milliseconds. Each student practised the task, and then responded to a total of 264 word and non-word forms on the screen. Half of the forms were words and half were non-words, half of the words were high-frequency words and half were low-frequency words, and half the words were similar to Indonesian alphabetic letter sequences and half were letter sequences not found in Indonesian but which occur in English.

The results of the experiment showed that English native readers were very fast on all words and just about as fast on recognising non-words, demonstrating full automaticity of word recognition in English. The Indonesian students, as a group, were slower than the native English readers, but were significantly faster than the Chinese students in word recognition. Both groups of L2 students recognised more-frequent words much more rapidly than the less-frequent words, showing the influence of word frequency on L2 word-recognition skills (and showing indirectly that practice and extensive exposure to print will improve recognition for more commonly repeated words). Finally, the Indonesian students recognised English words more rapidly when they matched letter sequences that also are allowed in Indonesian orthography.

This study provides evidence that differing experiences with L1 orthographies do have an impact on L2 word-recognition abilities, even when students are matched on general reading abilities (using a standardised reading measure). The questions that the researchers raised at the outset of their study were all answered in ways that demonstrate the influence of differing L1 experiences on L2 reading processes. By using a computer and recording response times on English L2 word

> **Quote 5.4**
>
> The results of this experiment demonstrated an effect of the L1 ortho-graphic system on L2 word recognition. The better performance of the Indonesian participants, relative to the Chinese participants, suggests that the Indonesian readers developed a relatively strong interletter associative network through their L1 reading experience, which they transferred to this task. In contrast, the Chinese readers, who were accustomed to pro-cessing primarily logographic characters in their L1, did not have the advantage of transferring such L1 knowledge to this task.
>
> Muljani, Koda and Moates (1998, p. 109)

recognition, the researchers demonstrated that students from different L1s engage in word recognition in different ways.

This research study reveals that we simply cannot assume that L2 students from different L1 backgrounds will carry out reading processes in the same ways. How such differences influence reading instruction is an interesting question that awaits further research by either profes-sional reading researchers or practising teachers engaged in action research.

5.2.3   A study on knowing enough words for academic success

One of the most important, but elusive, questions for fluent reading abilities is how many words a reader needs to know to read most texts fluently. This issue, raised in Chapters 2 and 3, is a source of ongoing debate. In an important study, Hazenburg and Hulstijn (1996) wanted to find out if the commonly cited argument among L2 researchers of 5,000 words was a realistic minimum number of words needed to understand beginning university text material in an L2. They were sceptical of this claim, and set out to answer the following question: What is the minimal number of words that a beginning university student needs to read successfully in an L2?

To answer this question, the researchers (Dutch L1 speakers) first wanted to determine the number of Dutch words needed to account for 95 per cent of the different words that had been collected in a 42 million word corpus of Dutch text material. They argued that 23,550 different **headwords** (from a good dictionary) provided 90 per cent coverage of the 42 million words. The researchers reasoned that about

5 per cent of the remaining 10 per cent of the corpus were proper nouns, technical terms or words not in general use. Assuming that most proper nouns can be learned directly from reading, they argued that 23,550 words (actually headwords) represented the *ideal* word knowledge needed for beginning university work, providing 90 per cent coverage of most reading material, plus approximately 5 per cent with proper nouns, for a total 95 per cent coverage.

They then collected a range of beginning university text materials and showed that the 23,550 words also covered 90 per cent of the words in those texts. But these results did not entirely satisfy them. They also wanted to know the *minimal* number of words needed for reading success rather than simply an ideal number. In the next stage of their study, they argued persuasively that 11,123 headwords would provide 89 per cent of word coverage for text material. (The large increase in number of words between 89 per cent and 90 per cent coverage of words in text material reflects a curvilinear growth rate because less frequent words are encountered.) Hazenburg and Hulstijn then argued that because university students could learn proper nouns easily, students might have reading fluency of almost 95 per cent of the words in the university texts (assuming again 89 per cent coverage with most frequent words and 5 per cent coverage with proper nouns). To test this assumption, they created a 140-item vocabulary test made up of a systematically selected set of words representing a broad range of word frequencies in university text materials. One hundred and thirty-seven Dutch-L2 students took the vocabulary test in addition to the university entrance reading exam for Dutch-L2 students. The L2 students who passed the reading test had an average word knowledge of 11,813 words based on their vocabulary-test performance. Some of the students had vocabulary scores below this average but still passed the reading test. Based on the range of students' test scores, the researchers concluded that an L2 student (at least in the Netherlands) would need a *minimum* of 10,000 headwords to read university-level texts successfully.

This study is important because it persuasively challenges the notion that 5,000 words is an appropriate vocabulary learning target for academically orientated L2 students. Hazenburg and Hulstijn may be optimistic in their arguments for 95 per cent word coverage with approximately 11,000 words; however, the 11,000-word estimate offers a more realistic picture of L2 vocabulary demands for fluent reading than do most L2 claims. In their research, Hazenburg and Hulstijn asked a key question that evolved into a good story as they tracked

> **Quote 5.5**
>
> We therefore estimate that L2 learners familiar with the 11,123 most frequent base words...would actually know one or two per cent more than 88.9 per cent of the word tokens of an average written text. Should they also be familiar with most of the proper names occurring in a text, then they might come very close to knowing 95 per cent, a percentage generally held desirable for a reasonable level of text comprehension.... [I]ndividuals with a vocabulary of fewer than ten thousand base words run a serious risk of not attaining the reading comprehension level required for entering university studies.
>
> Hazenburg and Hulstijn (1996, pp. 150, 158)

through many arguments and claims to present interesting results. They have certainly shown that L2 reading demands a large recognition vocabulary, and that teachers and curriculum developers need to consider how so much vocabulary can be learned by L2 students.

5.2.4   A study on the benefits of recognising discourse organisation

An important component of reading comprehension in academic settings is the ability to recognise discourse organisation in texts. Reading research in L1 contexts has demonstrated that students who recognise and follow a text's basic discourse organisation recall more information from it. This research has also shown that differing discourse organisational schemes, or rhetorical frames, in texts (e.g. comparison–contrast, cause–effect, description) can lead to different results in recall of information. These issues were explored by Patricia Carrell (1992) who wanted to see if L2 students performed in ways that were similar to the many L1 groups that have been studied. The questions that she asked were essential for understanding some of the contributions of discourse knowledge to reading comprehension: Do L2 students recognise and use discourse organisation information for differing types of texts? Do L2 students recall more information from certain types of discourse organisation? What is the relation between discourse organisation and recall of information more generally?

For this study, 45 high-intermediate ESL students (TOEFL 470–524) at a US university were recruited. The students read two texts, one a comparison–contrast text, the other a loose classification description. After reading each passage, students were asked to write down as much as they could remember. Two measures of awareness of text structure were used: (a) written recalls were reviewed to determine what pattern of organisation was used in the recall, and (b) an open-ended question was asked to get students to explain what plan the writer used to organise the passage they had just read. The recall was scored for the number of correct ideas, with differing values given for main ideas, supporting ideas and details. Two judges determined if the recall followed the organisation of the text and if students could correctly explain the discourse organisation of the texts. These two awareness measures classified students differently, with overt explanation of the text organisation being a more difficult awareness task than simply using the appropriate pattern of organisation in written recalls.

> **Quote 5.6**
>
> Those subjects who use the structure of the original passages to organize their written recalls recalled significantly more total ideas than did those who did not.... Those subjects who used the structure of the original passages in their written recalls recalled significantly more of the very top-level ideas units and the high-level ideas than those who did not use the structure in their recalls.
>
> Carrell (1992, pp. 12–13)

Results of the study showed that the two text structures created differences in recall of information only at the level of main ideas; otherwise, there was minimal difference between student performance on the two text types. More important, the students who used the same pattern of organisation in their recalls as was used in the text performed significantly better in their recalls than students who did not use the same pattern. Students who used the same pattern as the text, and who could also describe the pattern in the text, performed the best. About 40 per cent of the students could use the appropriate text organisation in recalls and perform well on recall of information, but they could not explain the pattern overtly. This study showed that better L2 readers recognise the discourse organisation of texts sufficiently well to use that pattern in their own understanding of the text and recall of information. The ability to explain the organisation of a text is a more difficult task for students, and it is not clear from Carrell's results if this latter ability will always lead to better reading performance.

> ### Quote 5.7
>
> This study and its results represent an extension of Carrell (1985), which demonstrated in a training experiment that explicit, overt teaching about the top-level rhetorical organization of texts could facilitate ESL students' reading comprehension.
>
> Carrell (1992, p. 16)

This study provides important answers to the questions posed. Students who used the discourse organisation of the original text in their written recalls comprehend better with either type of text. There were no overall differences in amount of recall between the two types of texts. Students who were aware of discourse organisation to the point that they used the organisation to recall information from texts were better readers. This study suggests that instruction which highlights the organisation of texts may be useful for the development of L2 reading abilities.

5.2.5   A study of strategies used by L2 readers

One of the most important issues in L2 reading is the development of reading strategy use among students. To examine this issue, Neil Anderson (1991) posed two important questions: Will there be differences in strategy use when students only read a passage versus when they take a reading test? Will weaker students differ from stronger students in their use of strategies while doing each task?

For the study, Anderson recruited 28 students to complete two tasks: (a) take a reading test and comment on strategies used during the test and (b) read a text and comment on strategies used while reading. Because Anderson wanted to know if strategy use would differ between weaker and stronger readers, he first gave all students a reading test (that required no student commentary). The results of this preliminary test allowed him to divide the students into three groups: high, intermediate and low level. Students were taught to give think-aloud comments on a reading task and were then tested individually. In the case of the experimental reading test, students were asked to comment on the strategies that they used while reading and answering comprehension questions at the end of each passage. Student comments were audiotaped, transcribed and then categorised according to a list of 47 possible reading strategies.

Results of Anderson's study showed that weaker students were quite different from stronger students in their reading abilities; students who were better readers reported using significantly more *total strategies* in their think-aloud comments. However, there was no difference in the number of *different* strategies used or on their reading test performance. (See Chapter 3, Concept 3.1 and Anderson, 1991, for common strategies used by skilled readers.) In comparing three students as case studies, Anderson showed that students tended to use similar types of strategies across ability levels and across tasks. He also noted that the weakest case-study student could comment on many strategies, but she did not seem particularly skilled at monitoring the success of these strategies. For this student, the issue was not if she knew strategies but rather how well she could use them. Overall, there did not seem to be any single strategy or small set that contributed significantly to reading success. Most students use a wide variety of strategies and, overall, students reported using quite a few strategies, both while reading and while taking a reading test.

Quote 5.8

The most significant finding from these data suggests that there is no single set of processing strategies that significantly contributes to success on these two reading measures. Readers scoring high and those scoring low appear to be using the same kinds of strategies while reading and answering the comprehension questions on either measure.... [S]trategic reading is not only a matter of knowing what strategy to use, but also the reader must know how to use a strategy successfully and orchestrate its use with other strategies. It is not sufficient to know about strategies; a reader must also be able to apply them strategically.

Anderson (1991, pp. 468–9)

This study provides an exploratory view of reading strategy use among 28 ESL students in the US. It is interesting that students reported similar strategy use across reading tasks, and that all students reported using similar strategies. The study also confirmed the usefulness of an extensive strategy list for exploring student strategy use. Most important, the study revealed that the key differences in strategy use between weaker and stronger readers do not depend completely on different types of strategies or the number of different strategies used, but are more likely to depend on total numbers of successful strategy uses. (Anderson does add a note of caution: Some of the differences in total number of strategies reported may have been due to differences in fluency of strategy reporting among the students.) Finally, Anderson has shown that there is no magic small set of strategies that separates good readers from weaker readers. There are not five strategies, for example, that good readers use but that weaker readers do not know about. These results suggest a more complex approach to reading strategy instruction. Anderson asked an important set of questions about strategy use among L2 readers. How he arrived at his answers provides an interesting story of research on reading strategies.

> **Quote 5.9**
>
> Future research also needs to investigate the role of teaching successful strategy use to readers. Simply knowing what strategy to use is not sufficient and thus an investigation into the orchestration of strategies should be closely examined.
>
> Anderson (1991, p. 471)

5.2.6   A study of mental translation as a reading strategy

The ability to use strategies to understand a text better is a basic goal of reading instruction and a major topic for reading research. As we saw in the previous study (Anderson, 1991), strategy use during reading seems to cover a wide range of possibilities and most students report using a large number of strategies while reading. Yet, not all the strategies that students use are recognised as particularly useful. One such case is the use of mental translation from the L2 back to the L1 while reading. Until recently, this strategy was seen as a 'bad habit' typical of weaker readers. However, a study by Richard G. Kern (1994) presented a more complex picture of mental translation as a reading strategy. In his study, Kern asked a specific question: How is mental translation used as a positive, even though sometimes limited, strategy for L2 reading comprehension? His argument was that mental translation might provide a way for L2 students to work out key portions of text meaning without overburdening memory capacity.

In his study, Kern recruited 51 intermediate French L2 students from a US university to participate in think-aloud interviews while reading a French text. The interviews were carried out at the beginning and end

> ### Quote 5.10
>
> Translation appears to serve as a means of maintaining concentration long enough for meaning to be integrated and assimilated. The reader remarks that if the sentence gets too long, her comprehension 'breaks', affecting her concentration and forcing her to reread the sentence from the beginning. Her comprehension difficulties likely stem from lack of automaticity in word recognition as well as working memory span limitations.
>
> Kern (1994, p. 448)
>
> Translation is here not so much a primary means of accessing general meaning of the texts as it is a way of troubleshooting when visual information from the text does not correspond to the reader's already formed hypotheses about the text's meaning. Translation in this case reflects the reader's need for precision in interpreting visual information, and may indicate a switch from automatic to controlled processing.
>
> Kern (1994, p. 451)

of the semester. The uses of mental translation varied with student ability level and decreased as students progressed through the semester. In particular, weaker students used translation differently at the beginning and end of the semester. At the end of the semester, more students were using translation in association with successful comprehension efforts. It should also be noted that better students used less mental translation overall.

In examining the functional benefits of student translation, Kern inferred from the think-aloud reports that students used translation to assist in semantic processing and consolidation of meaning with difficult texts. Mental translation helped maintain concentration and keep information active while students problem-solved and put ideas in a reasonable order. A final use of translation was to give students assurances that they really understood the passage; translation gave readers a sense that they understood the text precisely rather than vaguely.

Kern concluded that mental translation, although it may indicate a strategy of a weaker L2 reader, nonetheless works to support reading comprehension in at least three ways. It simplifies processing demands, lets readers problem-solve through comprehension difficulties, and provides a sense of accurate comprehension. Of course, mental translation can become a crutch for weaker readers, but the key to this study

> **Quote 5.11**
>
> Another reported strategic use of translation was to verify the accuracy of one's comprehension of a portion of text.... [T]his metacognitive use of translation as a comprehension check was often associated with accurate comprehension. Not surprisingly, this procedure was used primarily by readers in the high ability group.
>
> Kern (1994, p. 453)

is that Kern showed the potential usefulness of mental translation as a processing strategy with difficult texts.

5.2.7 A study on using previews and preview discussions before reading

A number of reading research studies have examined specific aspects of instruction to determine their effectiveness for reading development. Such studies may look at the effectiveness of comprehension questions, the impact of **graphic organisers** for learning information, the importance of discussion about the main ideas of texts for comprehension development, the influence of repeated reading on fluency development, and so forth. In the study reported here, Hsiu-Chieh Chen and Michael F. Graves (1995) examined two commonly used pre-reading activities: **previewing** a text and providing readers with appropriate background knowledge before reading. The researchers' question was straightforward: Does reading comprehension improve when students are given previews of the story, background knowledge of the reading or both supports in combination?

To find an answer to their question, Chen and Graves recruited 243 students from a Taiwanese university to read two passages: a fictional narrative and an autobiographical text by Mark Twain. Students were given a pre-test of background knowledge to ensure reasonable comparability. The students were divided into four groups. One group received previews of the passages in English before reading; a second group received general background information in English before reading; a third group received both treatments; and a fourth group was a control (beginning the lesson by reading the text, without any form of pre-reading intervention). Each pre-reading activity was guided by a 200-word script to ensure consistency and each passage was followed by 30 post-reading comprehension questions (15 short-answer questions and 15 multiple-choice items). Each week, students did one of the two readings and related activities in a 2-hour session. A two-part attitude questionnaire on the treatments that they received was also given to all participants.

Based on the post-reading short-answer comprehension questions, all three treatment groups performed better than the control group, and the previewing group and combined group performed better than the background information group. With the multiple-choice questions, the combined group scored significantly higher than the control group and the background knowledge group. The combined group did not score higher than the group with just previewing support. These results argue that providing a preview of what the text will be about is as effective as a preview combined with background knowledge. Moreover, providing a preview is significantly better than providing only background knowledge support or just asking students to read the text. Students' attitudes to the treatments indicated that most found the text preview to be very useful. Students also said that it was important to go over difficult words that would appear in the text. Because previewing alone was as effective as a combined previewing and background information presentation, previewing of text information is recommended as an effective pre-reading activity for reading instruction.

> ### Quote 5.12
>
> The results of this study have definite implications for classroom teachers. Previews offer a promising option for ESL teachers to use in helping students read English texts. Because previews are relatively easy to prepare and take little class time to present, teachers should be encouraged to use previews to assist students in reading.... Previews that include vocabulary instruction should be particularly facilitative for different selections and with less competent and confident readers.
>
> Chen and Graves (1995, pp. 681–2).
>
> Previewing provides support for L2 students when dealing with unfamiliar selections, particularly selections reflecting unfamiliar cultural information. As students become better readers and increasingly familiar with the culture reflected in the nonnative texts they encounter, previews generally become less necessary. At the same time, whenever upcoming selections are likely to be challenging for students, previewing is one viable option to increase their comprehension and enjoyment of what they read.
>
> Chen and Graves (1995, p. 682)

This study provides a clear answer to an interesting question. Even though the results may not be applicable to all contexts, they add important evidence for the effectiveness of previewing activities in classroom instruction. This study also represents a good story about how to learn about the usefulness of certain pre-reading activities. The key question was answered in a way that has direct implications for reading instruction. The study is also one that could be repeated on a smaller scale in any teacher's classroom. Although the statistical controls and comparison may not be available to teachers undertaking such a study, they could look at student results over a period of time to determine which pre-reading activities appear to work better.

5.2.8   A study on the benefits of extensive reading

One of the more significant issues for L2 reading is evidence that extensive reading can make a major difference in student reading development over time (cf. Cipielewski and Stanovich, 1992, and Guthrie, Wigfield, Metsala and Cox, 1999, in Chapter 4). A real difficulty with this topic is that the benefits of extensive reading cannot be seen in a relatively short period of time, and often L2 teachers and reading programmes abandon extensive reading as an integral component of the curriculum before they see its real impact. In an important study, Warwick B. Elley (1991) demonstrated persuasively the impact of extensive reading on improved L2 student reading performance. In a series of earlier studies on extensive reading (or, in this case, **book flood programmes**) in Fiji and Niue, Elley showed the importance of an extensive reading programme with experimental classes that received class libraries for extensive-reading use. In a major study, Elley builds on these earlier works and describes a comparison study carried out over three years in Singapore schools, comparing an audiolingual ESL method with the REAP (Reading and English Acquisition Program) curriculum. The question was simple: Would students engaged in an extensive reading curriculum centred on appropriate book-reading activities outperform a more traditional ESL curriculum?

The REAP curriculum was implemented in the first three grades of schooling (6 to 8 year olds); it emphasised a **shared reading approach**, a modified **language experience approach**, and class libraries for extensive reading, usually involving 200–250 books per class. Students from up to 132 schools were involved in some aspect of this large-scale study. At the end of three years, a battery of language tests was given for two controlled studies. The REAP students significantly outperformed the control classes in vocabulary knowledge, grammar, reading comprehension, listening comprehension and writing. This study did not use a pre- and post-test design so we do not know if all the students started out with the same abilities, but the study was sufficiently large that some assumptions of a normal range of abilities in each group could be expected.

> **Quote 5.13**
>
> This article outlines a set of recent little-known empirical studies of the effects of 'book floods' on students' acquisition of a second language in elementary schools. In contrast to students learning by means of structured, audiolingual programs, those children who are exposed to an extensive range of high-interest illustrated story books, and encouraged to read and share them, are consistently found to learn the target language more quickly. When immersed in meaningful text, without tight controls over syntax and vocabulary, children appear to learn the language incidentally, and to develop positive attitudes toward books.
>
> Elley (1991, p. 375)

This large-scale study certainly qualifies as an epic story. The question raised was important, and the outcomes were useful. Despite the fact that the results do not specifically tell teachers how much extensive reading students should be involved in, the study reveals the benefits of extensive reading and suggests its usefulness for language development.

5.2.9 A study of metacognition and the language threshold

One of the more complex issues facing L2 reading relates to efforts to separate the influences of L1 reading abilities from the influences of L2 proficiency on L2 reading abilities. These issues form the core of research on the 'language threshold', an issue unique to L2 settings. Commonly, researchers will take a group of L2 students and give them an L1 reading test, an L2 language proficiency test and an L2 reading comprehension test. The goal is to determine whether L1 reading abilities or L2 proficiency has a greater influence on L2 reading abilities. Consistently, it has been found that L2 proficiency has a greater influence on L2 reading than do L1 reading abilities.

However, much of this research has assumed that a single measure of L1 reading abilities would be sufficient for research purposes. Rob Schoonen, Jan Hulstijn and Bart Bossers (1998) instead developed a study that tested students' reading abilities in the same way in both languages, treating both abilities (i.e. L1 reading and L2 proficiency) as a more complex combination of language-specific vocabulary know-ledge and potentially shared metacognitive-strategy knowledge. In this way, they could examine which aspects of L1 and L2 reading know-ledge overlapped and which aspects were separable. The questions that they asked were complex but important: What are the contributions of vocabulary knowledge and **metacognitive knowledge** on L1 reading abilities? What are the contributions of vocabulary knowledge and metacognitive knowledge on L2 reading abilities? Do the ability com-binations appear similar across both languages or does L2 reading look different from L1 reading abilities? Will a language threshold effect arise with lower-proficiency L2 readers?

To find answers to these questions, the researchers recruited Dutch students (Dutch = L1, English = L2) from three grade levels: 6, 8 and 10 (ages 12–16). Four hundred and eighty-eight students, in total, completed tests for the study. All students took a test of Dutch L1 reading comprehension, but only students in grades 8 and 10 took a standardised test of L2 English reading comprehension. (The sixth graders did not take English tests because they were in their very first year of English studies.) Students were given sets of questions to measure their metacognitive knowledge for each language, their self-concept as readers and their knowledge of reading goals, text charac-teristics and reading strategies. These measures together formed an overall measure of metalinguistic knowledge. Students were also given vocabulary-knowledge tests in each language, with the exception of the sixth graders who only took the vocabulary-knowledge test in Dutch.

Quote 5.14

[Foreign language] vocabulary is the best predictor of FL reading compre-hension in both grades [8 and 10]. However, in grade 10, where students have reached a relatively high level of FL reading proficiency, the import-ance of vocabulary seems to decrease and the importance of metacogni-tive knowledge seems to increase.

Schoonen, Hulstijn and Bossers (1998, p. 89)

Of the four components of metacognitive knowledge, knowledge of text characteristics, knowledge of reading strategies, and, to a lesser extent, knowledge of reading goals... appear to be more important domains.

Schoonen, Hulstijn and Bossers (1998, p. 98)

Results showed that vocabulary knowledge and metacognitive knowledge accounted for a large proportion of L1 reading comprehension abilities (65 per cent of **shared variance** in sixth grade, 62 per cent in eighth grade, and 65 per cent in tenth grade; cf. Carver, 1997, discussed in Chapter 4). Vocabulary accounted for a greater proportion of the L1 reading abilities at sixth grade, whereas both vocabulary and metacognitive knowledge made strong contributions to L1 reading in the eighth and tenth grade. In L2 reading, the two measures (vocabulary and metacognitive knowledge tests) accounted for 76 per cent of L2 reading ability at eighth grade and 60 per cent at tenth grade, both very strong relationships. Vocabulary was the stronger predictor of L2 reading. By grade ten, however, metacognitive knowledge made a strong contribution as well.

This study demonstrates the strong connection between reading and vocabulary in both L1 and L2 contexts. The researchers found that vocabulary is important in accounting for reading abilities at all levels and in both languages. However, in comparing the factors contributing to L1 and L2 reading, the researchers found that vocabulary knowledge had a greater influence on L2 reading than on L1 reading, particularly at the lower grade level. Metacognitive knowledge contributed in important ways to L1 and L2 reading, yet metacognitive knowledge makes a bigger contribution to reading abilities at higher proficiency levels than it does at lower proficiency levels. Knowledge of text structure and knowledge of strategies were the best indicators of metacognitive knowledge associated with reading. The study also showed that metacognitive knowledge works in similar ways across L1 and L2 reading; vocabulary knowledge acts in a less similar manner across L1 and L2 readers.

These results show that both vocabulary and metacognitive knowledge contribute to L2 reading. The stronger role for vocabulary at lower proficiency levels demonstrates the likelihood of a language

---

Quote 5.15

[W]e found evidence for the so-called threshold hypothesis, according to which (metacognitive) knowledge of reading strategies, reading goals and text characteristics cannot compensate for a lack of language-specific knowledge if the latter remains below a certain threshold level. The limited FL knowledge 'short-circuits' the transfer of reading skills to the FL.

Schoonen, Hulstijn and Bossers (1998, p. 72)

threshold in L2 reading that must be accounted for in reading instruction. Two important implications emerge from this study: Language proficiency is an essential foundation of L2 reading abilities, and metacognitive instruction in text structure and reading strategies is likely to reinforce the emergence of strong metacognitive abilities that support more advanced reading. This research study represents a major venture to find a better way to understand L1 and L2 reading abilities using similar measures for both languages.

5.2.10   A study on becoming literate in a second language

Jill Sinclair Bell (1995) carried out an important diary study on becoming literate in a second language. Bell spent 12 months learning spoken and written Chinese in Canada and also studying her own language-learning processes. She was taught spoken Chinese (Cantonese) in a regular university foreign language classroom, and she hired a Hong Kong-born, bilingual and bicultural tutor to learn written Chinese, which is quite different from the spoken form. The question that she asked was whether she would learn Chinese, particularly written Chinese, in the same way that she assumed she had learned to read and write in English.

Quote 5.16

[I]t seems that the issue of transfer between literacies is not as straight-forward as we have tended to suppose. . . . I would suggest that [the] wholesale transfer of assumptions regarding L1 literacy to L2 literacy can introduce considerable complications into the process of being literate in an L2. . . . [Skills transfer] may or may not prove helpful in the new literacy.

Bell (1995, p. 690)

To document her literacy tutorials, Bell kept a journal of her experiences and audiotaped her literacy lessons. The literacy lessons were then transcribed so that she could examine them more objectively. Bell conducted a strictly qualitative analysis of lesson transcripts, journal entries and reflections on her successes and failures. She did not attempt to quantify her observations in any way. She found that she did not make the type of progress in Chinese literacy skills that she had expected based on previous language learning experiences and her own assumptions about how languages should be learned. The spoken language class fitted her assumptions, but the literacy tutorials did not. Her 'failure' with literacy learning led her to question her assumptions about language learning and literacy more specifically. (For more detailed coverage of Literacy, see Burns and Hammond, forthcoming.) It became clear to her that literacy skills in Chinese impose a different set of cultural values and expectations on its users. As a result of this study, Bell reassessed her views on literacy-as-reading and literacy-as-writing, cultural influences on literacy practices, the importance of the written form in learning, the notion of progress in literacy training, the need for consistent practice, the role of feedback for learning, the value of praise-as-encouragement and praise-for-achievement, the importance of holistic aspects of learning and the concept of the good learner.

> **Quote 5.17**
>
> [M]y basic belief was that all my English language and literacy knowledge could be transferred so that I saw the entire learning task as conquering these particular visual shapes [Chinese characters].... Most of my difficulties arose out of my mistaken assumption that literacy in English and Chinese was differentiated only by the shape of the squiggles on the paper. Consequently I used the same strategies and approaches for L2 literacy as had given me success in L1 literacy. The resultant failures left me baffled and frustrated. Had I realized I was attempting to develop a new way of thinking, learning a new way to present myself to the world, and developing a new set of values, I might have been more prepared for the impact this would have on my self of identity.
>
> Bell (1995, pp. 700–1)

Qualitative case studies such as Bell's are usually used to explore topics and gain insights rather than assemble extensive numerical evidence and look to make generalisations. In this way, qualitative case studies complement other studies that collect numerical data on groups of learners to make generalisable inferences. In this case, Bell came to important insights regarding her own assumptions about literacy, what it means to be skilled at writing and the limitations of an analytic approach with a language (and culture) that values more aesthetic and holistic orientations to literacy. Because Bell's qualitative study involved self-reflection, the results are offered as observations on her own experience rather than generalisations that would apply to others.

Nevertheless, the observations she makes raise questions and issues that deserve exploration by teachers in other settings, whether the teacher has the role of teacher or learner. Bell showed that teachers benefit from reflecting on their own learning experiences to understand better the cross-cultural demands placed on learners, and to reassess habitual assumptions that are seldom challenged otherwise. This study represents an important autobiographical story about changing values and assumptions based on qualitative analyses of data collected by the researcher.

5.3 Conclusion

The 10 studies presented in this chapter showcase a range of research topics pertinent to L2 settings and illustrate a number of different methods for conducting meaningful research. There was an individual diary study, several multiple case studies and a large-scale study with 132 schools. Numerous studies relied on qualitative analyses, whereas others were more quantitative in nature. One study used computers to collect data, and others used questionnaires, interviews, written recalls, a formal corpus, audiotaped and transcribed think-aloud comments, checklists and translation tasks. Three studies used control groups for the sake of comparison. Numerous studies used pre-tests to ensure comparability between or among participants and others used pre- and post-tests to compare student performance before and after the study. This list of research methods only begins to highlight the range of options that researchers have open to them.

This inventory of research options might lead us to believe that the 10 studies introduced here are quite different from one another. And indeed, at one level, the studies are quite distinct. Yet, at another level, they are quite similar to one another in that they all follow a similar story line. All the reseachers started out with good manageable questions; they then decided on ways to collect information that were controlled in useful and appropriate ways; this step was followed by an analysis of data to find evidence about the question posed; and finally, the researchers inferred a fair and reasonable answer to their questions based on the evidence and decided on the usefulness of the answer (and the research).

Whether researchers conduct research by looking at themselves, at their own students or at students in other teachers' classes, the basic sequence of events generally is the same. Most of the studies reported in this chapter (and the previous one) were conducted with students of other teachers. But this is not the only way to conduct research. For inquiring teachers who want to improve classroom instruction, doing a small-scale research study – with their own students and in their own classrooms – by asking manageable questions is a reasonable strategy. By understanding that a research study is much like a story, the steps to be followed are relatively simple. Any effort to carry out a small-scale research study, when following these basic steps, will evolve, much as a story will unfold through a series of episodes leading to a final resolution. This emphasis on teacher-initiated small-scale research is the primary goal of the next section of the book (Section III).

Further reading

For additional information on L2 reading research, refer to Chapter 10 (section 10.3). For more specific readings on the L2 areas introduced in this chapter, see the following: On *word-level issues in reading development*, see Coady and Huckin (1997), Koda (1997, 1999), Nation (2001), Schmitt (2000), Stahl (1999). On *discourse organisation and text comprehension*, see Grabe (1997), Grabe and Gardner (1995), Martin (1989), Mohan (1986), Reppen (1994/1995), Tang (1992). On *main idea comprehension and instructional routines*, see Aebersold and Field (1997), Anderson (1999), Day (1993), Silberstein (1994). On *extensive reading and motivation*, see Day and Bamford (1998), Dörnyei (2001a,b). On *topics unique to L2 reading settings*, see Urquhart and Weir (1998), Bernhardt (2000). On *social and cultural context influences on reading*, see Snow, Burns and Griffin (1998), Garcia (2000). On *assessment of reading*, see Alderson (2000), Read (2000).

III Researching reading in the classroom

Chapter 6

The reading teacher as classroom researcher

This chapter provides a rationale for teacher-initiated enquiry and introduces a flexible 12-step framework for conducting action research in reading classrooms. Of particular interest will be the following:

- a general introduction to action research that highlights its value and versatility
- a list of general reading-related topics that can be explored through action research
- a detailed, and easy-to-use, description of a 12-step action research process
- two sample action research projects that illustrate each step of the process

Those of us who are responsible for teaching reading find ourselves in a range of instructional settings, including classrooms devoted solely to reading, classrooms that emphasise integrated skills and classrooms with sheltered or other forms of content-based instruction. In all of these settings, we can guide students toward becoming better, more strategic readers. To be most effective, we need to go beyond superficial theories of reading, instructional fads, out-of-date perceptions of reading, loose intuitions based on our own experiences learning to read (as if one can really remember) and certain instructional procedures proposed by popular textbook series and curriculum guidelines. A current understanding of reading, both theory and practice, helps us improve our own teaching effectiveness and guides us to do the following:

1. Assess students' reading needs.
2. Define meaningful instructional goals and objectives.
3. Design (and redesign) courses.
4. Plan purposeful reading lessons.
5. Adopt, adapt and develop instructional materials and assessment instruments.
6. Provide feedback to students on various aspects of reading.
7. Adjust daily lessons in response to students' immediate needs, responses and attitudes.
8. Redefine and adjust curricular priorities to meet students' evolving needs.

In response to these responsibilities, we can work toward a better understanding of reading in a number of ways. We can read the professional literature (books such as this one), subscribe to professional journals (see Chapter 10), participate in professional development seminars on reading, attend conference sessions on reading-related topics and enrol in advanced degree programmes. We can also use our own classrooms, an often-neglected resource, as a window to a more profound understanding of reading. By means of systematic reflection on aspects of our teaching and our own students' learning, we can develop a keener understanding of reading, improve our use of instructional techniques that help students develop reading skills, and build student–teacher roles that support effective learning.

> **Quote 6.1**
>
> Action research takes its name from two processes that are central to it: a data-gathering component (the research element) and a focus on bringing about change (the action component).
>
> Richards (1998, p. 28)

The term *action research* is often used to describe the type of structured teacher reflection, or teacher-initiated research, in which teachers look critically at their own classrooms for the purposes of improving their own teaching and enhancing the quality of learning that takes place there. (See Burns, 1999, Edge, 2001 and Wallace, 1998, for a fuller description of action research for language teachers.) Action research helps teachers develop professionally through the systematic collection and analysis of relevant data and, then, the use of results as the basis for decisions about further professional actions.

> **Quote 6.2**
>
> Action research involves the collection and analysis of data related to some aspect of our professional practice. This is done so that we can reflect on what we have discovered and apply it to our professional action. This is where [action research] differs from other more traditional kinds of research, which are much more concerned with what is universally true, or at least generalisable to other contexts. [Action research] is a loop process, in the sense that the process can be repeated (reframing the problem, collecting fresh data, rethinking our analysis, etc.) until we have found a solution that satisfies us.
>
> Wallace (1998, pp. 16–17)

Action research provides many benefits for practising teachers; through action research, we become aware of what is really happening in our own classrooms. We begin to explore aspects of our teaching that either puzzle, intrigue or trouble us. Action research also helps us gain an understanding of our own attitudes about language and learning. Basically, action research gives us access to information about a wide range of classroom practices (e.g. classroom management, classroom interaction, the use of resources, the effectiveness of instructional techniques). For the purposes of this discussion, we will focus on the role that action research can play in heightening our understanding of reading, in general, and the effectiveness of reading instruction, more specifically.

Action research provides us with non-threatening means for reflecting on reading from a variety of perspectives and for a variety of purposes, as specified in Concept 6.1. This list of possibilities is not meant to be comprehensive; rather, it simply illustrates the potential of action research in relation to reading. In essence, through action research, we can investigate almost any aspect of reading instruction (or assessment) that we want to understand better or improve. The real appeal of action research is that it permits us to examine reading in

---

Concept 6.1 **Purposes for reading-related action research**

By means of action research, teachers can

- Examine instructional practices (e.g. the use of graphic organisers, Sustained Silent Reading) that appear to work well and determine why they work.

- Analyse instructional practices (e.g. paced readings, jigsaw readings) that do not work as effectively as expected, so that such practices can be remedied (rather than discarded).

- Monitor classroom behaviours to determine how they impact on reading improvement.

- Evaluate aspects of reading (e.g. rate, recognition, skimming, vocabulary) in relation to different instructional techniques to determine what works best.

- Determine the effectiveness of various instructional techniques (e.g. explicit vocabulary instruction, rereading, strategy training, teacher–student questioning, the use of graphic organisers) in relation to students' reading development.

- Examine the appropriateness of assigned reading passages in terms of abstract imagery, assumed background knowledge, cultural assumptions, grammatical complexity, length, text density, vocabulary and so forth.

- Evaluate student responsiveness to a range of text types, genres and topics.

- Assess the effectiveness of different purposes for reading (e.g. reading to search for simple information, reading to learn, reading to write, reading for general comprehension) to determine the real benefits derived by students.

- Determine the value of extensive reading in terms of student attitudes toward reading and student reading abilities.

- Evaluate alternative means of achieving instructional goals, experiment with them and evaluate their effectiveness.

---

practical terms and explore practical alternatives to reading instruction in our own classrooms, with our own students, at our own pace. The end result is not only an enhanced understanding of reading, but also improved instruction and more proficient student readers.

> **Quote 6.3**
>
> Action research offers a valuable opportunity for teachers to be involved in research which is felt to be relevant, as it is grounded in the social context of the classroom and the teaching institution, and focuses directly on issues and concerns which are significant in daily teaching practice.
>
> Burns (1999, p. 17)

6.1   Teachers investigating their own classrooms: 'How to' guidelines

The benefits of action research suggest that such enquiry should become a routine part of a teacher's life. As should be clear by now, action research can focus on many aspects of the reading classroom. Despite the fact that our options for action research are virtually limitless, the steps that we take to investigate our own classrooms typically follow a basic progression, like a predictable storyline (see Concept 6.2). What is particularly appealing about the process is that there is always room for simplicity, flexibility and practicality. And the potential usefulness of action research is ever present.

Although the process might appear to be lengthy because it involves 12 steps, action research need not require a lot of time (always a concern of busy teachers). In a simple, but meaningful, action research project, a teacher can observe herself for 1 or 2 days to see, for example, how she responds to students' questions about new vocabulary, or how she builds upon questions provided at the end of a textbook chapter to create more meaningful reading lessons. Or a teacher can devote every other Friday to a reading rate development routine that she wants to understand better. Or she can follow the progress of one student over the course of a week (or a month or a semester) to determine how one type of student (e.g. a motivated student, an unmotivated student, a fast reader, a slow reader) responds to a particular teaching technique, group activity or reading task. Because we are in control of our action research projects, we can design them to meet our own needs and conform to our own time constraints.

The 12-step process proposed here is fluid and adaptable. Although presented as separate steps, in reality the steps are interrelated, with

---

Concept 6.2   **Basic steps for action research**

Step 1: Establish a purpose and decide on a topic.

Step 2: Pose a specific question (narrowing the focus of enquiry).

Step 3: Anticipate outcome(s).

Step 4: Specify the type of data to collect.

Step 5: Determine way(s) to collect data.

Step 6: Consider issues related to time.

Step 7: Collect data systematically.

Step 8: Examine and analyse data.

Step 9: Reflect on results.

Step 10: Generate practical solutions.

Step 11: Experiment with solutions.

Step 12: Share insights with colleagues.

Quote 6.4

By collecting evidence in our own classrooms . . . we can begin to explore the actuality of what we do and say and what happens in response. Because we are investigating situations in which we ourselves are participants, we have the best possible opportunity of gaining access to the values and beliefs which underpin what we do and say.

Somekh (1993, p. 36)

---

considerable overlap among them. In an effective action research project, there is a dynamic relationship between the research question, determined by the teacher herself at the beginning of her research, and the way in which the project proceeds. Action research gives the teacher the flexibility (and power) to reconsider the question(s) posed, the data-collection techniques decided upon, and methods of analysis. The bottom line is that the teacher should, and can, make the project as meaningful, and as manageable, as possible.

In the sections that follow, each part of the 12-step process is introduced with general comments that highlight major goals; more specific details emerge in our description of two distinct, and what we believe to be realistic, reading-related action research projects. These two sample projects – one exploring vocabulary instruction in a reading class and the other exploring extensive reading – gradually unfold, like a story, as we move from step to step. We hope that the two examples, written in first person to demonstrate their real-world applicability, illustrate how manageable and worthwhile the action research process can be. It should be noted that these two model action research projects, as well as the many sample projects that follow in Chapters 7–9, could easily be modified to complement the concerns and interests of teachers in a variety of second language and foreign language settings, including K-12 classrooms, adult education programmes, English for Academic Purposes (EAP) programmes and English for Specific Purposes (ESP) programmes.

6.1.1 Establish a purpose for research and decide on a topic

When we identify some aspect of reading, our teaching, or students' learning that we would like to understand better or improve, we are, in essence, establishing a *purpose* for our research and defining a *topic*. Consider the following real-world examples.

Example 6-1

Purpose: I want to understand the extent to which I am teaching vocabulary directly because there is evidence that direct instruction can assist L2 students in developing their vocabulary and, in turn, help them become better readers.
Topic: Explicit instructional techniques for vocabulary expansion.

Example 6-2

Purpose: I recognise that extensive reading is one of the best ways to help students develop their reading abilities. Although I devote a lot of class time to reading-related activities, I don't think that my students engage in enough silent, extended reading. I want to determine how much extensive reading my students actually engage in.
Topic: Amount of extensive reading that students engage in.

6.1.2 Pose a specific question

To conduct a manageable action research project, we need to limit the focus of our enquiry by posing a question that will guide our research. To get started, we generally brainstorm possible questions related to the topic of interest. Then, in an effort to narrow the scope of the project, we select one (or a limited number) of our questions to guide our research. Because every action research project has the potential of being extended, the questions that result from brainstorming, in addition to others that are likely to emerge during the action research project itself, can serve as resources for future projects.

Consider the process of narrowing the scope of an action research project by examining these two examples.

Example 6-1a

Topic: Explicit instructional techniques for vocabulary expansion.
Possible questions include the following:

1. What instructional approaches do I use in class to assist students in learning new vocabulary?
2. To what extent do I integrate the use of definitions into my instruction?
3. How often do I use word-family exercises and word-analysis activities to promote vocabulary learning?
4. What kinds of games do I use to promote vocabulary expansion?
5. To what extent do I resort to translations to speed up the vocabulary-learning process?
6. How can I use the Word Wall concept (see Eyraud, Giles, Koenig and Stoller, 2000) as an explicit vocabulary-teaching technique?
7. Which explicit vocabulary-teaching techniques lead to better retention of vocabulary over a period of time?
8. What works better: using explicit vocabulary-teaching techniques *before* or *after* students have encountered a new word in context?

Preferred question: What instructional approaches do I use in class to assist students in learning new vocabulary? (question 1)

Example 6-2a

Topic: Amount of extensive reading that students engage in.
Possible questions include the following:

1. How much extensive reading do my students actually do in class?
2. How much extensive reading do my students claim to do at home?
3. What is the proper amount of time to devote to Sustained Silent Reading, as a form of extensive reading, in class?
4. How do students feel about the amount of extensive reading that they are engaged in?
5. Which books or magazines do students decide to read when they engage in extensive reading?
6. What are students' attitudes toward extensive reading?
7. To what extent does the school library collection meet the extensive reading needs of my students?
8. What types of follow-up activities do students enjoy the most after extensive reading?

Preferred question: What is the total amount of extensive reading students do in class and at home? (combination of questions 1 and 2)

6.1.3   Anticipate outcomes of action research

We should consider what we hope to gain from our research. This early reflection will help us decide what data to collect and how to collect them. Consider the examples below.

Example 6-1b

Topic: Explicit instructional techniques for vocabulary expansion.
Preferred question: What instructional approaches do I use in class to assist students in learning new vocabulary?
Anticipated outcome(s): After becoming more aware of the direct instructional techniques that I use in class, I hope to incorporate additional explicit vocabulary-building approaches into my teaching repertoire. In this way, I'll be able to add variety to my teaching and help my students expand their vocabulary.

Example 6-2b

Topic: Amount of extensive reading that students engage in.
Preferred question: What is the total amount of extensive reading students do in class and at home?
Anticipated outcome(s): After I determine how much extensive reading my students actually do each week (in and out of class), I will rethink my classroom activities and homework assignments to make sure sufficient time is being spent on extensive reading because it is so important for reading skills development.

6.1.4   Specify the type of data to collect

After deciding on a research question, we need to consider the type(s) of data that we should collect to answer the question. Careful consideration of the research question is likely to reveal various options, including the collection of **quantitative data** (i.e. numerical data, data that can be counted), **qualitative data** (i.e. data that cannot be counted, but that can be reviewed for noticeable patterns and insights into students and tasks) or both. For example, a teacher, guided by the desire to determine which of her students need additional work on rate development, may want to find out how fast her students read when they are reading for general comprehension. With the assistance of a record-keeping sheet, the teacher can systematically collect students' reading rates – in minutes and seconds – and comprehension scores – as the number correct over total possible. This quantitative data (numerical data) will help the teacher answer her action research question. Or imagine a teacher who wants to explore ways of helping students develop an appreciation and enthusiasm for reading-to-learn activities. That teacher might ask her students to write a series of brief reflective papers that require them to record the most important new information learned at the end of every week, based on a review of readings. An analysis of those reflective papers is likely to reveal students' attitudes about their readings (i.e. qualitative data), offering the teacher insights into students' perceptions of the value of reading-to-learn activities.

Many types of data can be collected (e.g. students' reading rates, an inventory of pre-reading tasks in a mandated textbook, lesson plans, student or teacher journal entries, student homework, reading exams, audiotaped lessons). What is key is that the data collected, when analysed, assist us in finding answers to our action research questions. Consider the following two examples, which showcase different types of data to be collected.

Example 6-1c

Topic: Explicit instructional techniques for vocabulary expansion.
Preferred question: What instructional approaches do I use in class to assist students in learning new vocabulary?
Type of data to collect: Inventory of explicit vocabulary instruction techniques used in class.

Example 6-2c

Topic: Amount of extensive reading that students engage in.
Preferred question: What is the total amount of extensive reading students do in class and at home?
Type of data to collect: A record of time (in minutes) that students spend reading in school and at home.

6.1.5   Determine ways to collect data

Important considerations in action research revolve around the kinds of data to collect (Step 4) in addition to *how*, *where* and *from whom* to collect the data. We can approach the data-collection task in many ways. We can choose individual approaches (which do not involve other teachers) or collaborative approaches (which involve others, often another teacher).

Quote 6.5

Action research is made more feasible, professionally exhilarating and relevant when conducted with a collaborative and supportive group of colleagues.

Burns (1999, p. 6)

We can devise data-collection procedures that complement normal classroom routines (and that cause no disruption whatsoever to class lessons), or we may use approaches that are viewed as intrusive because they are not part of the normal classroom routine (e.g. questionnaires administered during class time that are not part of regular instruction). Or we might choose approaches that do not impact on classroom instruction at all by, for example, gathering sets of documents that are relevant to the research question (e.g. lesson plans, student writing samples, completed homework assignments, textbooks). We have many data-collection options open to us; the key is to select a data-collection technique that is a natural outgrowth of the guiding research question (Step 2) and desired outcomes (Step 3). Concept 6.3 lists some commonly used data-collection techniques.

Concept 6.3   Data-collection techniques

Case studies: Investigation of an individual *case* (e.g. a learner, a student group, a teacher, a class).

Classroom observations: Attentive observation, supported by some form of record keeping (e.g. note taking, audiotaping, videotaping, filling out checklists) of aspects of one's own classroom (by the researcher herself or another person) or another teacher's classroom.

Document gathering: Collection of sets of documents (interpreted broadly) that are relevant to the research question (e.g. in-class exams; lesson plans; pre- and post-tests; software; student exercises, worksheets, writing assignments or projects; student records; textbooks).

Field notes: A written record of classroom events related to the research question (e.g. physical set up of classroom, student groupings, student movement, teacher–student interactions). Field notes are taken as the study proceeds, not after the fact. (Compare with *Journals* and *Teaching logs*.)

Interviews: Face-to-face interactions conducted by the teacher in a structured, semi-structured, or unstructured format with teachers, administrators, librarians, aides and parents. (Compare with *Teacher–student conferences*.)

Journals: Written record of teacher's opinions and reactions to research questions and related issues. Dated journal entries are usually completed after class. (Compare with *Teaching logs* and *Field notes*.)

Questionnaires: A set of written questions related to research that the teacher asks participants (e.g. students, other teachers, administrators, librarians, parents) to answer.

Record-keeping forms: Standardised forms (e.g. charts, checklists, grids, matrices, tally sheets, worksheets) used for systematic data collection.

Self-observation: Attentive observation of some select aspect of one's own teaching, utilising some form of record keeping (e.g. audiotaping, videotaping).

Simulated recall: Review of previously recorded data (e.g. an audiotape, videotape or transcription of a class or a teacher–student conference) to prompt responses from participants on events or activities being investigated.

Teacher–student conferences: Focused face-to-face interactions between teacher and student, often away from the rest of the class. (Compare with *Interviews*.)

Teaching logs: Written record of focal teaching events, usually completed after class. Dated log entries normally include factual information rather than more subjective reactions and opinions. (Compare with *Journals* and *Field notes*.)

Verbal reports: Verbal reflections on focus of research, often tape recorded.

Quote 6.6

Data collection methods used are generally multidimensional, allowing for a variety of data collection tools and methods as well as the perspectives of different participants in the research context. This means that the data can be 'triangulated' or, in other words, come from various sources which can be tested out against each other.

Burns (1999, p. 10)

Although the data-collection techniques described in Concept 6.3 are listed separately, we can (and often do) use more than one data-collection technique as part of our action research. Consider the examples below, each one making use of more than one type of data-collection technique.

Example 6-1d

Topic: Explicit instructional techniques for vocabulary expansion.
Question: What instructional approaches do I use in class to assist students in learning new vocabulary?
Primary way(s) to collect data: Self-observation and a record-keeping form (Figure 6.1).

Explicit vocabulary teaching technique	Week 1			Week 2			Week 3			Week 4		
	M	W	F	M	W	F	M	W	F	M	W	F
Analysis of word parts												
Anecdotes or stories highlighting word meaning												
Associations												
Cognate awareness												
Definitions												
Dictionary consultation												
Discussion of word meaning												
Games												
Glosses												
Illustrations/drawings on the blackboard												
Realia												
Semantic feature analysis												
Semantic mapping												
Synonyms/antonyms												
Translation												
Use of lexical sets												
Word family activities												
Other												

Figure 6.1 **Techniques for direct vocabulary instruction**

Example 6-2d

Topic: Amount of extensive reading that students engage in.
Question: What is the total amount of extensive reading students do in class and at home?
Primary way(s) to collect data: A record-keeping form for students to complete out of class (e.g. Figure 6.2), classroom observation and a record-keeping form for the teacher to fill out in class (e.g. Figure 6.3).

Student's name_____						
Date	Start time	End time	Total reading time (in minutes)	What did you read?	Homework reading (✓)	Pleasure reading (✓)
15/9/01	5:30	5:44	14 minutes	*Space Exploration,* pp. 7–11	✓	
	8:40	9:00	20 minutes	*Sports Illustrated*		✓

Figure 6.2   **Record of out-of-class reading, kept by students for a 2-week period**

Class: _____									
Date	Minutes of extensive reading in class								
	1–5	6–10	11–15	16–20	21–25	26–30	31–35	36–40	41–45	46–50

Figure 6.3   **Record of in-class extensive reading time, in 5-minute increments**

6.1.6   Consider issues related to time

Although action research need not take up a lot of time, time is required for all action research projects. When we decide to engage in action research, we must consider (and possibly calculate) the time demands of the project. In this way, before jumping into the project, we have a realistic sense about what we have committed ourselves to. The time demands of action research vary, depending on the nature of the task, data-collection procedures and analysis. In some projects, we have to devote time *before* actually starting our research, to prepare or locate appropriate materials (e.g. questionnaires, record-keeping sheets, worksheets, pre- and post-exams, comprehension questions, textbook reading passages, vocabulary items). In other cases, time may be needed *after* class sessions to reflect on classroom events (e.g. in a journal, in a teaching log or on a checklist) or to transcribe an audiotape of a class observation. Some action research projects necessitate in-class instructional time; these types of projects usually require us to devote some time before class in order to adjust our lesson plans, thereby accommodating our data-collection activities. In all action research projects, time will be needed to analyse data (Step 8), reflect on results (Step 9) and consider new ways of teaching in response to those results (Step 10). When we choose to share our insights with colleagues (Step 12), we have to allot additional time for such activity.

Also related to time are issues of *when*, *how often* and *how long* to gather data. As noted earlier, we may choose to observe ourselves during one single class session. Or we may collect data every Monday, Wednesday and Friday for an entire semester or academic year. Although action research can be shortened or lengthened at any point in time, deciding on an initial time frame is helpful. Consider the time issues in the examples below.

Example 6-1e

Topic: Explicit instructional techniques for vocabulary expansion.
Question: What instructional approaches do I use in class to assist students in learning new vocabulary?
Time needed: Before actually starting my research, I need to devote time to researching explicit vocabulary-teaching techniques and then creating a checklist (similar to Figure 6.1) for easy record keeping. Then I'll set aside time after class – for one month, every Monday, Wednesday and Friday – to fill out my checklist.

Example 6-2e

Topic: Amount of extensive reading that students engage in.
Question: What is the total amount of extensive reading students do in class and at home?
Time needed: I need to create two charts, one for student record keeping and the other for my own record keeping (see Figures 6.2 and 6.3). I'll need to set aside time in class to introduce the project to my students and show them how to keep records of their out-of-class extensive reading. Then I'll collect data over a 2-week period. After 2 weeks of daily record keeping, I'll determine if I need to collect more data. During the analysis stage, my in-class records will be easy to tabulate. Individual student records, on the other hand, may be more time-consuming to tabulate and interpret.

6.1.7   Collect data systematically

It is during the data-collection stage when the preceding steps (Steps 1–6) are put into action. How data are collected and how often they are collected are variable; what should remain constant, however, is *careful*, *regular* and *systematic* data collection. Consider the following examples.

Example 6-1f

Topic: Explicit instructional techniques for vocabulary expansion.
Question: What instructional approaches do I use in class to assist students in learning new vocabulary?
Data collection: During class, I'll pay careful attention to the ways in which I assist students in learning new vocabulary. Immediately following each Monday, Wednesday and Friday class for a month, I'll fill out my checklist (Figure 6.1) by indicating the instructional techniques used in class. If I use a technique that is not listed on my checklist, I'll add it to the list.

Example 6-2f

Topic: Amount of extensive reading that students engage in.
Question: What is the total amount of extensive reading students do in class and at home?
Data collection: Over a 2-week period, I'll time students while they are engaged in silent reading in class. I'll record the actual time spent reading, in 5-minute increments, on a record-keeping chart (see Figure 6.3). During the same time period, I'll ask students to record what they read and the amount of time that they spend reading at home, using a standardised record sheet (similar to the one in Figure 6.2). [Note: I'll recognise, from the very beginning, that student responses might not be entirely accurate. Some students may inflate their reported reading times, imagining that large time blocks might impress me; others might report less time, embarrassed about the time needed to complete homework assignments and any other reading they engage in.] After 2 weeks of daily record keeping, I'll determine if I need more data.

6.1.8   Examine and analyse data

During this important step of the action research process, we are likely to engage in a range of activities, with the goal being to *describe*, *display*, *interpret* and *explain* the significance of the data collected in light of the research question driving the project. The ultimate aim of the project, of course, is to use insights gained during this stage of the process to improve one's own classroom teaching and the learning that takes place there. The analysis stage is likely to require us to be involved in one or more of these activities:

1. *Assembling or transforming data* (e.g. transcribing videotapes or audiotapes, tabulating numerical data, organising student essays).

2. *Examining data* in search of recurring (a) *patterns* (e.g. both strong and weak readers benefit from the use of graphic organisers during pre-reading activities), (b) *trends* (e.g. students who are given the opportunity to select their own reading materials tend to read increasing numbers of pages over the course of a semester), (c) *characteristics* (e.g. slow readers use few, if any, pre-reading strategies on their own), (d) *sequences* (e.g. the assignment of descriptive passages before cause–effect passages seems to be more manageable for students), (e) *relationships* (e.g. students who use two or more vocabulary-collection techniques on their own are likely to have larger vocabularies than students who constantly use the same technique repeatedly), (f) *hierarchies* (e.g. students of all ability levels seem to value certain reading strategies – previewing the text, predicting the contents of the text, connecting text to background information – more than others – specifying a purpose for reading, checking predictions, rereading), or (g) *themes* (e.g. students enjoy reading non-fiction themes more than fiction).

3. *Categorising data* (e.g. dividing vocabulary words – identified by students as unfamiliar – into groups of content words and function words; or separating questions posed by the teacher into categories, such as questions that require (a) recall of information, (b) a summary, (c) an expansion of an original response, (d) an explanation, (e) an evaluation, (f) an application of information, (g) a judgement, (h) a personal response, (i) an inference, (j) an interpretation, (k) a prediction, (l) a restatement).

4. *Comparing data* (e.g. comparing findings from one class with findings from another class; comparing results of highly motivated and less motivated students; comparing students' receptiveness to one pre-reading activity and then another).

Consider our two example action research projects to see how data are analysed.

Example 6-1g

Topic: Explicit instructional techniques for vocabulary expansion.
Question: What instructional approaches do I use in class to assist students in learning new vocabulary?
Data analysis: After a month of data collection, I'll tabulate the check marks on my record-keeping sheet to determine which explicit vocabulary-teaching techniques I use and the extent of their use. The results should reveal my current preferences as well as techniques that are under-used or not used at all.

Example 6-2g

Topic: Amount of extensive reading that students engage in.
Question: What is the total amount of extensive reading students do in class and at home?
Data analysis: At the end of the data-collection period, I'll add up numbers on both sets of record-keeping charts: my own records (to determine in-class extensive reading time) and students' individual records (to determine how much time each student reports reading outside of class). I'll tabulate how much time each student reads per week (adding my numbers to theirs). I'll try to identify the characteristics (and reading abilities) of students who read the most and those who read the least. I'll compare the amounts of out-of-class reading completed by skilled student readers and less-skilled student readers to see if there are any transparent relationships between the two.

6.1.9   Reflect on results

This phase of the action research process, in reality, is hard to separate from the examination and analysis stage (Step 8). As we analyse our data, we naturally reflect on the importance and usefulness of our observations for the ultimate purpose of answering our research question, drawing conclusions and resolving the dilemma (or satisfying the curiosity) that led to the question. During this critical step of the process, we need to consider our topic and guiding research question to determine what we have learned. We try to develop theories that explain our interpretations and guide future actions or research projects. With an open mind, we can consider important questions such as these: What do these results mean? What have I learned about myself? About my students? About reading? About reading instruction? How can I use the insights gained to improve the teaching and learning that goes on in my classroom? Based on the results of this project, what aspects of my classroom instruction should remain the same and what should be modified?

Quote 6.7

Gaining insights into one's own teaching or discovering something about oneself as a professional that one didn't know before is the very essence of action research.

Wallace (1998, p. 44)

At this stage, we can also reflect on the action research project itself, asking questions such as these: What were the strengths and weaknesses of my study? What are the limitations to the study that I should take into account while reflecting on the results? Do I need to take this research one step further to learn even more about this topic? What new questions do I have now? Could these questions be used to structure a new action research project?

To gain more insights into this stage of the process, consider our two sample action research projects.

Example 6-1h

Topic: Explicit instructional techniques for vocabulary expansion.
Question: What instructional approaches do I use in class to assist students in learning new vocabulary?
Reflection on results: I'll think about the patterns that have emerged from my data and try to understand why I've been drawn to certain vocabulary-teaching techniques and why I've shied away from others. I've noticed that I often use definitions, synonyms and antonyms, illustrations and mime to define new vocabulary terms but rarely use techniques such as dictionary consultation, **analysis of word parts**, cognate awareness and use of **lexical sets**. Not even once did I use **semantic feature analysis** with my students! Now that I think about it, I probably had many opportunities to do so. I'm probably cheating my students by not exposing them to a broader range of vocabulary-learning techniques. I may be limiting myself

because I haven't had much experience with those other techniques. When I was a language student, my teachers mainly used translation, but that won't work in my multilingual classroom.

Although I've learned a lot about my students' vocabulary-building experiences in my own classes, I'm not really sure about the vocabulary-learning techniques my students are being exposed to, on a regular basis, in their other classes. I may need to interview my students' other teachers to find out the extent to which students are exposed to other vocabulary-learning techniques.

Example 6-2h

Topic: Amount of extensive reading that students engage in.
Question: What is the total amount of extensive reading students do in class and at home?
Reflection on results: As I might have predicted, the total amount of extensive reading my students engage in out of class varies greatly. Although I have to keep in mind that students' records may be over-inflated or under-reported, there are indications that the stronger readers in class read at least 20 minutes every day (even on weekends!). A few of the able readers (I could have predicted who they were) spend even longer periods of time with pleasure-reading materials taken out of the library. The weaker readers are hardly reading at all; they seem to be doing the bare minimum to complete their homework assignments. With just a few exceptions, my weaker readers are not involved in any ongoing pleasure reading.

What was particularly surprising, and even disturbing, is the limited amount of silent reading going on in class. I had thought we were spending a lot of time on reading lessons, but most time is devoted to a discussion of the reading assignments or vocabulary explanations. Little time is actually spent on reading. I wonder what the principal would say if he walked by the room and it was totally silent, with everyone reading!

The totals that I've tabulated convince me that I need to reorganise my lessons to make time for more extensive reading. In addition, I need to figure out a way to motivate my weaker readers to read more out of class.

6.1.10   Generate practical solutions

In one sense, the goal of action research is to arrive at this point in the process. That is, we normally engage in action research not only to gain a better understanding of our classrooms (Steps 1–9) but also to take practical steps to improve classroom instruction (Steps 10–11). One way to enhance classroom teaching and learning, after having reflected on the results of our research, is to generate practical solutions and a plan to implement them. It should be noted that in the 'search' for solutions, we should not assume that there is a single solution waiting to be discovered; rather, there are probably many practical options from which we can choose. We may try out a brand new approach, technique or set of materials (that we have read about or heard about at a conference) on an experimental basis, or restructure a tried and true technique. The critical issue is to use the research results (and insights from reading theory and other research) to take action, to try out new classroom practices.

Revisit our two case studies to discover some of the practical solutions generated in response to the questions posed.

Example 6-1i

Topic: Explicit instructional techniques for vocabulary expansion.

Question: What instructional approaches do I use in class to assist students in learning new vocabulary?

Practical solutions: The checklist designed to keep track of the vocabulary-teaching techniques that I commonly use in class will come in handy. I want to expand my repertoire of explicit vocabulary-teaching techniques by initially experimenting with four techniques listed on the checklist that I have never used: semantic feature analysis, in-class dictionary consultation, analysis of word parts and use of lexical sets. (I don't plan on experimenting with cognates at this time because my class is so multilingual.) It will be worth my time to experiment with these four vocabulary-teaching techniques for a number of reasons. First, research (not my own, but research by others) has indicated the value of explicit vocabulary teaching for developing readers; second, my students' reading is likely to improve when they have a more developed vocabulary. Third, I need to broaden my repertoire to assist my students with their vocabulary development.

To experiment with these four vocabulary-teaching techniques, I'll have to spend time predicting the words that my students are likely to have difficulties with and work out lesson plans, when appropriate, that make use of these new techniques. Because I've never used the techniques before, I'll try to work out all the details in my lesson plans so that I'm more likely to be successful with them.

At some time in the future, I'd be interested in interviewing some of my colleagues (those who teach the same students) to find out how they teach new vocabulary to our students.

Example 6-2i

Topic: Amount of extensive reading that students engage in.
Question: What is the total amount of extensive reading students do in class and at home?
Practical solutions: The results of my action research project reveal that I need to increase the time students spend reading in and out of class. Although my students who are strong readers already read a fair amount, they too will benefit from reading more. The real beneficiaries of my plan, however, will be my weaker readers, those who are spending very little time reading.

First, to increase the amount of time that students spend reading silently in class, I'm going to experiment with a Sustained Silent Reading (**SSR**) programme 2 days per week, for an entire semester. Second, to increase the amount of reading done out of class, I'll focus on the weaker readers in class. I need to motivate them to spend more time reading at home. I'll hold teacher–student conferences during which I can talk to them about their reading and build their confidence and self-image as readers. I will also schedule a meeting with the principal of my school to tell him about my proposed SSR programme so that he'll understand the rationale for the programme and be supportive of my efforts. Because he is a strong proponent of communicative classrooms, I need to help him understand the benefits of a quiet classroom, with students working on their own, at their own desks, silently engaged in interesting reading. Some time in the future, I'll work with the school librarian to identify pleasure-reading books that might be of interest to my weak students.

6.1.11   Experiment with solutions

At this point in the process, we become eager to implement practical solutions to our action research question, with the goal of enhancing the effectiveness of classroom instruction. The insights gained from our research and the practical solutions generated through reflection usually represent a source of excitement and positive challenge because they are so closely tied to reality: our real world, real classroom, real students and real needs. When we try out our practical solutions, however, we are wise to view our efforts as experimental. Because we cannot possibly know how effective proposed solutions will be, it is natural to consider initiating a follow-up action research project to determine their effectiveness. Of course, this entails going back to Steps 1 and 2 to begin the process again.

What we learn from the action research process, at this point, is that it is never conclusive, nor is it static or self-contained. In exploring a narrow area of a larger topic, we inevitably encounter new questions, leading to new action research projects. The dynamic nature of action research creates multiple opportunities for new and manageable action research projects.

Once again, let's return to our two case studies to see how this step unfolds.

Example 6-1j

Topic: Explicit instructional techniques for vocabulary expansion.

Question: What instructional approaches do I use in class to assist students in learning new vocabulary?

Experimentation with practical solutions: When appropriate, I'll experiment with four new vocabulary-teaching techniques (i.e. semantic feature analysis, dictionary work, analysis of word parts and use of lexical sets). When I am able to integrate these new techniques into my lesson plans (at points where they complement the texts and vocabulary under consideration), I'll be sure to observe students' responses to the techniques and the adjustments that I make to my plans in order to accommodate their needs and reactions. To evaluate the effectiveness of the techniques and the ways in which I integrate them into my classroom, I'll keep an after-class journal, noting my reactions and my students' reactions to the techniques (as part of a follow-up action research project). I'll also jot down notes on my lesson plans to reflect the changes made, if any.

Around the same time, I'll schedule short, relatively informal interviews with my colleagues to identify the explicit vocabulary-teaching techniques they use in class, if any (as a follow-up action research project). Before the actual interviews, I'll talk to my colleagues casually and explain my reasons for wanting to interview them. Hopefully they'll become interested in the topic and be willing to cooperate. I'll use my own checklist of techniques as a springboard for our conversations. I'll take notes at the interviews to keep a record of responses. When I've collected data from everyone, I'll analyse the results of my interviews to try to determine the vocabulary-learning experiences that my students are having across the curriculum.

Example 6-2j

Topic: Amount of extensive reading that students engage in.
Question: What is the total amount of extensive reading students do in class and at home?
Experimentation with practical solutions: Because it wouldn't be realistic to experiment with all of my practical solutions at once (I'm simply too busy), I'll start out with the two solutions that are most closely related: the implementation of SSR and a meeting with my principal to explain my rationale for SSR. At a later date, I'll schedule teacher–student conferences with my weaker readers and begin to work with the school librarian more closely to identify books that might motivate my weaker readers.

During the semester in which I experiment with SSR, I'll subscribe to standard SSR procedures: student-selected reading materials, regularly scheduled SSR sessions, teacher participation by reading silently along with students and the absence of explicit instruction, evaluation and interruptions. I'll start with 5-minute sessions and gradually extend their length to no more than 15 minutes. I'll keep track of the time allotments and make notes about student concentration, attitudes and restlessness to ascertain the best time allotment to sustain student interest (as a follow-up action research project). I know that, at first, there will be some confusion and some resistance, but I'll work through that.

When I meet the school principal to explain my reasons for implementing SSR, I'll explain the importance of extensive reading for developing readers and the role SSR can play in a reading curriculum.

6.1.12   Share insights with colleagues

In the final stages of an action research project, we have the option of sharing what we have learned from the project with interested colleagues. We can share findings, practical solutions, insights about the action research process and new theories about our topic with colleagues in our own institutions and with professionals outside our institutions at professional conferences – as part of informal discussions, formal presentations, interactive workshops or poster sessions. We can also share insights through written publications in school or district newsletters, in professional journals or as part of Internet chat groups. (See Burns, 1999, Chapter 7, for helpful guidelines for writing up reports of action research. See Wallace, 1998, Chapters 3 and 10, for comments on the ethics of reporting and issues of confidentiality.)

There are many benefits to disseminating action research findings. Although we often work in the isolation of our own classrooms, we experience similar challenges (and similar joys). The concerns of one teacher are often the concerns of her colleagues; the frustrations of one teacher often represent the frustrations of others. Similarly, the action research questions that one teacher poses are often similar to the action research questions of other teachers. Because of common concerns and aspirations, we are normally interested in the insights of colleagues who have been engaged in action research. Although it takes time to disseminate information, the effort is worthwhile because of the so-called **multiplier effect**. When we share what we have learned with others, increasing numbers of students become the beneficiaries of the research. When other teachers experiment with practical solutions or theories introduced by teachers who have been engaged in action research, efforts to improve classroom instruction and student learning are more far-reaching. The potential for the multiplier effect to operate here extends the impact of a single action research project, enhancing the teaching and learning in multiple classrooms.

Consider the ways in which insights are disseminated in our two model projects.

Example 6-1k

Topic: Explicit instructional techniques for vocabulary expansion.
Question: What instructional approaches do I use in class to assist students in learning new vocabulary?
Sharing of insights with colleagues: After I interview my colleagues to find out what vocabulary-teaching techniques they use on a regular basis, I'll have a better sense of which techniques are being used and which aren't being used with our students. If my colleagues are not using semantic feature analysis, dictionary work, analyses of word parts or the use of lexical sets (the four techniques that I'll be experimenting with), I'll share ideas about those techniques with them. Because vocabulary is so critical for all language students, I am considering creating a poster, to be displayed at a local teachers' conference, that highlights the ways in which I integrate one of the vocabulary techniques (the one I'm most successful with) into my lessons.

Example 6-2k

Topic: Amount of extensive reading that students engage in.
Question: What is the total amount of extensive reading students do in class and at home?
Sharing of insights with colleagues: I intend to share the insights that I gain from my experimentation with SSR with other teachers in my school. I feel that this is important because students at all levels of instruction can benefit from uninterrupted extensive reading. I'll probably start out by talking informally with teachers in my own area because I know them well and know that they are concerned about the reading abilities of their students. Then I'll write up a general set of teacher guidelines, outlining the general principles of SSR, its standard procedures and some of the pitfalls that I experience, along with possible solutions to those problems. I plan to present the guidelines to my colleagues at a faculty meeting and organise a discussion that may lead to a department-wide (or possibly school-wide) commitment to SSR (or at least experimentation with it).

6.2   Conclusion

Quote 6.8

We agree that teachers are in the best position to explore their own practice and to make sense of the classroom worlds 'because they are full-time inhabitants of those settings rather than episodic visitors'.

Shulman (1997, p. 21, cited in Baumann and Duffy-Hester, 2000, p. 94)

The 12-step action research process outlined in this chapter should be seen as a flexible framework for teacher-initiated research and structured teacher reflection. The framework represents a manageable tool that we can use to understand the complexities of our own classrooms and to generate practical solutions to classroom-based issues. Those of us responsible for teaching reading can use action research to explore a wide range of reading-related topics. In the three chapters that follow, we focus on seven major areas for possible exploration:

Chapter 7	Chapter 8	Chapter 9
• Vocabulary	• Strategic reading	• Reading instruction
• Fluency	• Discourse	• Student affect
• Rate development	organisation	

In Chapters 7, 8 and 9, we outline the key features of nine manageable action research projects, for a total of 27 detailed projects. These sample projects should be seen as adaptable models that can be modified, in small or large ways, for different instructional settings. To assist interested teachers, we have listed additional questions in each chapter that can be used to suggest meaningful action research on various aspects of reading.

Further reading

Readers interested in further information on action research should consult Chapter 10 (sections 10.6 and 10.9). For a detailed discussion of *steps involved in collaborative action research projects*, see Burns (1999). For a detailed discussion and description of *data collection techniques*, see Wallace (1998, chapters 3–8). See Richards and Lockhart (1994) for a description of seven *action research case studies* (at the end of chapters 4–9) and *guidelines for conducting action research* (Appendix 7 of chapter 1).

Vocabulary, fluency and rate development: Action research projects

This chapter will showcase nine easy-to-use action research projects related to vocabulary, fluency and reading rate development. The particular focus of the chapter will be the following:

- key questions that can guide meaningful reading-related action research projects
- model action research projects that can be adapted for many classroom settings
- steps that teachers can take to engage in teacher-initiated enquiry
- different data collection and analysis techniques

Vocabulary, reading fluency and reading rate are central to skilled reading; for that reason, reading teachers regularly engage in action research projects around these broad topics. Reflective teachers concerned about their students' progress in these areas often ask themselves practical questions: How well am I facilitating vocabulary learning? Reading fluency? Reading rate development? Do my students read fast enough? Do my students know enough vocabulary to understand classroom assignments? How did my students do today with respect to vocabulary/fluency/rate? Despite the value of such queries, they are too broad to be useful for meaningful action research projects. More manageable questions, like the ones listed below, narrow down the topic and target select aspects of these broad areas. (Note that the questions with a check mark ✓ in front of them are explored in further detail later in this chapter.)

Specific questions related to *vocabulary* include, but are not limited to, the following:

✓ What percentage of words (and which words) in one chapter of our mandated textbook is unfamiliar to my students?

✓ What do I do when students ask me the meaning of an unknown word (either in front of the whole class or one-on-one)?

✓ How can I help my students become more efficient using an English–English dictionary?

✓ How effective are glosses in assisting students in comprehending a reading passage in a timely fashion?

✓ What word-collection techniques can I introduce to students to encourage autonomous vocabulary learning? Which techniques do students like best?

How often can students gain an understanding of an initially unfamiliar lexical item by rereading a passage?

How can I free students from over-dependence on the dictionary?

How can I help students begin to understand multiple meanings of words?

Specific questions related to *reading fluency* and *reading rate* include the following:

✓ Which of my students have difficulties with rapid word recognition?

✓ How fast do my students read when they read for general comprehension?

✓ What rate should I set for initial paced-reading activities?

✓ Which students should be paired for the most effective use of paired rereadings in class?

Which rereading activities work best in my class?

When should I integrate recognition exercises into a reading lesson, before or after students are asked to read a passage?

What type of teacher signal works best to indicate a reading rate to students during paced-reading exercises?

Questions such as these represent a small sampling of the questions that we can pose to guide action research projects about vocabulary, fluency and rate. The questions that we can ask of ourselves are virtually limitless; what is important for the purposes of teacher-initiated enquiry is that we pose questions that are meaningful for our own teaching contexts. Whether we pose questions about our own teaching effectiveness, the appropriateness of mandated or supplementary materials, students' abilities, classroom procedures or select instructional techniques, the key is to ask questions that will lead to a better understanding of our own classrooms and suggest solutions to specific classroom-related issues.

> **Quote 7.1**
>
> I would strongly recommend action research to all teachers. The process is rewarding because it validates classroom observation and encourages you to value your own judgements.... While traditional forms of professional development can be very stimulating, it is sometimes difficult to relate the theory with which teachers are presented to the reality of the classroom. Action research is refreshing as it is concerned with the classroom as it really is.
>
> Ross, cited in Burns (1999, p. 11)

7.1 Model action research projects

In this chapter, we outline nine action research projects that are likely to be of interest to teachers who are responsible for teaching reading. We focus on the questions marked with a ✓ above. For each model project, we (a) describe its purpose, (b) specify the key research question, (c) state anticipated outcomes, (d) identify primary way(s) to collect data, (e) enumerate methods for data collection, (f) describe techniques for data analysis, (g) consider the time required and (h) list necessary resources. Teachers who would like to pursue similar projects can modify these 'plans', in small or grand ways, so that the resulting projects complement the settings in which they work and the specific issues of concern to them. The action research projects outlined here serve at least two purposes: They present ideas for manageable action research projects and they offer an actual starting point for readers interested in the sample questions discussed in this chapter.

The first five action research projects relate to vocabulary issues; the last four are related to fluency and rate (see Figure 7.1). It should be noted that the research questions guiding these model projects could be approached from many different angles. Action research is flexible; thus interested teachers should feel free to adapt these models in

Model action research project	Page(s)	Topic	Primary way(s) to collect data
7.1.1	186–187	Percentage of familiar/unfamiliar words in mandated textbook	In-class vocabulary checklist
7.1.2	188	Teacher responses to student queries about unknown vocabulary	Audiotaped lessons and a teaching log
7.1.3	188–190	Use of dictionaries	Pre- and post-tests, teacher–student conferences
7.1.4	190–191	Effectiveness of glosses	Timed readings and post-reading comprehension questions
7.1.5	191–194	Students as collectors of words	Pre- and post-questionnaires
7.1.6	194–195	Student difficulties with word recognition	Word-recognition exercises and student record sheets
7.1.7	196–197	Student reading rate when reading for general comprehension	Record-keeping sheet
7.1.8	197–199	Initial rate for paced-reading activities	Observation of students, record keeping
7.1.9	199–201	Paired rereadings	Teaching log

Figure 7.1   **Model action research projects presented in Chapter 7**

whatever ways will assist them in obtaining answers that are meaningful to them (and their students).

7.1.1   Percentage of familiar/unfamiliar words in mandated textbook

Purpose: Reading fluency generally requires that a reader know 95 per cent or more of the words encountered in a text for independent comprehension. If students do not know 95 per cent of the words in assigned readings, they may experience reading difficulties. For this reason, it is valuable to try to determine the percentage of words in mandated materials that are likely to be unfamiliar to one's students.

Key question: **What percentage of words (and which words) in one chapter of our mandated textbook is unfamiliar to my students?**

Anticipated outcome(s): After determining which words are unfamiliar to the majority of students, a set of vocabulary-building activities can be devised that introduces students to words that are critical for comprehension of the chapter. These activities, when integrated into the pre-reading component of a reading lesson, will prepare students for the reading of the chapter.

Primary way to collect data: In-class vocabulary checklist.

Data collection: Collect data using a vocabulary checklist that includes 25 content words (or phrases) and 10+ function words from a chapter that students have not yet read. (See Figure 7.2 for a sample exercise.) Ask students to judge their familiarity with the word by indicating whether the word is unknown, seen before but not understood, understood but not used in their active vocabulary or known and used in their active vocabulary.

Data analysis: Tabulate the results of the vocabulary checklist to determine how familiar students are with the targeted words. Although not all students will be entirely truthful in their responses, words that the majority of students do not understand are likely to emerge from the data set.

Time needed: Design a vocabulary checklist that can be administered easily, well before the target chapter is actually going to be assigned. If limited time is available, make a list of lexical items for students to judge (much like in Figure 7.2.). With more extended time, create a checklist that presents target words in context. *Between* collecting data and assigning the target chapter, evaluate student responses and identify the vocabulary items that should be introduced by means of pre-reading vocabulary-building activities.

Resources needed: Mandated textbook.

How familiar are these words?	I don't know this word.	I've seen this word but I don't understand it.	I know this word but do not use it.	I know this word and use it.
Example: Their				✓
1. Voluntary				
2. Global				
3. Planet				
4. Population				
5. Growth				
6. Rate				
7. Overcrowded				
8. Traffic jams				
9. Nearly				
10. However				

Figure 7.2 Checklist to determine students' level of familiarity with select vocabulary items

7.1.2   Teacher responses to student queries about unknown vocabulary

Purpose: We often respond to students' queries about unknown vocabulary by providing students with an answer – in the form of a definition, synonym, translation, example, illustration, anecdote and so forth – instead of introducing students to strategies that they can use to figure out the meaning of words independently. Our natural impulse is often just to answer students' questions, mainly to save class time. Keeping track of how we deal with students' queries about vocabulary can be useful.

Key question: **What do I do when students ask me the meaning of an unknown word (either in front of the whole class or one-on-one)?**

Anticipated outcome(s): The results of this research may make it easier to move away from simply giving students an answer to their questions about unfamiliar vocabulary, and move toward introducing students to strategies for figuring out word meanings themselves.

Primary way to collect data: Audiotaped lessons and a teaching log.

Data collection: When reviewing instructional materials and planning classes over a month-long period, identify lessons in which students are likely to encounter unknown vocabulary. Audiotape those class sessions, with a small voice-activated recorder, as a way of keeping track of responses to student questions. As soon after class as possible, review the audiotape and note responses in a teaching log. (If it is possible to listen to the tape shortly after class, it will not be necessary to listen to the entire tape; save time by fast forwarding the tape to segments that include student questions and teacher responses.)

Data analysis: Review teaching-log entries to identify the ways in which students' questions about unfamiliar vocabulary are answered. Group similar teacher responses in an attempt to see patterns that may emerge. (Indications of a move away from direct responses to student questions may be due to an interest in introducing students to strategies for dealing with new words.)

Time needed: After audiotaped class sessions, listen to and make notes from tapes in a teaching log. After a month of data collection, set aside time to analyse data.

Resources needed: Voice-activated tape recorder and cassettes.

7.1.3   Use of dictionaries

Purpose: Students often spend a lot of time wading through dictionary entries when looking up definitions of unfamiliar words. When doing so, reading is interrupted, thinking disturbed and comprehension disrupted. Students could probably become more efficient in dictionary use with some systematic in-class training.

Key question: **How can I help my students become more efficient using an English–English dictionary?**

Anticipated outcome(s): After familiarising students with English–English dictionaries and introducing them to strategies for efficient dictionary use, students may be able to use their dictionaries more efficiently, ultimately spending more time reading and less time plodding through dictionaries entries.

Primary way to collect data: Pre- and post-tests, teacher–student conferences with a subset of students.

Data collection: Collect data during Spring term by means of pre- and post-tests. The tests, designed around two different 400-word passages, will evaluate students' use of the dictionary before and after systematic English–English dictionary training. Each test will be divided into two parts. In the first part, students will be asked to read a passage (with their dictionaries closed). Passages selected for the tests will meet two requirements: they must be of potential interest to the class and they must include at least eight vocabulary items that are unfamiliar to students. Equal numbers of words unknown to the majority of the class (approximately eight) will be underlined in each passage. After students have finished reading the passage, they will be asked to look up all underlined words and then write down appropriate dictionary definitions. Students will time themselves from the beginning to the end of the dictionary-consultation component of the test (the second part of the test) as a way to measure their efficiency and accuracy in using the dictionary. Pre-test scores will serve as baseline measures.

After the pre-test, conduct at least one 10-minute lesson per week, for the remainder of the term, to familiarise students with the dictionary and strategies for using it efficiently. Toward the end of the term, when training is complete, administer the post-test. Afterwards, meet a random sample of students for teacher–student conferences, during which students will be asked to recall the strategies that they used to complete the post-test. Take notes during (or audiotape) the teacher–student conferences.

Data analysis: Tabulate the results of pre- and post-tests to determine both time needed to complete the tests and number of correct answers. Compare pre- and post-test results for each student. Improved test scores will suggest that students have benefited from instruction on dictionary use. If students (or subsets of students) do not show improvement between the pre- and post-tests, consult student attendance records, other performance measures and teacher–student conference notes, if applicable, to try to determine why there was no improvement.

Time needed: Construct two parallel tests (a pre- and post-test) that will assess the effectiveness of students' dictionary use. Plan a series of 10-minute lessons to familiarise students with various dictionary features (e.g. pronunciation keys, part-of-speech indicators, definitions, usage notes, synonyms, abbreviations, spelling options, collocations) and strategies for using the dictionary (e.g. determining part of speech of unfamiliar word, selecting correct definitions of words with multiple meanings, determining when and when not to look up a word, choosing correct headwords, finding idiomatic expressions). If necessary, look over study skills textbooks to see how dictionary skills are introduced and reviewed.

Resources needed: Two 400-word passages that include at least eight words that students do not know; a class set of English–English dictionaries (if students do not have their own).

7.1.4   Effectiveness of glosses

Purpose: A limited vocabulary usually prevents students from achieving satisfactory reading comprehension. It would be interesting to find out if adding glosses to reading passages helps students with their comprehension and reading rates.

Key question: **How effective are glosses in assisting students in comprehending a reading passage in a timely fashion?**

Anticipated outcome(s): The results of this small-scale action research project should reveal the role that glosses play in assisting student readers with unfamiliar words. The results can help teachers decide whether or not to add glosses to primary readings that are assigned to future classes.

Primary way to collect data: Timed readings and post-reading comprehension questions.

Data collection: When teaching two sections of the same course, conduct an informal experiment. Designate one section as the control class and the other as the experimental class. Determine students' initial comprehension abilities by using scores of a reading comprehension test that students have already taken or by asking students to read a 400–500 word passage and answer 10 comprehension questions. The results of the pre-test measure will serve as simple baseline data. Once initial reading abilities have been determined, collect data during 5–6 class sessions. During each session, ask the control class to read a passage *without* glosses, and ask the experimental class to read the same passage *with* glosses. Ask both sets of students to answer an identical set of comprehension questions. Students will record the amount of time spent on reading and answering questions on their answer sheets. Collect answer sheets for later analysis.

Data analysis: Analyse results (comprehension scores and times) from the last three sessions (assuming that the early sessions serve as opportunities for training) to see if there is a difference in performance between the control and experimental classes. Consult baseline data to identify the students who started out as strong readers, and those who started out as weak readers, and then compare their pre- and post-test scores to see if the glosses made a difference for either group. The results of the analysis should give an indication of the usefulness of glosses in assisting students' reading comprehension.

Time needed: Find 5–6 reading passages that include words that are likely to be unfamiliar to students. Create two versions of each passage: one version with glosses of unfamiliar words and the other without. On the glossed versions, select a word to gloss every 4–8 lines. For each passage, write a set of comprehension questions to assess the usefulness of the glosses in helping students understand the text.

Resources needed: Five–six reading passages, with comprehension questions that require some understanding of the glossed words; a classroom clock (so that students can time their own reading); a 400–500 word passage, with 10 comprehension questions, to be used as a pre-test if scores from another test are not available.

7.1.5   Students as collectors of words

Purpose: Although direct instruction of vocabulary has an important place in L2 classrooms, students need to take some responsibility for learning and reviewing words on their own. Some students are natural collectors of words, while others need to be introduced to different techniques for collecting words. As part of this action research project, teachers introduce students to different ways of collecting words and then determine which techniques students like the best. Hopefully, students will discover and become comfortable with at least one technique that complements their own learning styles.

Key question: **What word-collection techniques can I introduce to students to encourage autonomous vocabulary learning? Which techniques do students like best?**

Anticipated outcome(s): The results of this action research project are likely to lead to insights about students' responsiveness to different types of word-collection techniques. This knowledge will influence the teacher's selection and sequencing of vocabulary-learning strategies for classroom practice. An added benefit may be an introduction to less traditional word-collection techniques – which students have devised on their own – that can be added to a teacher's vocabulary-teaching repertoire.

Primary way to collect data: Pre- and post-questionnaires.

Data collection: At the beginning of this project, ask students to complete a questionnaire (see Figure 7.3) on which they will indicate the ways in which they collect vocabulary words that they want to learn and review on their own. Then formally introduce students to the techniques listed on the questionnaire, one at a time, over the course of the semester. (If students list additional techniques on their questionnaires that might be useful for everyone to try out, add them to the list of word-collection options.) Give students the opportunity to experiment with each technique for a 2-week period.

At the start of each 2-week period, spend about 10 minutes discussing the targeted vocabulary-collection technique as a class. Give the technique a name, review procedures, discuss the benefits of the technique and practise using it in meaningful ways. As part of the introduction, ask students who have already had experience with the technique to share insights with classmates. Active student participation in the process of promoting different vocabulary-collection techniques is likely to have a more positive impact than a teacher-centred endorsement.

Over the 2-week period, devote five 10-minute sessions (for a total of 50 minutes of class time) to the collection of student-selected vocabulary using the targeted technique; the class should practise using the technique when most applicable (as part of pre-, during- or post-reading activities) to demonstrate its versatility. At some point during that two-week period, encourage students to use the vocabulary that they have collected (e.g. on index cards, in notebooks) as part of vocabulary-related games and select writing activities. For example, during a summary writing activity, ask students to use at least two vocabulary words from their index-card collection.

After covering all word-collection techniques in this way, ask students to complete a new questionnaire (see Figure 7.4) on which they will rank order the word-collection techniques practised in class, from most to least favourite. Ask students to provide a rationale for their

How do you collect words that you want to learn on your own? Read the statements on the left. Place a check mark (✓) in the appropriate space to the right.

	Never	Always	Sometimes
1. I write new words and their translations on index cards.	____	____	____
2. I keep a running list of new vocabulary words in my notebook. Next to each word, I write a definition. I add to the list whenever I hear or read a new word that I want to remember. I usually write down where I first saw/read the word.	____	____	____
3. I fill out index cards with new words, their definitions, an example sentence and something special to help me remember them.	____	____	____
4. I keep separate lists of new nouns, verbs, adjectives, adverbs and idioms in a special vocabulary notebook. Next to each word, I write the original sentence with the word and then I write a sentence of my own.	____	____	____
5. I organise new words that are interesting to me by topic. I have a separate page in my notebook for each topic.	____	____	____
6. Other _____	____	____	____

Figure 7.3   Sample questionnaire items designed to determine what techniques students use to collect vocabulary items on their own

ratings (or perhaps just for their most favourite technique, if time doesn't permit responses for all techniques).

Data analysis: Collect initial student questionnaires and review them immediately to determine which vocabulary-collection techniques are familiar to them. Use questionnaire results to make decisions about how to sequence the presentation of different techniques; start with techniques that students are already familiar with. Make use of questionnaire responses to identify students who might be asked to make comments during introductory activities. Later, analyse the results of the second questionnaire. Tabulate numerical responses to identify the students' favourite and least favourite vocabulary-collection techniques. Review written responses for insights into students' preferences.

Time needed: Write pre- and post-questionnaires (like Figures 7.3 and 7.4). Plan introductions to each vocabulary-collection technique and hands-on sessions during which students can practise techniques with

Consider the vocabulary-collection techniques (listed below) that we've used in class. Which one do you like the best? Which one do you like the least? Rank order these vocabulary-collection techniques (1 = my favourite; 6 = my least favourite). Provide a reason for your ranking decisions.		
Rank (1–6)	Vocabulary-collection techniques	Reason for ranking decision
	I write new words and their translations on index cards.	
	I keep a running list of new vocabulary words in my notebook. Next to each word, I write a definition. I add to the list whenever I hear or read a new word that I want to remember. I usually write down where I first saw/read the word.	
	I fill out index cards with new words, their definitions, an example sentence and something special to help me remember them.	
	I keep separate lists of new nouns, verbs, adjectives, adverbs and idioms in a special vocabulary notebook. Next to each word, I write the original sentence with the word and then I write a sentence of my own.	
	I organise new words that are interesting to me by topic. I have a separate page in my notebook for each topic.	
	Other:	

Figure 7.4   **Sample questionnaire items that will indicate student preferences for different vocabulary-collection techniques**

important words that have come up in class activities. Set aside class time early and late in the project to administer and then analyse questionnaires.

Resources needed: Pre- and post-questionnaires.

7.1.6   Student difficulties with word recognition

Purpose: Skilled readers possess good recognition skills. Students need to be able to recognise letters, letter groups, word parts, words and phrases very quickly to become good readers. There are many benefits to finding out which students have difficulties with word recognition.

Key question: **Which of my students have difficulties with rapid word recognition?**

Anticipated outcome(s): After administering a set of word-recognition exercises (that will be used as evaluation tools) to one's students, it is possible to identify the students who might benefit most from additional word-recognition practice. Students with weak word-recognition abilities will be assigned a set of recognition exercises, designed to include words from major reading assignments.

Primary way to collect data: Word-recognition exercises and student record sheets.

Data collection: Create a set of 20-item recognition exercises, including key words that students are likely to encounter in class readings. (See Figure 7.5 for a sample format.) During one class session, with about 15 minutes of class time, introduce students to procedures for completing recognition exercises (including timing, correction and record-keeping procedures). At that time, students will practise with a few trial exercises. The next day (for about 10 minutes), ask students to complete four recognition exercises. Have students time themselves, correct their own work and record their time and accuracy for each exercise on a record sheet.

Data analysis: Evaluate the results of the second, third and fourth exercises to identify students who might benefit from additional word-recognition practice (either because their rate is slow or because their accuracy is weak). Consider the first exercise to be a warm up; do not include it in the analysis.

Time needed: Write up two sets of four recognition exercises, one set for practice and one set for evaluation purposes. Create a record-keeping sheet with easy-to-manage sections to indicate time and accuracy for each word-recognition exercise. Set aside two 10–15 minute class sessions for word-recognition activities. Toward the conclusion of the project, create new word-recognition materials for independent student use.

Resources needed: Three sets of word-recognition exercises and a record-keeping sheet. (See Stoller, 1993, for suggestions on writing recognition exercises and using them in class.)

Key word					
1. **direct**	distinct	donate	di/rect	detect	desire
2. **trial**	entail	serial	trail	trial	frail
3. **through**	through	though	thorough	borough	thought

Figure 7.5   **Sample word-recognition exercise format (and response marking)**

7.1.7   Student reading rate when reading for general comprehension

Purpose: Good readers read at a reasonable rate, though the pace varies depending on the reader's purpose for reading. Determining how fast one's students read for general comprehension makes it easier to identify those students who might benefit from additional work on rate development.

Key question: **How fast do my students read when they read for general comprehension?**

Anticipated outcome(s): After determining students' average reading rates (when reading for general comprehension), it is possible to identify the slow readers in the class, those who might benefit from additional work on rate development. Once slow readers are identified, a reading rate development plan can be created for individual students in need.

Primary way to collect data: Record-keeping sheet.

Data collection: Integrate a series of timed-reading exercises into classroom instruction. Use materials like those in the Spargo (1989, 1998) series where readings are equal in length, with equal numbers of post-reading comprehension questions, for ease of record keeping. Early in the project, devote class time to (a) a discussion of reading speed and its relationship to skilled reading; (b) an introduction to procedures for timed readings, comprehension checks and record keeping; and (c) practice. After five or six introductory lessons and practice sessions, begin to collect data (student rates – in minutes and seconds – and comprehension scores – as number correct over total possible) from at least four different readings, recognising that the topics of the readings will be different and that students are likely to read more familiar topics at a somewhat faster pace. Record student data on a record-keeping sheet (see Figure 7.6).

Data analysis: To calculate students' average reading rates for general comprehension, only consider rates where students achieve 70 per cent or more (i.e. 7/10 or higher) on comprehension. For students who comprehend 70 per cent or more of the text on a fairly consistent basis, add up all acceptable reading times and then divide that number by the number of readings considered. Then divide the length of the four reading passages (e.g. 400 words per passage) by the average reading time to determine how many words students read per minute. (See Figures 7.6 and 7.7 for a sample calculation.) Students who receive comprehension scores of 60 per cent or lower on a regular basis can be given alternative (easier) reading materials immediately and the opportunity to work on rate building during individualised instruction time.

Student	Time (minutes: seconds) for 400-word passages				Average reading rate	Words per minute
	Reading 1 Rate Comp	Reading 2 Rate Comp	Reading 3 Rate Comp	Reading 4 Rate Comp		
Maria H.	4:15 7/10	4:30 8/10	4:05 9/10	3:30 6/10	4:17	92

Figure 7.6   **Sample reading rate and comprehension record-keeping sheet**

To calculate *average reading rate*, add up reading rates where student achieved 70 per cent or more on comprehension: 4:15 + 4:30 + 4:05 = 12:50; then divide by the number of readings considered: 12.50 ÷ 3 = 4:17. (Note that the 3:30 rate is not included in these calculations because the student's comprehension was under 70 per cent.)

To calculate *words per minute* (wpm), convert the seconds (of the average reading rate) to the nearest percentage equivalent, and then move the decimal two places to the right. Then divide the average length of reading passages by average time percentage.

Seconds   Percentage equivalent

:10 = .17

:20 = .33

:30 = .50

:40 = .67

:50 = .83

For example, 4:17 is closest to 4 minutes and 20 seconds; convert 4:17 to 4.33. Move the decimal two places to the right to get 433. Then divide 400 (average length of reading passages) by 433 (average time percentage). Thus, 400 ÷ 433 = 92 wpm.

Figure 7.7   **Sample reading-rate calculation for Maria H**

Time needed: Compile sets of timed readings and create a simple record-keeping sheet.

Resources needed: Class sets of timed readings, student record sheets.

7.1.8   Initial rate for paced-reading activities

Purpose: Reading rates vary for individual readers, depending on the nature of the text one is reading, one's reason for reading and one's reading proficiency. There are rates, however, that are simply too slow for general comprehension. Many language learners read too slowly for good comprehension; these students could probably benefit from direct attention to rate building in class. Reading speed can be developed in numerous ways in the classroom. Timed-reading activities (activities in which students work individually to improve their reading rates) are popular with students. Paced-reading activities (activities in which the teacher sets a reading rate for the entire class) represent an alternative means for rate building. Teachers who have never used paced readings face the challenge of determining what pace to set for the class as a starting point. The goal is to identify a pace that pushes the majority of students to read faster than they normally would on their own, but that is not too challenging for the weakest readers in class.

Key question: **What rate should I set for initial paced-reading activities?**

Anticipated outcome(s): This action research project should reveal a reading rate that can be used to systematise an in-class paced-reading programme. Other insights (e.g. into the logistics of implementing a paced-reading programme, the challenges that students will encounter and the time required for in-class paced-reading sessions) are likely to emerge as well.

Primary way to collect data: Observation of students, record keeping.

Data collection: After introducing students to a rationale for paced-reading activities and procedures for completing them, set a 100 words-per-minute pace for the initial practice exercise (the initial pace can be modified, depending on the students). For some students, that pace is likely to be too fast; for others, it may be too slow. Use a 400-word passage, similar to those in Spargo (1989, 1998), indicating, after every 60 seconds, that students should be at the next 100-word mark, in-dicated in the margin of the text. (See Figure 7.8 for a pace-setting guide.) When students hear the signal (e.g. a light tap on the desk), they will know that they have to adjust their reading speed to match the pace established for the class. Do three consecutive paced readings at 100 wpm. (If adjustments need to be made at this point, make them.) At the end of each reading, students answer simple comprehension questions. After going over answers, ask students to indicate, with a show of hands, who thought the pace was too fast, too slow or just right. Make notes about student reactions on a record-keeping sheet. Note whether or not students are able to answer basic comprehension questions following the pacing exercise.

The goal of finding an appropriate reading pace for the class will probably require a series of attempts. Records and observations are likely to reveal whether the 100-wpm pace is too slow or too fast for

75	80
80	75
To set a pace of 100 words per minute (wpm), signal every 60 seconds.	
125	48
150	40
175	34
200	30
225	26
250	24
275	22
300	20

Figure 7.8 **Pace-setting guide**

the majority of the class. If it is too slow, try something like 125 wpm during the next class session (signalling every 48 seconds). If the 100-wpm pace is too fast, slow down to 80 wpm (signalling every 75 seconds). Through the process of trial and error, find a pace that will meet the needs of the majority of the class. During each paced reading, observe the students to see how well they handle the pace. Note any important observations on the record-keeping sheet.

Data analysis: Analyse data as it is collected. By means of ongoing data analysis, work toward determining a good pace for the majority of students. From that point, work toward building students' reading rates by increasing the pace incrementally every few class sessions. Note which students appear to struggle with the post-reading comprehension questions.

Time needed: The only time needed is class time. The first paced-reading session will require more time due to the need to integrate a rationale and introduction to procedures into the lesson. After the introductory lesson, class time will need to be dedicated to paced readings.

Resources needed: Paced-reading passages, ideally of equal or similar length, that conclude with basic comprehension questions.

7.1.9   Paired re-readings

Purpose: Numerous research studies have demonstrated the benefits of reading fluency training. Students can develop fluency by reading a lot (i.e. extensive reading in and out of class) and by engaging in a number of fluency building activities, including different re-reading exercises (e.g. re-reading by oneself, paired re-readings, re-reading with a tape, re-reading along with a teacher or group of students), rate building exercises (e.g. timed readings, paced readings), word and phrase recognition exercises and read alouds. For the purposes of this project, teachers can experiment with one re-reading technique, specifically paired re-readings. Later, they may experiment with other techniques with an eye toward adding them to their teaching repertoire.

Key question: **Which students should be paired for the most effective use of paired re-readings in class?**

Anticipated outcome(s): This action research project will result in insights into pair work, in general, and pair work for re-reading activities, more specifically. Teacher experience has shown that for some types of language learning activities, it is wise to have mixed-level ability groups; for others, it is effective to group students with similar abilities. This action research project will help determine the best ways to pair students for re-reading activities (of the type described here).

Primary way to collect data: Teaching log.

Data collection: Follow standard procedures for paired re-readings. Students will work in pairs. Student A will read a passage aloud for 60 seconds, as quickly and as accurately as possible. While Student A is reading aloud, Student B will follow along and assist Student A if necessary. At the end of 60 seconds, Student A will mark the end point of his read aloud. Then Student A and B will switch roles. Student B will read the exact same passage as Student A, starting at the very same point. After 60 seconds, Student B will also mark the end point of his read aloud. The students will then repeat the procedure for a second round, re-reading the same exact text, from the same starting point. The goal is to advance further in the text in the second round. Records of the number of words increased on the second reading will be kept.

Follow the same procedures every time students are asked to engage in paired re-readings, but experiment with different student pairs. First, pair students with similar reading abilities; then, pair students with different reading abilities (i.e. strong and weak readers); and finally, pair students with different motivational levels and attitudes toward reading (even if they have similar reading abilities). In a teaching log, keep track of student pairs and make notes about student enthusiasm for the exercise, their cooperation with one another, their fluency improvement (based on how far they get in the text), their willingness to help each other and any other behaviours that are worth noting.

Data analysis: Review teaching log entries to determine which student pairs result in the most effective use of paired re-reading exercises.

Look for the pairing configuration that leads to fluency improvement, cooperation between students and the most positive attitudes toward reading.

Time needed: This project will not require too much time. Initially, set aside class time to orientate students to the activity and 'sell' them on the importance of fluency activities. After an introduction to basic procedures, designate 10 minutes (or less) for each paired re-reading session. Ten minutes should allow for teacher comments and encouragement after each 'round' in addition to record keeping.

Resources needed: Short reading passages.

7.2 Conclusion

In this chapter, we have showcased nine action research projects related to vocabulary, reading fluency and reading rate development. These projects, which represent a small sampling of action research possibilities, are meant to model the steps that teachers can take to engage in teacher-initiated enquiry. Teachers can pursue adapted versions of these projects – or use other questions, such as those posed at the beginning of the chapter – to guide their own action research.

Further reading

Teachers who want to engage in action research on vocabulary, fluency and rate development should consult Chapter 10 (section 10.4) for further information. For additional information, refer to the following: For readings on *repeated reading*, see Dowhower (1987, 1994), Rasinski (1990), Rasinski, Padak, Linek and Sturtevant (1994), Samuels, Schermer and Reinking (1992). For further information on *glosses*, see Jacobs (1994). For information on *dictionary use* while reading, see Knight (1994), Luppescu and Day (1993). For two textbooks that have systematically integrated *word-recognition exercises* into instruction, see Rosen and Stoller (1994) and Stoller and Rosen (2000).

Chapter 8

Strategic reading and discourse organisation: Action research projects

This chapter will introduce nine model action research projects focusing on strategic reading and issues related to discourse organisation and reading. Of particular interest will be the following:

- a set of research questions that can guide meaningful action research projects
- steps that teachers can follow to implement classroom-based research
- easy-to-use data-collection instruments that can be adapted for many instructional settings
- model action research projects that can be adapted by interested teachers

In Chapter 7, we proposed a set of action research projects that centres around issues related to vocabulary, reading fluency and reading rate development. In this chapter, we propose additional action research projects that focus on two different aspects of reading and reading instruction, specifically strategic reading and discourse organisation. Reflective teachers, in an effort to understand the effectiveness of their classroom instruction, often ask themselves questions about these two topics:

- What is the difference between teaching reading strategies and training students to become strategic readers?
- Which reading strategies are most useful for beginning readers?
- Which reading strategies, if any, are best reserved for more advanced courses?

- To what extent do students pay attention to the organisation of the passages that they are reading?
- Do students use their knowledge of text structure to make sense of what they are reading?

Questions such as these are provocative, but they are too broad to be useful for busy teachers who want to engage in action research. By narrowing down the focus of these questions, we can generate more realistic research questions and more manageable action research projects. Specific questions related to *strategic reading* include, but are not limited to, those listed below. (Questions with a check mark ✓ in front of them are explored in greater detail in the remainder of the chapter.)

✓ To what extent am I supporting the development of strategic reading behaviour?

✓ To what extent do my students use common reading strategies?

✓ Can I raise my students' awareness of reading strategies by explicitly modelling strategic reading behaviours while reading aloud to the class?

✓ What strategies can I introduce to my students to help them make sense of densely written texts?

✓ How well do I incorporate student self-reflection into the end of reading lessons, as a way of promoting metacognitive strategy use?

How often do I ask students to reread a text? For what reasons are students asked to reread?

How helpful do my students think metacognitive strategies (e.g. planning, monitoring, repairing) are?

How can I help students learn to use titles, subtitles, captions, headings and illustrations to orientate themselves to the text? To locate information? To predict contents of the text?

How successful are students in identifying the strategies that they use when they read difficult texts?

What strategies do students use when they read for the main idea?

How can group tasks contribute to effective strategy instruction?

How can L1 skills and strategies become positive support for L2 reading development?

How can I train my students to assess what types of reading skills and strategies would be most appropriate in various circumstances?

Specific questions related to *discourse organisation* include the following:

✓ How can I raise my students' awareness of patterns of rhetorical organisation through visual displays and graphic organisers?

✓ When is it more beneficial to discuss text structures with students: as part of pre-reading activities or post-reading activities?

✓ How can I use graphic organisers to help students make sense of challenging texts? How can students use graphic organisers to make sense of challenging texts on their own?

✓ How can I help students learn to identify sequence and contrast markers in the texts that they are reading?

How can I help students see the hierarchical organisation of the texts that they are reading?

How can I train myself to become more aware of text structure and discourse organisation so that I can integrate these topics into my instruction?

What are some previewing techniques that I can use in class that will guide students in identifying key words that signal text structure?

How can I use outlines to help students identify main units of a text?

How can I use summary writing activities to guide students in understanding the discourse organisation of texts that they are reading?

To what extent does the use of scrambled sentences and paragraphs assist students in understanding conventions for discourse organisation?

To what extent does the use of cloze passages, with transition words and phrases removed, assist students in learning the meaning of different signal words?

Questions such as these represent just a sampling of the questions that can guide action research projects related to strategic reading and discourse organisation. The best questions, of course, are those that help us understand the effectiveness of our own classroom instruction, the usefulness of certain teaching techniques, student responsiveness to different classroom procedures, student grasp of materials and so forth.

> ### Quote 8.1
>
> Action research applies a systematic process of investigating practical issues or concerns which arise within a particular social context.... Action research is driven by practical actions from which theories about learning and teaching can be drawn.
>
> Burns (1999, p. 31)

8.1   Model action research projects

In this chapter, we outline nine action research projects that are likely to be of interest to practising reading teachers. We approach these projects in the same way that we approached those in Chapter 7. The projects described here should not be viewed as rigid templates; rather, they should be viewed as flexible models that can be adapted, in small or large ways, for different instructional settings. We hope that teachers who read over these model projects will be inspired to pursue action research on their own, either about the topics showcased here or in response to other questions, such as those listed earlier in the chapter. Figure 8.1 lists the topics developed in the chapter.

8.1.1   Emphasising strategic reading behaviour

Purpose: Reading instruction that emphasises strategic reading behaviour frequently includes certain supportive characteristics (see Figure 8.2). Determining the extent to which teachers incorporate these characteristics into their teaching can be instructive.

Key question: **To what extent am I supporting the development of strategic reading behaviour?**

Anticipated outcome(s): At the end of this project, it is assumed that teachers will have a better understanding of the characteristics of their reading lessons. Based on this understanding, teachers should be able to alter the ways in which they teach to create an environment more conducive to the development of strategic reading behaviours.

Primary way to collect data: Class observation; set of worksheets.

Data collection: At the end of every class session, for the duration of one entire thematic unit, evaluate the extent to which the development

Model action research project	Page(s)	Topic	Primary way to collect data
8.1.1	205–207	Emphasising strategic reading behaviour	Class observation, teacher's worksheets
8.1.2	208–209	Using common reading strategies	Student questionnaire, teacher–student conferences, student read-alouds
8.1.3	210–212	Modelling of strategic reading behaviours	Lesson plan scripts, checklists, journal
8.1.4	212–214	Using reading strategies for dealing with densely written texts	Lesson plans, teaching log
8.1.5	214–216	Incorporating self-reflection, as a metacognitive strategy, into reading lessons	Journal
8.1.6	216–219	Raising awareness of patterns of rhetorical organisation through visual displays to enhance comprehension abilities	Lesson plans, teaching log, student-generated visual displays
8.1.7	219–220	Discussing text structures as part of pre- and post-reading activities	Lesson plans, teaching log, student assessment measures
8.1.8	220–221	Training students to use graphic organisers to make sense of challenging texts	Journal, teacher-generated graphic organisers, teacher-guided graphic organisers, student-generated graphic organisers
8.1.9	222–224	Focusing on the identification of signal words indicating sequence and contrast	Pre- and post-tests, teaching log

Figure 8.1   Model action research projects presented in Chapter 8

of strategic reading behaviours is being supported. Use a worksheet (like the one in Figure 8.2) to record supportive practices that have occurred in class. Feel free to modify teaching practices (even in the midst of this action research project) when it becomes apparent that certain aspects of a strategic reading classroom are being neglected.

Data analysis: At the end of the thematic unit, review record-keeping worksheets to identify common practices that support strategic reading as well as neglected aspects of a strategic reading classroom. Pay special attention to written comments to determine how attitudes toward

Teacher's Worksheet

Date: _____   Class:_____

Characteristics of courses that emphasise strategic reading behaviour	Presence of characteristic	Comments
1. The teacher explains what strategies are and why they are important.	Yes No	
2. Students discuss what strategies are and why they are important.	Yes No	
3. Students are encouraged to use and practise specific strategies.	Yes No	
4. The teacher reads and thinks aloud, modelling expert reading behaviour.	Yes No	
5. Students read and think aloud, experimenting with different strategies.	Yes No	
6. Students receive feedback on their strategy use.	Yes No	
7. Students are reminded of the benefits of strategy use and are asked to explain how they use strategies to process texts.	Yes No	
8. The class has a content base; students use strategies while reading to learn content information.	Yes No	

Figure 8.2   **Characteristics of courses that emphasise strategic reading behaviour**

and approaches to strategic reading have changed over time. Consider findings with an eye toward determining which classroom practices should be continued and what types of modifications could be made to support strategic reading behaviours to a greater extent.

Time needed: Create a worksheet, similar to Figure 8.2, for data collection purposes. Set aside 5–10 minutes at the conclusion of each class to fill in the worksheet. At the end of the thematic unit, evaluate the whole set of worksheets and plan for improved teaching in the future.

Resources needed: A set of worksheets for teacher use.

8.1.2   Extent to which students use common reading strategies

Purpose: Expert readers are able to use a variety of strategies flexibly and in conjunction with one another. Determining the extent to which students are using certain common reading strategies in class can be useful for teachers interested in helping students become more strategic readers.

Key question: **To what extent do my students use common reading strategies?**

Anticipated outcome(s): This action research project should reveal the strategies that students think they are using while reading. The results of the questionnaire will expose under-used strategies that can be emphasised in future classes through teacher modelling, classroom discussion and explicit opportunities for student practice.

Primary way to collect data: Student questionnaire, teacher–student conferences, taped student read-aloud.

Data collection: Conduct this project during a semester when a commitment to strategy instruction can be made. During the semester, introduce students to a range of strategies (see Figure 8.3) through explicit teacher modelling, whole-class discussions and student practice. Toward the end of the semester, administer a questionnaire (similar to Figure 8.3) once per week (for a period of 4–5 weeks) at the conclusion of class sessions with extended in-class reading. Students should know ahead of time if they are going to be filling out the questionnaire. In this way, they will be more conscious of the strategies that they use. (Before being asked to complete the questionnaire the first time, students should be given multiple opportunities to answer similar questions. The skill needed to answer questionnaire items can be developed through ongoing classroom discussion of how and when to use specific strategies.)

Late in the semester, schedule teacher–student conferences during which students can be interviewed about their strategy use and their perceptions about the effectiveness of strategic reading. Students can be asked to read a passage aloud, after which the teacher and student can discuss strategies observed and used. Read alouds and teacher–student discussions should be taped for later reference.

Data analysis: At the end of the semester, there should be 4–5 questionnaires from each student. Analyse the questionnaires from two perspectives: (a) from the perspective of individual students to determine each student's strategy use and changing perceptions about strategy use over a 4–6 week period and (b) from the perspective of the class as a whole. Itemise the strategies used by students into one of two categories:

Student name_____ Title of reading _____

While reading, did you use these strategies? For the strategies that you did use, comment on the following questions: How did you use the strategy? How did the strategy help your reading?

Identifying a purpose for reading	Yes	No	_____
Previewing	Yes	No	_____
Predicting	Yes	No	_____
Asking questions to yourself	Yes	No	_____
Checking your predictions	Yes	No	_____
Finding answers to a question you've asked	Yes	No	_____
Connecting text to background knowledge	Yes	No	_____
Summarising	Yes	No	_____
Connecting one part of the text to another	Yes	No	_____
Paying attention to text structure	Yes	No	_____
Rereading	Yes	No	_____
Looking up a word in the dictionary	Yes	No	_____
Using discourse markers to see relationships	Yes	No	_____
Taking steps to repair faulty comprehension	Yes	No	_____

Figure 8.3   **Student questionnaire on reading strategy use**

Category 1: Strategies that the majority of students use appropriately.

Category 2: Strategies that the majority of students under-utilise or use inappropriately.

Listen to tapes of teacher–student conferences to gain more insights into students' strategy use. Based on the results of an analysis of all data, create activities that model the strategies falling into Category 2; then provide students with opportunities to practise those strategies.

Time needed: Create a questionnaire (similar to Figure 8.3) that includes the strategies that have been introduced, modelled and practised in class. Toward the end of the semester, for a 4–5 week period, set aside class time to administer student questionnaires. Arrange time to conduct brief teacher–student conferences. Time will be needed to analyse questionnaires and audiotaped teacher–student conference data.

Resources needed: Questionnaire, tailored to the class; class time; reading passage(s) for read aloud during teacher–student conference.

8.1.3   Teacher modelling of strategic reading behaviours

Purpose: Skilled readers use a range of strategies while reading. There is evidence that students who have a heightened awareness of strategies use them more often and more effectively to enhance their understanding of a text and to monitor their comprehension. It has been suggested that teachers can raise students' awareness of strategies by modelling strategic behaviour while reading aloud to the class. (See Janzen, 1996, for a description of an English for Academic Purposes class in which she modelled strategic reading behaviours through teacher read alouds.)

Key question: **Can I raise my students' awareness of reading strategies by explicitly modelling strategic reading behaviours while reading aloud to the class?**

Anticipated outcome(s): After being exposed to various reading strategies over time, it is hoped that students will begin to incorporate the same strategies into their own read alouds and maybe even their own silent reading. Research findings could provide insights that will help teachers with the planning of future strategy training.

Primary way to collect data: Lesson plan scripts, checklists and journal.

Data collection: Plan a two-part action research project. In the first part, incorporate explicitly stated strategies into teacher read alouds. In essence, verbalise strategic reading behaviours (e.g. predicting, asking questions, summarising, establishing a purpose for reading, checking predictions, connecting text to background knowledge, drawing inferences) that can be used to comprehend texts. Start out by modelling one or two strategies and then gradually build up the number of strategies that are modelled. Write out verbal comments in a lesson plan **script** to control the strategies that are introduced and then recycled. Keep an additional record of the strategies used by marking a checklist after each read-aloud session (see Figure 8.4). This phase of the project will require a considerable number of weeks.

Students should know ahead of time that they will be listening for teacher strategies. At the end of each read aloud, ask students to identify the strategy or strategies that were modelled. Over time, the students and teacher will create a wall poster listing the strategies that students identify and the purpose for their use. The poster will serve as a convenient reference tool for students in subsequent classes. Comment on student responses, student reactions and teacher assessment of the read-aloud session in a journal immediately following class.

Strategy	Date of class				
Specifying a purpose for reading					
Planning what to do/what steps to take					
Previewing the text					
Predicting the contents of the text or section of text					
Checking predictions					
Posing questions about the text					
Finding answers to posed questions					
Connecting text to background knowledge					
Summarising information					
Making inferences					
Connecting one part of the text to another					
Paying attention to text structure					
Rereading					
Guessing the meaning of a new word from context					
Using discourse markers to see relationships					
Checking comprehension					
Identifying difficulties					
Taking steps to repair faulty comprehension					
Critiquing the author					
Critiquing the text					
Judging how well objectives were met					
Reflecting on what has been learned from the text					
Other					

Figure 8.4 **Strategy checklist**

In the second part of the action research project, ask students to take turns reading short sections of a text aloud; ask students to incorporate a few explicitly stated strategies into their read alouds. Fill out a checklist, similar to the one in Figure 8.4, to track the strategies that students use. The class as a whole should briefly discuss the strategies that classmates have incorporated into their read alouds. Post-reading discussions will bring strategy use to the conscious level of all students in class.

Data analysis: At the conclusion of the first part of the study, lesson-plan scripts, a checklist and journal entries will be available for analysis.

Start with the checklists because they will be most straightforward to interpret, revealing the range and frequency of strategies introduced and recycled. Lesson-plan scripts will bring to mind the specifics of the read-aloud sessions, while journal entries will document more subjective information (i.e. teacher and student attitudes about the lessons).

At the conclusion of the second part of the study, an additional checklist will be ready for analysis. That checklist will reveal the range and frequency of strategies used by students in their own read alouds. Compare the results of both checklists to see if there is a gradual carry over from teacher modelling to student use. Rethink the presentation of strategies that were modelled but that students failed to use in their own read alouds.

Time needed: During the first part of the study, set aside weekly 15-minute periods for read alouds in class. Beforehand, work out a script for each read-aloud session that systematically introduces and recycles strategies. During the second part of the study, structure lessons so that there is time for students to take turns reading aloud. Before starting the project, create two strategy checklists (similar to the one in Figure 8.4) to record teacher and student strategy use, respectively.

Resources needed: Two strategy checklists and reading passages for read alouds. (Because students benefit from multiple exposures to a given text, feel free to use texts that have been or will be assigned for other purposes in the course.) Over time, a wall poster will be created (during class discussion) that lists the strategies that students have noticed in teacher read alouds. Every time a new strategy is introduced, a new item will be added to the poster. Students can use the poster to guide their listening to read alouds and comments during class discussions.

8.1.4   Reading strategies for dealing with densely written texts

Purpose: Densely written texts are often difficult for L2 readers to process. L2 students benefit from being introduced to strategies that they can eventually use on their own for making sense of dense text.

Key question: **What strategies can I introduce to my students to help them make sense of densely written texts?**

Anticipated outcome(s): This action research project can lead to the development of two sets of procedures: one for introducing students to strategies for coping with densely written texts and the other for guiding students in the efficient use of those strategies. These procedures can eventually become a regular part of a teaching repertoire; with

Simplify the text by

- breaking it down into two or more sentences, deleting conjunctions
- asking who, what, where, when and how questions
- underlining unfamiliar words
- identifying cohesive elements (e.g. pronouns) and determining what each refers to
- finding noun phrases and eliminating pre- and post-modifiers
- identifying the verbs and using the 'who or what does what?' technique to find the subject and object of each
- identifying discourse markers (e.g. therefore, however) to clarify relationships among text components
- rereading the passage

Figure 8.5 **Strategies for making sense of dense texts**

time, the hope is that students will use the strategies on their own and at the right times.

Primary way to collect data: Lesson plans and teaching log.

Data collection: First, make a list of strategies for dealing with dense text that can be used as a reference tool when planning strategy lessons (see Figure 8.5). Then, when reviewing class readings, watch out for portions of assigned texts that are densely written and that will likely cause comprehension difficulties for students. When appropriate, set aside time in class lessons to use challenging texts as springboards for strategy training. Initiate the lessons by writing a select number of difficult sentences (or clusters of sentences) on the blackboard and introducing students to strategies for making sense of them. As a class, follow systematic steps for making sense of dense text by using the most appropriate strategies listed in Figure 8.5. Immediately after each strategy training session, record the strategies introduced and the steps taken in a teaching log. As the semester progresses, give students more responsibility for selecting appropriate strategies and determining the steps that they can take to understand dense text. In the teaching log, jot down reflections on student decisions and success rate.

Data analysis: Look over lesson plans and corresponding teaching log entries in an effort to determine (a) the strategies that students found most useful, (b) the strategies that students found most difficult to manage, (c) training procedures that students found most helpful, (d) the most efficient sequencing of strategies for training purposes, (e) the impact of recycling strategies and (f) students' success rate in deciphering dense texts. Insights gained can be incorporated into future lessons on strategy use.

Time needed: Compile a list of strategies that can be used as a reference tool. Review assigned reading passages to identify chunks of text that are densely written and worthy of in-class attention. Work through various strategies for simplifying dense text with students in class, and make entries in a teaching log after each strategy session.

Resources needed: List of strategies to consult and teaching log.

8.1.5   Incorporating self-reflection, as a metacognitive strategy, into reading lessons

Purpose: Developing readers benefit from reflecting on reading experiences to identify strategies that worked for them and those that did not work so well. The explicit incorporation of student self-reflection, as a metacognitive strategy, into reading lessons might be worthwhile. Future action research projects can focus on other metacognitive strategies.

Key question: **How well do I incorporate student self-reflection into the end of reading lessons, as a way of promoting metacognitive strategy use?**

Anticipated outcome(s): This action research project has the potential for leading to an understanding of ways to stimulate student self-reflection at the end of reading lessons. Because students are likely to react to self-reflection differently, one of the goals of a project such as this will be to determine how to motivate all students to participate in the self-reflection process. In addition to learning about teaching techniques that can be used in the future, a more immediate result of the project will be students' heightened awareness of the value of self-reflection in reading.

Primary way to collect data: Journal, based on a set of guided questions.

Data collection: Ask students to reflect on their reading experiences at the end of reading lessons, every Tuesday and Thursday, for a month. Ask questions that require some degree of self-reflection (see Figure 8.6). Keep a journal – using questions, such as those listed in Figure 8.7, to guide journal entries – to document students' self-reflection activities, their responses to questions and the teacher's role in those endeavours. If recall is difficult, tape record the end of targeted reading sessions and listen to the tape to complete journal entries.

Data analysis: After collecting data for 4 weeks, analyse journal entries to (a) determine self-reflection techniques and corresponding questions that work with different types of students, (b) identify the types of students that might need special encouragement, (c) discover the type of language required for self-reflection and (d) explore students'

How much of this reading assignment did you understand? 100%   80%   60%
40%   20%   0%

How easy was the assignment for you? Very easy   Easy   Difficult   Very difficult

Which parts of the text were easy for you? Why were they easy?

Which parts of the text were difficult for you? Why were they difficult?

What did you learn from this reading assignment?

What did you learn about yourself as a reader?

What strategies did you use to complete this assignment?

In what ways did the strategies help your reading?

Did you try any new strategies? What were they? Would you use them again?
Why/why not?

What will you do next time to be a better reader?

Other

Figure 8.6   **Possible questions to ask students to encourage self-reflection**

What steps did I take to encourage students' self-reflection?

How much time did we spend on the self-reflection activity?

Was the time allotted enough? Too little? Too much?

How did the self-reflection activity work?

How much student participation occurred?

Which students responded to my questions?

Which students were hesitant to get involved?

To what extent did students' language abilities prevent them from participating fully?

To what extent did students understand the value of the exercise?

What will I do differently next time?

Other

Figure 8.7   **Possible questions to guide journal entries about student self-reflection activities**

attitudes about self-reflection activities. If journal entries do not provide enough information in one or more of these targeted areas, continue the data collection process and focus on the neglected areas in new journal entries. Use the insights gained from the analysis to improve the ways in which self-reflection activities are incorporated into teaching.

Time needed: Fine-tune two sets of questions before beginning the action research project: one set to guide student reflections (Figure 8.6) and the other to guide an evaluation of self-reflection activities

(Figure 8.7). Then set aside time, after every Tuesday and Thursday reading lesson for a month, to write in the journal.

Resources needed: Questions to guide student reflection and teacher evaluation.

8.1.6 Raising awareness of patterns of rhetorical organisation through visual displays to enhance comprehension abilities

Purpose: A number of studies argue persuasively that student awareness of text structure and discourse organisation enhances reading comprehension. To narrow down the focus of this action research project, one could focus solely on issues related to patterns of rhetorical organisation (Figure 8.8). Future projects can be devoted to other aspects of text structure and discourse organisation (e.g. genre features, text markers that signal different organisational patterns). Although rhetorical patterns can be explored in numerous ways (e.g. through critical readings, group analysis of texts, model texts), this research will be conducted by exploring rhetorical organisation with students by means of visual displays (i.e. graphic organisers) such as time lines, Venn diagrams, compare/contrast matrices, flow charts, bar graphs, pie charts, grids, family trees. (See Figure 8.9 for sample graphic organisers.)

Key question: **How can I raise my students' awareness of patterns of rhetorical organisation through visual displays?**

Anticipated outcome(s): Effective ways of introducing patterns of rhetorical organisation through visual displays can be discovered with this action research project. The identification of visual displays that make it easy for students to distinguish varied patterns of organisation would be ideal. Students' heightened awareness of rhetorical patterns is likely to help them improve their reading (and writing) abilities.

Cause and effect

Classification

Comparison and contrast

Definition

Description

Narrative sequence of events

Problem and solution

Procedures

Figure 8.8 **Common rhetorical patterns, as frames**

Graphic representations are visual illustrations of verbal statements. Frames are sets of questions or categories that are fundamental to understanding a given topic. Here are shown nine 'generic' graphic forms with their corresponding frames. Also given are examples of topics that could be represented by each graphic form. These graphics show at a glance the key parts of the whole and their relations, helping the learner to comprehend text and solve problems.

Spider Map

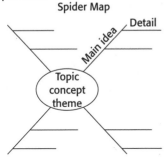

Used to describe a central idea: a thing (a geographic region), process (meiosis), concept (altruism) or proposition with support (experimental drugs should be available to AIDS victims). Key frame questions: What is the central idea? What are its attributes? What are its functions?

Series of Events Chain

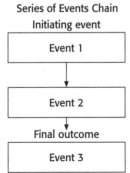

Used to describe the stages of something (the life cycle of a primate); the steps in a linear procedure (how to neutralise an acid); a sequence of events (how feudalism led to the formation of nation states); or the goals, actions and outcomes of a historical figure or character in a novel (the rise and fall of Napoleon). Key frame questions: What is the object, procedure or initiating event? What are the stages or steps? How do they lead to one another? What is the final outcome?

Continuum/Scale

Low		High

Used for time lines showing historical events or ages (grade levels in school), degrees of something (weight), shades of meaning (Likert scales) or ratings scales (achievement in school). Key frame questions: What is being scaled? What are the end points?

Compare/Contrast Matrix

	Name 1	Name 2
Attribute 1		
Attribute 2		
Attribute 3		

Used to show similarities and differences between two things (people, places, events, ideas, etc.). Key frame questions: What things are being compared? How are they similar? How are they different?

Problem/Solution Outline

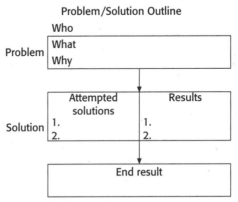

Used to represent a problem, attempted solutions and results (the national debt). Key frame questions: What was the problem? Who had the problem? Why was it a problem? What attempts were made to solve the problem? Did those attempts succeed?

Figure 8.9   **Sample graphic organisers**

Network Tree

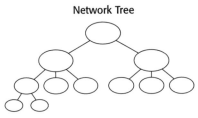

Fishbone Map

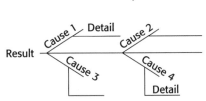

Used to show causal information (causes of poverty), a hierarchy (types of insects), or branching procedures (the circulatory system). Key frame questions: What is the superordinate category? What are the subordinate categories? How are they related? How many levels are there?

Used to show causal interaction of a complex event (an election, a nuclear explosion) or complex phenomenon (juvenile delinquency, learning disabilities). Key frame questions: What are the factors that cause X? How do they interrelate? Are the factors that cause X the same as those that cause X to persist?

Human Interaction Outline

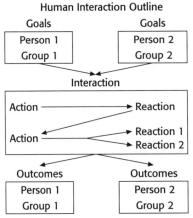

Cycle

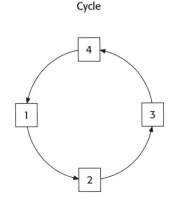

Used to show the nature of an interaction between persons or groups (European settlers and American Indians). Key frame questions: Who are the persons or groups? What were their goals? Did they conflict or cooperate? What was the outcome for each person or group?

Used to show how a series of events interact to produce a set of results again and again (weather phenomena, cycles of achievement and failure, the life cycle). Key frame questions: What are the critical events in the cycle? How are they related? In what ways are they self-reinforcing?

Figure 8.9   Continued. Copyright 1988 by the North Central Regional Educational Laboratory. All rights reserved. Reprinted with permission

Primary way to collect data: Lesson plans, teaching log entries and student-generated visual displays.

Data collection: Introduce students to visual displays that highlight the differences among patterns of rhetorical organisation in texts or segments of texts. Lesson plans can serve as one form of record keeping; a teaching log – with notations about teaching techniques, student questions, student reactions and student responsiveness to the visual displays introduced in the lessons – can serve as another form of record keeping. Assign readings, over a period of time, that tend to highlight select rhetorical patterns or that include rhetorically identifiable segments. Ask students to work with and then create simple visual displays that reveal the text structure of each. Collect students' work.

Data analysis: Review lesson plans and teaching log entries to identify the different ways in which rhetorical patterns and corresponding visual displays are introduced to the class. Pay close attention to the questions that students asked, their reactions and their responsiveness to diverse instructional approaches and different visuals. Try to determine why students might have felt the way they did. Then evaluate students' work in relation to the readings assigned to see if they grasped the notion of rhetorical patterns and the differences among the texts assigned. The insights gained from lesson plans, teaching log entries and student work ought to provide ideas for improving future instruction.

Time needed: Compile readings that typify or include basic rhetorical patterns. Focus on patterns that students are likely to encounter in their textbooks and other classes. (This may require a review of textbook passages to identify commonly used rhetorical patterns.) Design a set of lessons that ties the introduction of visuals to different rhetorical patterns and then another set of lessons that requires students to create simple visual displays on their own.

Resources needed: Sets of texts representing different rhetorical patterns.

8.1.7   Benefits of discussing text structures as part of pre- and post-reading activities

Purpose: Research studies argue persuasively that student awareness of text structure (e.g. patterns of rhetorical organisation, text markers, different genres, discourse conventions that require known information to precede new information) enhances comprehension abilities. Student awareness of text structure can be raised through class discussion. The question, however, is when to bring in discussion of these matters.

Key question: **When is it more beneficial to discuss text structures with students: as part of pre-reading activities or post-reading activities?**

Anticipated outcome(s): Based on this study, insights into the effectiveness of incorporating discussions of text structure into the beginning and end of reading lessons are likely to be gained.

Primary way to collect data: Lesson plans, teaching log, student assessment measures.

Data collection: During a semester when teaching two separate reading classes, incorporate discussions of relevant text structure into pre-reading activities with one class and into post-reading activities with the other. After each class, record notes in a teaching log about students' grasp of issues related to text structure, their responsiveness to the lesson and the types of questions that students ask. For each teaching log entry, note the type of text used, the text structure(s) highlighted and teaching approach. At the end of the semester, ask both classes to read two or three reading passages that are organised differently. Request that students comment, in writing, on text-structure features that distinguish one text from the others to assess their level of awareness.

Data analysis: At the end of the semester, three data sources will be available for analysis: lesson plans, teaching log entries and students' written work. Start out by evaluating students' written work to see if one of the classes seems to grasp issues related to text structure more fully than the other. If one class does appreciably better than the other, it could suggest that discussions of text structure are better incorporated before or after a reading assignment. If there are no significant differences between the two classes, it is possible to conclude that discussions of text structure can be integrated in both pre- and post-reading activities. With the analysis of students' written work in mind, review lesson plans and teaching log entries to recall what took place in each class. The lesson plans and teaching log will help reconstruct class sessions and identify useful instructional practices.

Time needed: Plan two versions of similar reading lessons, one with discussion of text structures as part of pre-reading activities and the other with discussion of text structures as part of post-reading activities. Account for the fact that a number of lessons will be necessary for students to develop the ability to analyse text structures. Compile a set of four or five readings, which exhibit different text features, that can be used as assessment measures. Set aside time after each class session to make teaching log entries.

Resources needed: Two versions of a set of reading lessons, four or five different readings with identifiable text features that can be used for assessment purposes, a teaching log.

8.1.8   Training students to use graphic organisers to make sense of challenging texts

Purpose: Graphic organisers are versatile tools: They reveal relationships among ideas, clarify lexical items and their relationships, link new with known content, organise and summarise information, and so forth. (See Figure 8.9.) Students can use graphics to help them make sense of challenging texts. In instructional settings where graphics have not been used for this purpose, it is worthwhile to train students to use simple graphics through a series of exercises that will move them from teacher-generated graphics, to teacher-guided student graphics and finally to student-generated graphics.

Key question: **How can I use graphic organisers to help students make sense of challenging texts? How can students use graphic organisers to make sense of challenging texts on their own?**

Anticipated outcome(s): At the conclusion of a series of training sessions that initially involves teacher-generated graphics and then moves to teacher-guided student graphics, students should be able to create simple graphics on their own to make sense of a challenging text. This project will oblige the teacher to experiment with new teaching techniques and new graphic organisers. The insights gained are likely to help with the planning of future classes.

Primary way to collect data: Journal, teacher-generated graphic organisers, teacher-guided graphic organisers, student-generated graphic organisers.

Data collection: Keep a journal outlining the steps that are taken to train students in the use of graphics. Start with simple guided outlining because students are likely to be familiar with it. Maintain one file folder with the graphics that the teacher creates for these purposes and one folder for graphics that students create with teacher guidance. At the end of the training process, ask students to construct simple graphics on their own. Collect (and then evaluate) student graphics.

Data analysis: Initially, examine the graphics that students create on their own to see if the students have been able to use them to make sense of a difficult text, or portions of a challenging text. Review journal entries and file folders of graphics to reconstruct the instructional steps taken, with an eye toward identifying procedural improvements for the future.

Time needed: From the very beginning of this action research project, recognise that the project may need to develop over an extended period of time. Plan a series of lessons, around challenging texts, that moves students from teacher-generated graphics, to teacher-guided student graphics, to student-generated graphics. Create graphics for the early stages of this intervention.

Resources needed: Challenging texts and accompanying graphics.

8.1.9   Instruction focusing on the identification of signal words that indicate sequence and contrast

Purpose: Good readers are able to identify text markers (i.e. signal words) that help them understand how information is organised and that give them clues about what is important in a text. Signal words fall into different categories. There are words that signal cause and effect, comparison and contrast, conclusion, continuation, emphasis, examples, hedging, sequence, time and so forth. (See Figure 8.10.) Because proficient reading requires the ability to pick up clues provided by these signal words, developing readers can benefit from instruction that focuses on the identification of important text markers and their functions. To make this action research project manageable, only two categories (specifically, sequence and contrast signal markers) will be explored. Future action research projects can focus on other categories.

Key question: **How can I help students learn to identify sequence and contrast markers in the texts that they are reading?**

Anticipated outcome(s): Two important outcomes from this action research project are anticipated. Because of the extra attention paid to sequence and contrast signal words, students are likely to develop an ability that is critical for proficient reading, specifically the ability to pick up clues that will signal how information is organised and what is important in a text. At the same time, the teacher will learn about different ways for bringing signal words to the conscious attention of students, thereby expanding the teacher's repertoire of teaching techniques.

Primary way to collect data: Pre- and post-test, teaching log.

Data collection: To begin with, hand out a reading passage that includes sequence and contrast markers. Ask students to read over the text and *underline* sequence markers (i.e. words or phrases that signal a special order to the ideas) and *circle* contrast markers (i.e. words that signal differences, different points of view, changes in argumentation). This activity will serve as a pre-test and an indicator of student familiarity with sequence and contrast markers. Then, as the semester progresses, the class will focus on sequence and contrast markers as they emerge in class readings; instruction will entail paying special attention to the markers by identifying them, discussing them and exploring their textual functions as they are found. Ask students to keep a running list of the markers that they encounter in their notebooks. Periodically, collect notebooks to make sure that students' lists are accurate; also ask students to compare lists with an eye toward identifying markers that

Cause, condition or result signals: as, because, but, consequently, due to, for, from, if, in that, resulting from, since, so, so that, that, then, therefore, thus, unless, until, whether, while, without, yet

Comparison–contrast signals: also, although, analogous to, and, best, better, but, conversely, despite, different from, either, even, even though, half, however, in contrast, in spite of, instead of, less, less than, like, more than, most, much as, nevertheless, on the contrary, on the other hand, opposite, or, otherwise, rather, same, similar to, still, then, the opposite, though, too, while, worse, worst, yet

Conclusion signals: as a result, consequently, finally, from this we see, hence, in closing, in conclusion, in sum, in summary, last of all, therefore

Continuation signals: a final reason, again, also, and, and finally, another, first of all, furthermore, in addition, last of all, likewise, more, moreover, next, one reason, other, secondly

Emphasis signals: above all, a central issue, a distinctive quality, a key feature, a major development, a major event, a primary concern, a significant factor, a vital force, by the way, especially important, especially relevant, especially valuable, important to note, it all boils down to, more than anything else, most noteworthy, most of all, of course, pay particular attention to, remember that, should be noted, the chief outcome, the crux of the matter, the most substantial issue, the principal item

Example signals: for example, for instance, in the same way as, much like, similar to, specifically, such as, to illustrate

Hedging signals: alleged, almost, could, except, if, looks like, maybe, might, nearly, probably, purported, reputed, seems like, should, some, sort of, was reported

Non-word emphasis signals: bold type, exclamation point, italics, graphic illustrations, numbered points (1, 2, 3), quotation marks, underlining

Sequence signals: A, B, C; after; always; before; during; earlier; first, second, third; in the first place; last; later; next; now; o'clock; on time; since; then; until; while

Spatial signals: about, above, across, adjacent, alongside, around, away, behind, below, beside, between, beyond, by, close to, east, far, here, in, in front of, inside, into, left, middle, near, next to, north, on, opposite, out, outside, over, right, side, south, there, toward, under, upon, west

Time signals: after, after awhile, already, at the same time, during, final, following, immediately, lately, little by little, now, once, then, when

Figure 8.10 **Signal words (adapted from Fry, Kress and Fountoukidis, 1993)**

they should add to their own lists. After a month or two, basically after students have encountered markers numerous times and in numerous contexts, administer a post-test. Similar to the pre-test, students will be given a reading passage and asked to underline sequence markers and circle contrast markers. Students will be asked to explain the function of each signal word that they encounter on a separate piece of paper. During the time between the pre- and post-tests, keep a running tally of the signal words that are encountered by the class (identifying the date of the first encounter with the words and the dates of repeat encounters). Jot down comments that might be helpful with regard to the ways in which certain words are explained, as well as the questions and difficulties that students have.

Data analysis: First, compare students' pre- and post-test scores to determine if they have developed a better familiarity with and understanding of sequence and contrast signal words.

The post-test should reveal signal words that need more explicit instruction time. Review teaching log notations, with test results in mind, to determine what techniques worked and what techniques did not work so well. Apply (and adapt, if necessary) findings to future classes.

Time needed: Find two level-appropriate reading passages, one for the pre-test and one for the post-test. Both passages must have numerous examples of sequence and contrast signal words. Read all other passages that will be assigned in class with an eye toward identifying useful sequence and contrast signal words that can be discussed when encountered in class.

Resources needed: Reading passages with sequence and contrast signal words, teaching log.

8.2 Conclusion

In this chapter, we have presented nine model action research projects that centre around select issues related to strategic reading and discourse organisation. These projects, a sampling of the options open to reading teachers, can be modified easily for different instructional settings. Teachers interested in other aspects of strategic reading and discourse organisation could use many of the ideas for data collection and data analysis presented here to devise their own action research projects.

Further reading

Teachers who are interested in engaging in action research that focuses on issues raised in this chapter can benefit from consulting sources listed in Chapter 10 (sections 10.4, 10.5 and 10.8). Additional resources include the following: For a discussion of *strategies*, see Anderson (1991), Chamot and O'Malley (1994), Duffy (1993), Janzen and Stoller (1998), Li and Munby (1996). Of particular interest in the N. J. Anderson (1991) volume is the *list of 47 strategies* that can be introduced and practised in class (p. 463). On *graphic organisers*, see Hyerle (1996), Jones, Pierce and Hunter (1988/1989), Tang (1992).

Chapter 9

Reading instruction and student affect: Action research projects

This chapter will introduce nine model action research projects focusing on select aspects of reading instruction and issues related to student affect, including student motivation, student attitudes and student interests. Of particular interest will be the following:

- a set of practical questions that can guide meaningful teacher-initiated enquiry
- detailed steps that teachers can follow (with or without modification) to carry out classroom-based action research
- helpful charts and graphs that can be used as data collection instruments
- model action research projects that can be adapted with ease

The effectiveness of reading instruction is dependent on a large number of instructional and motivational factors including appropriateness of lesson objectives; sequencing of classroom activities and tasks; clarity of instructions; suitability of materials and corresponding tasks; teacher flexibility and responsiveness to student needs; student attitudes, interest and motivation; pacing and time allotments; and teacher/student preparedness. Reflective teachers ask themselves questions about the effectiveness of their classroom instruction on a regular basis. Below we offer a sampling of questions related to classroom effectiveness that we feel can lead to manageable action research projects. We have divided the questions into two groups: the first group centres around specific aspects of reading instruction and the second group focuses on issues related to student affect (i.e. motivation, interest and attitudes).

Questions with a check mark ✓ in front of them are explored in greater detail later in the chapter. Specific questions about *reading instruction* can include the following:

✓ For what purposes are students reading in-class assignments?

✓ What kinds of pre-reading activities do I use? Which seem to work well? Which don't seem to work well?

✓ What are the different ways in which I check students' understanding of a text? What types of questions do I ask? What do the questions require of my students?

✓ What are the goals of the post-reading exercises included in required reading materials?

✓ What difficulties are students likely to encounter with required course readings?

✓ How often are students exposed to **non-linear texts** (e.g. charts, diagrams, figures, graphs, illustrations, maps, tables) in mandated reading materials?

How can I integrate graphic organisers into my teaching, specifically into pre-reading activities?

How effective are the **reading-to-write tasks** that I assign to my students?

What role do I play during post-reading discussions: teacher or evaluator?

How often do I probe to find out why students have given a particular answer so that, if need be, I can help them see where they have gone wrong?

What benefits do students derive from using **reading guides**?

Which segments of a reading lesson are best served by group work?

How can I give students sufficient feedback on their reading in a large class?

How do I handle students' answers that are incorrect?

How can I use **jigsaw-reading activities** to maximise student involvement in my reading lessons?

How can I teach students to synthesise information from multiple texts?

Which reading skills are students practising with in-class reading assignments?

To what extent is there a mismatch between reading tasks in our language class and the reading tasks that will be assigned to students in mainstream classes?

Specific questions related to *student motivation*, *interest* and *attitudes* include, but are not limited to, the following:

✓ What supplementary topics will motivate my students to read more?

✓ How can I build students' images of themselves as readers?

✓ What are students' attitudes toward reading?

To what extent will reluctant student readers become more motivated to read by charting their progress on individual student record-keeping sheets?

To what extent do my students identify with being readers? What is their self-concept as readers?

To what degree does student motivation increase when students are given the opportunity to select some of their own readings?

To what extent does creating a print-rich environment encourage students to read more? What kinds of print displays are most interesting to students?

How effective am I in creating a supportive, nonjudgemental and constructive atmosphere in my reading lessons?

How can I help students become more autonomous, independent readers?

Quote 9.1

Action research . . . represents what I would call an 'inside out' approach to professional development. It represents a departure from the 'outside in' approach (i.e. one in which an outside 'expert' brings the 'good news' to the practitioner in the form of a . . . workshop or seminar). In contrast, the inside out approach begins with the concerns and interests of practitioners, placing them at the centre of the enquiry process. In addition to being centred in the needs and interests of practitioners, and in actively involving them in their own professional development, the inside out approach, as realised through action research, is longitudinal in that practitioners are involved in medium to long-term enquiry.

Nunan (1993, p. 41)

This list of action research questions could easily be expanded; there are countless aspects of classroom instruction and student affect that are worthy of investigation. This list should simply be viewed as a sampling of options that teachers have available to them for meaningful action research.

9.1 Model action research projects

In this chapter, we outline nine action research projects that can easily be adapted to different instructional settings. Much as in Chapters 7 and 8, these projects should be seen as flexible models that can be modified, in small or large ways, depending on the teacher's purpose for engaging in enquiry. Figure 9.1 lists the topics of the action research projects highlighted in the remainder of the chapter.

Model action research project	Page(s)	Topic	Primary way(s) to collect data
9.1.1	230	Purposes for reading	Tally sheet
9.1.2	230–232	Effectiveness of different types of pre-reading activities	Annotated lesson plans and after-class reflection worksheet
9.1.3	232–233	Checking students' understanding of a reading passage	Audiotaping of class, record-keeping sheet
9.1.4	233–236	Post-reading exercises included in required reading materials	Document gathering and tally sheet
9.1.5	236–238	Demands placed on student readers by course readings	Document gathering and record-keeping checklist
9.1.6	238–239	Exposure to non-linear text in mandated reading materials	Document gathering and tally sheet
9.1.7	239–240	Topics of student interest	Student questionnaire
9.1.8	240–242	Students' self-images as readers	Student writing assignments, student portfolios, grade book annotations
9.1.9	242–244	Student attitudes toward reading	Student questionnaire

Figure 9.1   Model action research projects developed in Chapter 9

9.1.1   Purposes for reading

Purpose: A comprehensive reading development program should give students opportunities to read for multiple purposes. An analysis of students' in-class reading experiences can lead to an inventory of the reasons for which students are reading.

Key question: **For what purposes are students reading in-class assignments?**

Anticipated outcome(s): The inventory that results from this action research project will reveal different aspects of students' reading experiences, more specifically, the purposes for reading that are addressed in class and those that are neglected by the curriculum. The knowledge gained from this action research can be used in the future (a) to ensure that the most important reading purposes receive sufficient attention and (b) to fine-tune the reading curriculum by creating new sets of reading activities that expose students to a larger variety of purposes for reading.

Primary way to collect data: Tally sheet.

Data collection: For a one-month period, evaluate all assigned reading materials and accompanying tasks with an eye toward identifying the purposes for which students are reading. Keep a tally of purposes on a table similar to the one in Figure 9.2. Instead of conducting this evaluation as part of lesson planning (prior to class), do so after the fact since what is actually done in class may not reflect original plans or the intentions of the textbook and materials writers.

Data analysis: After 4 weeks of record keeping, count up tally marks to determine which areas of reading are being addressed and which are being neglected. Results should assist the teacher in restructuring students' reading experiences so that they have opportunities to read for as many purposes as possible or focus more attention on the most important purposes.

Time needed: Spend time at the end of each school day evaluating readings and accompanying tasks and then filling in the tally sheet.

Resources needed: Tally sheet.

9.1.2   Effectiveness of different types of pre-reading activities

Purpose: Many reading methodologists support the use of pre-reading activities to tap students' background knowledge, provide information that students are not likely to have but need to comprehend the text, build up student expectations and/or stimulate student interest in the topic.

Purposes for reading	Week 1	Week 2	Week 3	Week 4
Reading to search for simple information				
Reading to skim quickly (to get some idea of the text)				
Reading to learn from texts				
Reading to integrate information				
Reading to write (or search for information needed for writing)				
Reading to critique texts				
Reading for general comprehension (school texts)				
Reading for general comprehension (pleasure reading)				
Reading to use information for other tasks				
Other				

Figure 9.2 **Purposes for reading: Tally sheet**

Key question: **What kinds of pre-reading activities do I use? Which seem to work well? Which don't seem to work well?**

Anticipated outcome(s): This classroom-based research can lead to a better understanding of the pre-reading segments of reading lessons. Insights into the kinds of pre-reading activities that work well with certain readings are likely to be gained. An understanding of why certain activities do not work well may emerge as well. The knowledge gained can be used to plan better lessons in the future, minimising an over-reliance on pre-reading activities presented in the textbook.

Primary way to collect data: Annotated lesson plans and after-class reflection worksheet.

Data collection: For a 4-week period, write out lesson plans with detailed notes for the pre-reading portion of the lesson (including intended purpose, rationale, questions to be asked, instructions to be given and so forth). At the end of each class session, annotate lesson plans to indicate the ways in which original plans were altered and the reasons for modifications. Fill out a worksheet (similar to the one in Figure 9.3) to document aspects of the pre-reading activities that might not be included explicitly in lesson plan annotations.

Date of class:_____   Reading passage/task_____

1. What, if anything, did I do during pre-reading activities to tap students' background knowledge?
    a. What worked? Why?
    b. What didn't work? Why?
    c. What should I do the next time I try this?

2. What, if anything, did I do during pre-reading activities to provide necessary background information?
    a. What worked? Why?
    b. What didn't work? Why?
    c. What should I do the next time I try this?

3. What, if anything, did I do during pre-reading activities to build up student expectations?
    a. What worked? Why?
    b. What didn't work? Why?
    c. What should I do the next time I try this?

4. What, if anything, did I do during pre-reading activities to stimulate student interest?
    a. What worked? Why?
    b. What didn't work? Why?
    c. What should I do the next time I try this?

Figure 9.3   **After-class reflection worksheet for the teacher**

Data analysis: With annotated lesson plans and worksheets side by side, analyse each class session to determine which pre-reading activities worked, which did not work, and why. Look for patterns that might lead to useful insights about teaching effectiveness, in general, and the value of particular pre-reading activities, more specifically.

Time needed: Before each class, write detailed lesson plans (at least the pre-reading portions of the lesson plans). After each class, annotate lesson plans and fill out the worksheet.

Resources needed: Set of worksheets for after-class reflection.

9.1.3   Checking students' understanding of a reading passage

Purpose: Many reading passages assigned to students are not accompanied by post-reading comprehension questions. Teachers often find themselves asking simple yes/no and short-response questions to check students' understanding of such texts. Unfortunately, this approach to checking reading comprehension is deceptive, robbing the teacher of a realistic assessment of a student's reading abilities and cheating students of the experience of having to be accountable for their reading and responses. Moving beyond yes/no and short-response questions helps teachers assess students' level of understanding and assists students in developing reading and critical thinking abilities.

Key question: **What are the different ways in which I check students' understanding of a text? What types of questions do I ask? What do the questions require of my students?**

Anticipated outcome(s): To conduct this action research, experiment with different ways of checking students' reading comprehension. The goal is to move beyond simple questions and to move toward questions that hold students accountable for their responses and that encourage critical thinking of various sorts. The process of experimentation itself is likely to increase the number of questioning techniques used. The analysis of concrete data that are collected by audiotaping select class sessions will make the project even more valuable since it will help determine the value of different questioning techniques.

Primary way to collect data: Audiotaping of class, record-keeping sheet.

Data collection: To collect data, audiotape one reading class per week for one month; audiotape classes that are expected to have extended post-reading question and answer sessions.

Data analysis: Listen to the audiotapes with a pen and paper in hand, or at a laptop computer. For each question asked as part of the post-reading question and answer period, determine how students interpreted the questions by the nature of their responses. Keep a tally of the types of student responses made, on a worksheet similar to Figure 9.4. On the same sheet, record the exact wording of questions posed, logging them in the boxes that correspond to the type of response they generated. Analyse the resulting 'inventory' of questions with an eye toward finding patterns that lead to different types of student responses. Consider using similar question types in future lessons to provide students with a broad range of experiences.

Time needed: Plan post-reading activities that incorporate different types of comprehension checks. More time-consuming will be the transcription of select portions of the audiotapes and the categorisation of question types.

Resources needed: Tape recorder, tapes and worksheet.

9.1.4 Post-reading exercises included in required reading materials

Purpose: Post-reading activities serve many purposes. Often teachers structure post-reading activities around the exercises included at the end of each reading passage in the class textbook without really thinking about the author's original intentions. This action research project will

Types of student responses to post-reading questions	Tally of responses	Actual questions asked
Apply information		
Evaluate information		
Expand original response		
Explain		
Infer		
Interpret		
Judge		
Personalise		
Predict		
Restate		
Summarise		
Other		

Figure 9.4   **Worksheet to track reading comprehension questions and responses**

help teachers (a) identify the goals of post-reading exercises in the course textbook and (b) discover post-reading emphases that may be neglected because of the limitations of the textbook. This project will focus on required reading materials; a follow-up project could involve surveying other L2 reading textbooks to discover new types of post-reading activities that might be adapted for later classroom use.

Key question: **What are the goals of the post-reading exercises included in required reading materials?**

Anticipated outcome(s): At the conclusion of this project, teachers will have a better understanding of the post-reading activities that are included in required reading materials. Insights gained will guide teachers in supplementing current materials with new exercises and activities so that students have a more complete reading experience.

Primary way to collect data: Document gathering, tally sheet.

Data collection: Begin the action research project by surveying post-reading activities included in the course textbook that have already been used in class (in the last month or two). Identify the goal(s) of each activity (see Figure 9.5). Keep a tally of primary goals, or if more specificity is desired, keep a tally of sub-goals. If the amount of data compiled in this way turns out to be minimal, continue collecting data by evaluating reading materials that are currently being used and/or those that will be used in the future.

Data analysis: Review the completed tally sheet to determine the range and frequency of different post-reading exercise types. Use the results to think about ways of improving and supplementing post-reading activities so that students practise a wider range of reading skills and strategies.

Time needed: After creating a record-keeping tally sheet, collect data by surveying reading materials used in class. Then set aside time for analysis procedures.

Resources needed: Tally sheet.

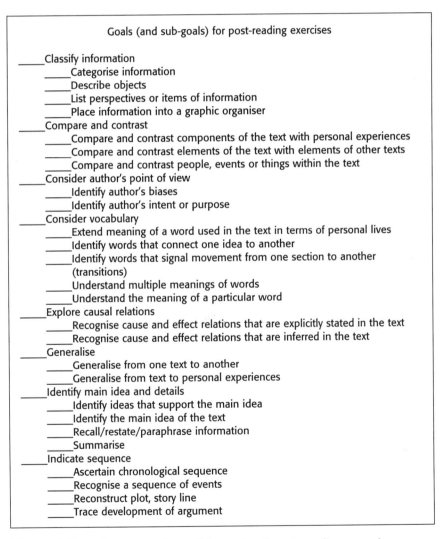

Goals (and sub-goals) for post-reading exercises

_____Classify information
     _____Categorise information
     _____Describe objects
     _____List perspectives or items of information
     _____Place information into a graphic organiser
_____Compare and contrast
     _____Compare and contrast components of the text with personal experiences
     _____Compare and contrast elements of the text with elements of other texts
     _____Compare and contrast people, events or things within the text
_____Consider author's point of view
     _____Identify author's biases
     _____Identify author's intent or purpose
_____Consider vocabulary
     _____Extend meaning of a word used in the text in terms of personal lives
     _____Identify words that connect one idea to another
     _____Identify words that signal movement from one section to another (transitions)
     _____Understand multiple meanings of words
     _____Understand the meaning of a particular word
_____Explore causal relations
     _____Recognise cause and effect relations that are explicitly stated in the text
     _____Recognise cause and effect relations that are inferred in the text
_____Generalise
     _____Generalise from one text to another
     _____Generalise from text to personal experiences
_____Identify main idea and details
     _____Identify ideas that support the main idea
     _____Identify the main idea of the text
     _____Recall/restate/paraphrase information
     _____Summarise
_____Indicate sequence
     _____Ascertain chronological sequence
     _____Recognise a sequence of events
     _____Reconstruct plot, story line
     _____Trace development of argument

Figure 9.5   Tally sheet of possible goals of post-reading exercises

_____Make connections
      _____Establish connections with other readings on the same topic
      _____Link content of text with personal experience or background knowledge
      _____Suggest practical applications of ideas in the text
_____Make judgements
      _____Consider significance of text
      _____Distinguish fact from opinion
      _____Draw conclusions
      _____Elicit personal response from readers (like/dislike; agree/disagree)
      _____Evaluate characters, incidents, ideas, arguments
      _____Evaluate usefulness, truthfulness, etc.
      _____Extend interpretation
      _____Recognise bias
      _____Understand what is implied versus what is stated
      _____Weigh evidence
_____Predict
      _____Speculate about what happened before
      _____Think ahead to what may happen in the future
_____Show understanding of grammatical relations
      _____Consider role of impersonal subjects
      _____Explore role of definite and indefinite articles as information signalling
        devices
      _____Find main clauses in complex sentences
      _____Identify relative clauses
      _____Understand complex tense uses
      _____Understand the role of modal verbs
      _____Understand uses of complex noun phrases in subject position
      _____Understand uses of passive structures
      _____Understand what or who specific pronouns refer to
_____Other

Figure 9.5   **Continued**

9.1.5   Demands placed on student readers by course readings

Purpose: Course readings can challenge students for different reasons. Difficulties often stem from students' lack of familiarity with the topic, but other text characteristics place demands on student readers as well: abstract imagery, assumed background knowledge, clarity of writing, cultural assumptions, formatting, grammatical complexity of sentences, length of sentences, organisation, text length and vocabulary. Because one of the goals of reading teachers is to make texts accessible to students, teachers must vary their reading lessons in response to the demands placed on the reader by the text itself. In planning meaningful lessons, teachers should preview passages that are to be assigned with an eye toward identifying the difficulties that their students might face and the causes of those difficulties.

Key question: **What difficulties are students likely to encounter with required course readings?**

Anticipated outcome(s): This action research project could lead to several useful outcomes. A careful analysis of reading passages before they are actually assigned, with an eye toward identifying characteristics of the text that are likely to cause difficulties for students, will make it easier to make texts accessible to students. Instead of following a standard template for planning reading classes, classes can be planned by focusing on aspects of the text that are likely to be challenging. By addressing difficulties head on, the teacher will be able to help students, over the course of a semester, develop strategies for making sense of difficult texts on their own. In addition, this new perspective on students' reading experiences will help the teacher be more understanding and compassionate in grading and the feedback that is given to students.

Primary way to collect data: Document gathering, record-keeping checklist.

Data collection: Begin by assessing the key reading passages in each chapter of the textbook. Use a separate checklist (like the one in Figure 9.6) to record the sources of potential difficulty of each passage. If there is time, follow similar steps with secondary passages and supplementary readings.

Data analysis: Analyse the checklists from three perspectives: the challenges of individual reading passages, the sequence of reading experiences that students are going to have in relation to those challenges and the students' overall reading experience. Initially, review checklists one at a time to determine the most formidable challenges that students are likely to face with each passage. At this stage, jot down ideas about how a lesson focusing on each passage might address potential difficulties to make the passage more accessible to students.

Then sketch out, on something like a time line, the challenges that students are likely to face as they progress through the semester. Consider questions such as these: Do passages become more cognitively challenging as the semester progresses? Do similar challenges surface repeatedly? Should the order of reading assignments be altered in some way so that students progress from less to more difficult passages? Do I need to devote extra instructional time to certain readings because of their levels of difficulty?

Then think about the students' overall reading experiences, from early to late semester. Consider questions such as these: Are the readings challenging enough or too challenging? With this set of readings, will students be exposed to different types of challenges and associated strategies for dealing with them? Is the level of difficulty going to cause

Title of reading passage:

Source(s) of potential difficulty for students
_____Abstract imagery
_____Assumed background knowledge by the author
_____Clarity of writing
_____Cultural assumptions
_____Demanding topic
_____Formatting
_____Grammatical complexity of sentences
_____Length of sentences
_____Length of text
_____New conceptual knowledge presented
_____Organisation
_____Vocabulary
_____Other_____

Figure 9.6 Checklist for recording potential sources of difficulty of key readings

unnecessary student anxiety and frustration? Should I supplement key readings with easier readings or more challenging readings? The answers to questions such as these should assist in the planning of individual lessons and the design of a more cohesive reading curriculum.

Time needed: Fine-tune the checklist (Figure 9.6), if necessary, and then make multiple copies of it. Read and then evaluate key reading passages in the textbook from the multiple perspectives set forth on the checklist; much of this work could be done before the semester begins.

Resources needed: Multiple copies of the standard checklist.

9.1.6 Exposure to non-linear text in mandated reading materials

Purpose: Skilled readers are able to process linear texts as well as non-linear texts (e.g. charts, diagrams, figures, graphs, illustrations, maps, tables). A quick inventory of non-linear texts in mandated textbooks and workbooks can help teachers assess the range and frequency of non-linear texts that are likely to be encountered by students. Once this project is done, teachers can conduct a follow-up project that examines what students are actually asked to do with the non-linear texts.

Key question: **How often are students exposed to non-linear texts (e.g. charts, diagrams, figures, graphs, illustrations, maps, tables) in mandated reading materials?**

Anticipated outcome(s): After creating an inventory of the non-linear texts included in the mandated textbook and workbook, teachers will

Non-linear text types	Chapter 1		Chapter 2		Chapter 3		ROW TOTALS
	Textbk	Workbk	Textbk	Workbk	Textbk	Workbk	
Charts							
Diagrams							
Figures							
Graphs							
Illustrations							
Maps							
Tables							
Other							
COLUMN TOTALS							

Figure 9.7   Tally sheet for inventory of non-linear texts in required textbook and workbook

have a better sense of the range of reading experiences that students are having. The inventory will reveal non-linear text types that are not represented, or that are under-represented, in the curriculum. Later, when compiling supplementary texts for class and individualised reading assignments, teachers can attempt to find (or create) non-linear text types that are poorly represented in the curriculum, thereby ensuring varied reading experiences for the class.

Primary way to collect data: Document gathering, tally sheet.

Data collection: Create an inventory of non-linear texts by filling out a grid (similar to the one in Figure 9.7) while paging through the chapters of the class textbook and accompanying workbook. Insert tally marks in the appropriate columns and rows to complete the inventory.

Data analysis: Tabulate row and column totals. Analyse results to find out the range and frequency of non-linear texts in the class textbook and workbook. Determine which types of non-linear texts are well represented and which are poorly represented in classroom materials.

Time needed: After finalising a tally sheet, review required materials.

Resources needed: Tally sheet.

9.1.7   Topics of student interest

Purpose: Everyone agrees that students are likely to read more if they are interested in the topics of their assigned readings. In many classroom settings, reading topics are determined largely by textbook chapters and mandated curricula. The identification of supplementary topics of interest, which might motivate students to read more, can prove to be a worthwhile endeavour.

Key question: **What supplementary topics will motivate my students to read more?**

Anticipated outcome(s): After determining students' interests, sets of supplementary readings can be compiled to motivate students to read more. Extra readings can be used in a variety of ways (e.g. for classroom use, homework assignments, individual student projects, pleasure reading options). Students can be asked to help gather sets of supplementary readings during school-library visits.

Primary way to collect data: Student questionnaire.

Data collection: For each mandated curricular theme, brainstorm a list of related topics. Create a questionnaire that lists new topics under each theme. Ask students to circle topics of special interest.

Data analysis: Merge student questionnaire responses to identify the most popular class topics for each curricular theme. Equally important, pay attention to the topics that do not seem to interest anyone in class.

Time needed: Create an easy-to-manage and easy-to-comprehend student questionnaire with lists of supplementary topics that complement the curriculum. Set aside time in class for students to complete the questionnaire. (Students can be asked to complete the questionnaire out of class, but it is preferable to keep students focused on the task by asking them to complete it during class time.) The most time-consuming aspect of this project will be locating and assembling appropriate sets of supplementary readings *after* student questionnaires have been analysed.

Resources needed: Familiarity with curricular themes and related topics.

9.1.8   Students' self-images as readers

Purpose: Students who identify themselves as readers and who enjoy reading are more likely to develop into skilled readers. This is due, in part, to their willingness to read and their openness to reading instruction and related activities. Teachers who understand how their students feel about themselves as readers can use classroom time to build students' self-images as readers.

Key question: **How can I build students' images of themselves as readers?**

Anticipated outcome(s): As a result of this action research, teachers can expect to understand students' attitudes about reading and their self-image as readers. Learning *what* students like to read, *where* they like to read and *when* they like to read in addition to *which* students really do not like to read at all can be useful when working with students individually and as a whole class. Equipped with such valuable information, teachers can work toward building students' perceptions of themselves as readers.

Primary way to collect data: Student writing assignments, student portfolios, grade book annotations.

Data collection: At the beginning of the school year, talk about yourself as a reader with students. Share information that reveals *what* you like to read, *when* you like to read and *where* you like to read. Encourage students to ask whatever questions they may have about your reading preferences and habits. After this interactive introduction, ask students to complete a simple (and brief) writing task. Ask them to choose *one* of the following topics and respond to it in writing: What do you like to read and why? When do you like to read and why? Where do you like to read and why? (Alternatively, ask them to respond to one of these prompts: Write about an enjoyable book you've read; Write about a place where you enjoy reading; Write about a time when you remember enjoying reading.) Ask students to reflect on the question of their choice, jot down a few notes, write up their responses and then talk about their responses, either in groups or as a class (depending on the time available and the size of the class).

While students are speaking, make a mental note of students' comments that reveal an interest or lack of interest in reading; in order to be able to recall relevant student comments, jot them down besides students' names in a grade book (or some easily accessible record-keeping device). Ask students to place their written (and dated) responses in their portfolios. Pose the same (or similar) questions once per month, over a 4-month period. Collect student portfolios at the end of the 4-month period.

Data analysis: Review grade book annotations and students' written work to discover insights into students' evolving views about themselves as readers. Look for words, phrases and anecdotes that indicate either a positive, negative or neutral orientation toward reading. Pay careful attention to information about the types of books that students like to read, where they like to read and when they like to read. Use this information to encourage reading and to devise in-class activities that will help build students' self-images as readers.

Time needed: Before data collection begins, set aside class time to share your own reading preferences and habits with students, followed by a question and answer period. Later, allot class time for student writing. During the first class session in which students are asked to reflect on their own reading experiences, take time to orient them to the task. As students become familiar with the task, they may need less time to explain their views or they may want additional time to express their evolving opinions about reading. After all data are collected, review grade book annotations and student portfolios.

Resources needed: None.

9.1.9 Student attitudes toward reading

Purpose: Students bring different attitudes about reading to the class-room and these attitudes influence students' willingness to involve themselves in reading lessons and related activities. Students' attitudes about reading are often linked to previous experiences with reading, the exposure that they have had to people who read and their percep-tions about the usefulness of reading. An understanding of students' attitudes can help teachers structure their lessons and the feedback that they give to individual students. Because information on students' atti-tudes toward reading is rarely available in school records or revealed on reading tests, action research to gather such information can prove to be useful.

Key question: **What are students' attitudes toward reading?**

Anticipated outcome(s): An action research project like this can lead to a better understanding of students' backgrounds and perceptions about the usefulness of reading. Teachers can use their new found knowledge in many ways: To individualise teacher–student conferences, tailoring comments and questions to each student; to structure reading lessons to reach more students; to lead class discussions about reading more effectively, knowing something about students' attitudes toward and experiences with reading; to be more strategic with the oral and written feedback given to students. Insights gained from this project – which may be as important, if not more important, than test scores – will help teachers understand why some students are excelling in reading and why others are not.

Primary way to collect data: Student questionnaire.

Data collection: After students have grown to know and trust you (the teacher), administer a questionnaire on attitudes toward reading (see Figure 9.8 for sample items). Encourage students to be as honest as possible and reinforce the fact that there are no right or wrong answers. Model the procedure on the blackboard, so that students who are

	Yes/ Always			No/ Never
	1	2	3	4
Think about your past experiences with reading.				
I did well in reading last year.	1	2	3	4
I like to read books that make me think.	1	2	3	4
I like having the teacher say I read well.	1	2	3	4
I visit the library with my family.	1	2	3	4
I like to read on rainy Saturdays.	1	2	3	4
I remember family members reading to me.	1	2	3	4
Think about people you know who read.				
Members of my family like to read.	1	2	3	4
I know people who can help me with my reading.	1	2	3	4
My brothers and sisters sometimes read to me.	1	2	3	4
My friends like to read.	1	2	3	4
My friends and I like to share books.	1	2	3	4
I talk to my friends about what I am reading.	1	2	3	4
Think about reading. How useful is it?				
I can learn a lot from reading.	1	2	3	4
I have favourite subjects that I like to read about.	1	2	3	4
I read to learn new information about topics of interest.	1	2	3	4
I like to read about new things.	1	2	3	4
I can use my reading to help me with schoolwork.	1	2	3	4
I sometimes read to my parents.	1	2	3	4

NB: Some questionnaire items included in Figure 9.8 have been adopted from Wigfield and Guthrie, 1997.

Figure 9.8   Sample questionnaire to determine students' attitudes about reading

unfamiliar with the 1–2–3–4 rating scheme will become comfortable with it before starting the questionnaire. Collect questionnaires when students have completed them.

Data analysis: Analyse each section of the questionnaire separately to obtain three different scores for each student. The first score (from Section I of the questionnaire) will indicate attitudes toward reading based on previous experiences with reading; the second score (from Section II) will indicate attitudes toward reading based on exposure to people who read; the third score (from Section III) will indicate attitudes toward reading based on students' perceptions about the usefulness of reading. To calculate scores, add up students' numerical responses to each item in the section and divide by the total number of items in the section. Average scores will range from 1 to 4. Low numbers will suggest more positive attitudes toward reading; higher scores will suggest more negative attitudes. Once all scores are calculated, look at individual student profiles and then a whole-class profile. Try to capitalise on positive attitudes and improve negative ones through whole-class and individualised reading instruction.

Time needed: Design a questionnaire (using Figure 9.8 as a starting point) that complements the classroom setting. If need be, consult articles (e.g. at the bottom of Figure 9.8) to look over other validated questionnaire items. Little time will be needed to administer the questionnaire. More time will be needed for the analysis stage.

Resources needed: Student questionnaire.

9.2 Conclusion

In this chapter, we have sketched out nine action research projects that showcase some ways in which reading teachers can investigate select aspects of reading instruction and student affect in their classrooms. Action research projects on these two broad areas are virtually limitless. We hope that the model projects presented here, as well as the additional questions listed at the beginning of the chapter, motivate teachers to become involved in action research.

Further reading

Teachers who want to engage in meaningful action research projects related to reading instruction and student affect might consider looking at resources listed in Chapter 10 (sections 10.4, 10.5 and 10.7). For additional readings on a number of key issues in this chapter, see the following: For *validated questionnaire items* (that can be adapted for a questionnaire on student attitudes on reading), refer to McKenna, Kear and Ellsworth (1995). For a description of *jigsaw reading procedures and other reading-related classroom activities*, see Nuttall (1996). For *guidelines for teaching reading in English for academic purposes (EAP) settings*, see Grabe and Stoller (2001). For *a description of pre-reading, during-reading and post-reading activities* that can be adapted to many reading classroom settings, see Stoller (1994b). For *a qualitative study that investigates the incorporation of different types of reading texts into a writing course*, see Hirvela (2001).

Section

IV Resources

Chapter 10

Resources for action research

In this chapter, we have listed select resources related to the teaching and researching of reading. (Other resources appear in the References section at the end of the book.) These resources can assist teachers in improving instruction in their classrooms and can guide them in conducting meaningful action research. We have divided the resources into the following ten sections:

- Journals[1] dedicated to reading and related issues

- Journals[1] that report studies related to reading and other topics

- Journals[1] that periodically have articles related to the teaching of L2 reading

- L2 teacher resource books on reading and related topics

- L1 teacher resource books with good ideas for L2 teachers

- Teacher resources on action research

- Web sites for reading teachers

- Web sites on graphic organisers

- Web sites on action research

- Professional organisations of interest to reading teachers

---

[1] Journal titles followed by web site addresses indicate sites that include mechanisms for scanning Tables of Contents of current and past issues.

10.1 Journals dedicated to reading and related issues

Journal of Adolescent & Adult Literacy (formerly *Journal of Reading*)
Journal of Literacy Research (formerly *Journal of Reading Behavior*)
   www.coe.uga.edu/jlr/index.html
Journal of Research in Reading
Reading and Writing
Reading & Writing Quarterly
Reading in a Foreign Language
Reading Psychology
Reading Research and Instruction
Reading Research Quarterly
Scientific Studies of Reading
   www.gse.utah.edu/edst/sssr/

10.2 Journals that report studies related to reading and other topics

Applied Linguistics
   http://www3.oup.co.uk/applij/contents/
Applied Psycholinguistics: Psychological Studies of Language Processes
Australian Review of Applied Linguistics
Canadian Modern Language Review
   http://www.utpress.utoronto.ca/journal/CMLR/cmlr.htm
Elementary School Journal
   http://www.journals.uchicago.edu/ESJ/home.html
Journal of Educational Psychology
   http://www.apa.org/journals/edu.html
Language Learning: A Journal of Research in Language Studies
Language Teaching Research
   http://www.arnoldpublishers.com/Journals/Journpages/
   13621688.htm
Modern Language Journal
   http://polyglot.lss.wisc.edu/mlj/
Studies in Second Language Acquisition
TESOL Quarterly
   http://www.tesol.org/pubs/magz/tq.html

10.3   Journals that periodically have articles related to the teaching of L2 reading

Applied Language Learning
English for Specific Purposes
English Language Teaching Journal (ELT Journal)
   http://www3.oup.co.uk/eltj/contents/
English Teaching Forum
   http://exchanges.state.gov/forum/
Foreign Language Annals
Internet TESL Journal
   http://www.aitech.ac.jp/~iteslj/
The Language Teacher
   http://langue.hyper.chubu.ac.jp/jalt/pub/tlt/
Prospect: A Journal of Australian TESOL
   http://www.nceltr.mq.edu.au/prospect/prospect.htm
System
TESL-EJ. Teaching English as a Second or Foreign Language: An Electronic Journal
   http://www-writing.berkeley.edu/TESL-EJ/
TESL Canada Journal/La Revue TESL du Canada
   http://members.home.net/teslcanada/Abstracts.htm
TESOL Journal
   http://www.tesol.org/pubs/magz/tj.html

10.4   L2 teacher resource books on reading and related topics

Aebersold, J.A. and Field, M.L. (1997) *From reader to reading teacher: Issues and strategies for second language classrooms.* New York: Cambridge University Press.

Anderson, N.J. (1999) *Exploring second language reading: Issues and strategies.* Boston, MA: Heinle & Heinle.

Carter, R. (1998) *Vocabulary: Applied linguistic perspectives* (2nd edn). New York: Routledge.

Day, R. (ed.) (1993) *New ways in teaching reading.* Alexandria, VA: TESOL.

Day, R. and Bamford, J. (1998) *Extensive reading in the second language classroom.* New York: Cambridge University Press.

Feurerstein, T. and Schcolnik, M. (1995) *Enhancing reading comprehension in the language learning classroom*. Burlingame, CA: Alta Book Center.

Hatch, E. and Brown, C. (1995) *Vocabulary, semantics, and language education*. New York: Cambridge University Press.

Hess, N. (1991) *Headstarts: One hundred original pre-text activities*. New York: Addison Wesley Longman.

Krashen, S. (1993) *The power of reading: Insights from the research*. Englewood, CO: Libraries Unlimited.

McCarthy, M. (1990) *Vocabulary*. New York: Oxford University Press.

Mikulecky, B. (1990) *A short course in teaching reading skills*. Reading, MA: Addison-Wesley.

Morgan, J. and Rinvolucri, M. (1986) *Vocabulary*. New York: Oxford University Press.

Nation, I.S.P. (ed.) (1994) *New ways in teaching vocabulary*. Alexandria, VA: TESOL.

Nation, I.S.P. (2001) *Learning vocabulary in another language*. New York: Cambridge University Press.

Nuttall, C. (1996) *Teaching reading skills in a foreign language* (new edn). Oxford: Heinemann.

Schmitt, N. (2000) *Vocabulary in language teaching*. New York: Cambridge University Press.

Schmitt, N. and McCarthy, M. (eds) (1997) *Vocabulary: Description, acquisition, and pedagogy*. New York: Cambridge University Press.

Silberstein, S. (1994) *Techniques and resources in teaching reading*. New York: Oxford University Press.

Urquhart, A.H. and Weir, C. (1998) *Reading in a second language: Process, product and practice*. New York: Longman.

10.5   L1 teacher resource books with good ideas for L2 teachers

Bellanca, J. (1990) *The cooperative think tank: Graphic organizers to teach thinking in the cooperative classroom*. Palatine, IL: IRI/Skylight Training.

Bellanca, J. (1992) *The cooperative think tank II: Graphic organizers to teach thinking in the cooperative classroom*. Palatine, IL: IRI/Skylight Training.

Fry, E.B., Kress, J.E. and Fountoukidis, D.L. (1993) *The reading teacher's book of lists* (3ʳᵈ edn). Englewood Cliffs, NJ: Prentice Hall.

Gaskins, I. and Elliot, T. (1991) *Implementing cognitive strategy instruction across the school.* Brookline, MA: Brookline Books.

Graves, M., Watts-Taffe, S. and Graves, B. (1998) *Essentials of elementary reading.* Boston, MA: Allyn & Bacon.

Heimlich, J. and Pittelman, S. (1986) *Semantic mapping: Classroom applications.* Newark, DE: International Reading Association.

Mandel Glazer, S. (1992) *Reading comprehension: Self-monitoring strategies to develop independent readers.* New York: Scholastic.

McKenna, M.C. and Robinson, R.D. (1997) *Teaching through text: A content literacy approach to content area reading* (2ⁿᵈ edn). New York: Longman.

Miller, W.M. and Steeber de Orozco, S. (1990a) *Reading faster and understanding more*, Book 1 (3ʳᵈ edn). Glenview, IL: Scott, Foresman/Little Brown.

Miller, W.M. and Steeber de Orozco, S. (1990b) *Reading faster and understanding more*, Book 2 (3ʳᵈ edn). Glenview, IL: Scott, Foresman/Little Brown.

Nagy, W. (1988) *Teaching vocabulary to improve reading comprehension.* Newark, DE: International Reading Association.

Parks, S. and Black, H. (1992) *Organizing Thinking: Graphic organizers*, Book I. Pacific Grove, CA: Critical Thinking Press & Software.

Parks, S. and Black, H. (1990) *Organizing Thinking: Graphic organizers*, Book II. Pacific Grove, CA: Critical Thinking Press & Software.

Pittelman, S., Heimlich, J., Berglund, R. and French, M. (1991) *Semantic feature analysis: Classroom applications.* Newark, DE: International Reading Association.

Pressley, M. and Woloshyn, V. (1995) *Cognitive strategy instruction that really improves children's academic performance* (2ⁿᵈ edn). Cambridge, MA: Brookline Books.

Readence, J.E., Bean, T.W. and Baldwin, R.S. (1998) *Content area literacy: An integrated approach* (6ᵗʰ edn). Dubuque, IA: Kendall/Hunt.

Stahl, S.A. (1999) *Vocabulary development.* Cambridge, MA: Brookline Books.

Tierney, R.J. and Readence, J.E. (1999) *Reading strategies and practices: A compendium* (5ᵗʰ edn). Boston: Allyn & Bacon.

Vacca, R. and Vacca, J. (1998) *Content area reading* (6ᵗʰ edn). New York: Addison Wesley.

10.6 Teacher resources on action research

Burns, A. (1999) *Collaborative action research for English language teachers.* New York: Cambridge University Press.

Burns, A. and Hood, S. (eds) (1995) *Teachers' voices: Exploring course design in a changing curriculum.* Sydney, NSW: National Centre for English Language Teaching and Research.

Edge, J. (ed.) (2001) *Action research: Case studies in TESOL.* Alexandria, VA: TESOL.

Edge, J. and Richards, K. (eds) (1993) *Teachers develop teachers' research: Papers on classroom research and teacher development.* Portsmouth, NH: Heinemann.

Educational Action Research (refereed international journal).

Freeman, D. (1998) *Doing teacher research: From inquiry to understanding.* Boston, MA: Heinle & Heinle.

Kemmis, S. and McTaggart, R. (1988) *The action research planner* (3rd edn). Geelong, Australia: Deakin University Press.

Nunan, D. (1990) Action research in the language classroom. In J.C. Richards and D. Nunan (eds), *Second language teacher education* (pp. 62–81). New York: Cambridge University Press.

Wallace, M.J. (1998) *Action research for language teachers.* New York: Cambridge University Press.

10.7 Web sites for reading teachers

Repository for information on extensive reading:
http://www.kyoto-su.ac.jp/information/er/

Extensive list of vocabulary references:
http://www.vuw.ac.nz/lals/staff/paul_nation/vocrefs.htm

Coxhead academic word list:
http://www.vuw.ac.nz/lals/staff/averil_coxhead

International Reading Association Literacy Links (including links of interest to students and teachers of English as a second language):
http://www.reading.org/links/lit_tp.html

ELAN (English Language Arts Network) web sites for English language arts and media teachers:
http://www.elan.on.ca/langlink.htm#

Northwest Regional Educational Laboratory: Library in the Sky Teacher Resources:
http://www.nwrel.org/sky/teacher.html

National Literacy Trust (UK) reading teacher resources:
http://www.literacytrust.org.uk/
Federal Resources (free) for Educational Excellence (US), including a section on reading:
http://www.ed.gov/free/
Practical teaching ideas on reading from National Council of Teaching English (NCTE):
http://www.ncte.org/teach/read.shtml
Practical teaching ideas on vocabulary from National Council of Teaching English (NCTE):
http://www.ncte.org/teach/vocab.shtml
What is Reading?: expanded definitions of many terms related to reading. Links to many other sites:
http://www.sil.org/lingualinks/library/literacy/glossary/cjJ459/krz809.htm
Activities for teaching reading, with procedures and suggestions for teachers:
http://www.sil.org/lingualinks/library/literacy/fre371/vao852/fre218/krz768/index.htm
Information on how to create and manage a literacy programme in developing countries:
http://www.sil.org/lingualinks/library/literacy/index.htm
Language & Literacy: A Canadian Educational E-Journal (online journal for educators interested in a broad range of literacy issues encompassing research and teaching in multimedia, print and oracy):
http://educ.queensu.ca/~landl/main.htm
International Literacy Explorer: A teacher training tool for basic education:
http://www.literacyonline.org/explorer/
Resource database with references to articles and publications on national and international literacy programmes, research and projects:
http://www.literacy.org/

10.8   Web sites on graphic organisers

Inventory of different graphic organisers, with multiple links:
http://www.graphic.org/goindex.html
http://www.sdcoe.k12.ca.us/SCORE/actbank/torganiz.htm
http://www.ncrel.org/sdrs/areas/issues/students/learning/lr1grorg.htm

http://www.macropress.com/1grorg.htm

Teacher guidelines for designing graphic organisers:
http://www.wm.edu/TTAC/articles/learning/graphic.htm

Critical Issue: building on prior knowledge and meaningful student contexts/cultures, with many links:
http://www.ncrel.org/sdrs/areas/issues/students/learning/lr100.htm

Introduction to K-W-L-H technique (K stands for helping students recall what they KNOW about the subject; W stands for helping students determine what they WANT to learn; L stands for helping students identify what they LEARN as they read; H stands for HOW we can learn more):
http://www.ncrel.org/sdrs/areas/issues/students/learning/lr1kwlh.htm

Example of an 'Anticipation/Reaction' grid used to assess students' knowledge before they begin a lesson:
http://www.ncrel.org/sdrs/areas/issues/students/learning/lr1anti.htm

Guide to Venn diagrams, with links to many other web sites:
http://tlc.ai.org/vennindx.htm

Semantic mapping for concept formation:
http://www.ilt.columbia.edu/k12/livetext/docs/semantic.html

Information about graphic organisers for instructional use:
http://www.fno.org/oct97/picture.html
http://www.angelfire.com/ks/teachme/graphicorganizers.html

Using tables or matrices to help students organise information:
http://www.squires.fayette.k12.ky.us/library/research/problem6.htm

Guide to using graphics in a reading class:
http://smasd.k12.pa.us/pssa/html/Reading/rihnd23b.htm

Inventory of web sites related to graphic organisers:
http://www.goto.com/d/search/p/netscape/?Keywords=graphic+organizers&Partner=netscapebox

10.9 Web sites on action research

"Opening the insider's eye: Starting action research" by S. Mann. 1999 article from The Language Teacher Online:
http://langue.hyper.chubu.ac.jp/jalt/pub/tlt/99/dec/mann.html

"Action research: A tool for improving practice in EFL classrooms" by A.Hayman. 1999 article from The Language Teacher Online:
http://langue.hyper.chubu.ac.jp/jalt/pub/tlt/99/dec/hayman.html
Site with action research tools for practising teachers:
http://www.actionresearch.org/actionresearch/
NETWORKS: An On-Line Journal for Teacher Research. On-line journal dedicated to teacher research:
http://www.oise.utoronto.ca/~ctd/networks/
"Action research for second language teachers – going beyond teacher research" by Graham Crookes. From (1993), *Applied Linguistics*, 14(2), 130–44:
http://www.lll.hawaii.edu/esl/crookes/acres.html
Internationally linked site on action research with lengthy list of relevant articles and other resources:
http://www.cudenver.edu/~mryder/itc_data/act_res.html

10.10   Professional organisations of interest to reading teachers (see web sites for affiliate organisations)

American Educational Research Association (AERA):
http://www.aera.net/
Association Internationale de Linguistique Appliquée/International Association of Applied Linguistics (of particular interest might be the AILA Scientific Commission on Literacy link):
http://www.aila.ac
Australian Council of TESOL Associations:
http://www.acta.edu.au/index.htm
International Association of Teachers of English as a Foreign Language (IATEFL):
http://www.iatefl.org/iatefl.html
International Reading Association (IRA):
http://www.reading.org/
The Japan Association of Language Teaching:
http://www.jalt.org/
National Reading Conference (NRC):
http://www.oakland.edu/~mceneane/nrc/nrcindex.html

Regional English Language Center (RELC) (Associated with the Southeast Asian Ministers of Education Organisation, SEAMEO, located in Singapore):
http://www.relc.org.sg/noframe.htm

Teachers of English to Speakers of Other Languages (TESOL):
http://www.tesol.org

Glossary

Note: Page number in parentheses after each term indicates the first significant use of the term. Words in italics can be found elsewhere in the glossary.

action research (p. 3) Type of teacher-initiated research. Teachers look critically and systematically at their own classrooms for the purposes of improving their own teaching and enhancing the quality of learning that takes place.

alphabetic principle (p. 100) Principle that written spellings systematically represent spoken words. One can transfer sound–letter knowledge to new words.

analysis of word parts (p. 174) Vocabulary-building activity in which students break down words into their smallest parts to identify prefixes, suffixes and stems.

automaticity (p. 21) Ability to carry out a skill accurately and rapidly, without being able to reflect on the processes involved, and without being able to suppress the skill.

background knowledge (p. 12) Prior knowledge that readers utilise in interpreting a text. This includes general, cultural and topic-specific knowledge.

book flood programme (p. 144) A reading programme in which students are provided with large amounts of interesting reading material, designed to be read, discussed and shared in a variety of ways.

bottom–up models of reading (p. 32) Metaphorical depiction of reading as a mechanical process in which the reader creates a unit-by-unit mental translation of the information in the text, with little interference from the reader's own background knowledge.

case study (p. 117) Research method that involves gathering and analysing data about an individual example as a way of studying a broader phenomenon. A case may be a single student, a group of learners, a whole class.

cognates (p. 47) Words, related in origin, with similar forms and meanings in another language.

comparison study (p. 110) Research method designed to compare two groups or two other phenomena.

comprehension accuracy (p. 122) Ability to construct an accurate understanding of a text.

concepts about print (p. 100) Preliminary knowledge of how text works: for example, opening a book properly, recognising the beginning of a book, knowing the direction in which print is read, having some elementary knowledge of the orthography.

connectionist theories (p. 35) Theories of how cognitive processes work, reflecting likely psychological correlates to the brain's neurological structure. In their most current versions, they provide strong accounts for word-recognition processes, vocabulary knowledge and learning and the development of syntactic knowledge (see Ellis, 1999, for an introduction).

constructivist models of reading (p. 34) Models of reading comprehension and interpretation that derive from the perspective of the reader. Since readers actively construct the comprehension of the text, the text meaning is essentially what the reader determines the text to mean. These theories are useful for understanding how literary texts can be understood in multiple ways and at multiple levels by different readers. However, as theories of reading development, they offer no detailed explanation for the development of reading abilities; rather, they assume acceptable comprehension and interpretive levels from the outset. Nor do they offer explanations for how expository texts are used for learning new material or how procedural texts are to be understood appropriately.

control group (p. 100) A group (of students) used as a standard of comparison in a controlled experiment that does not receive the *treatment* that the researcher is interested in. A group that, ideally, differs from the experimental group only in terms of the single factor that the researcher is investigating.

discourse knowledge (p. 43) Knowledge of *discourse organisation*.

discourse organisation (p. 27) Structural framework of discourse. Patterns and features of discourse that reflect *genre*, writers' intentions, flow of information, *text structure* and types of information being presented. (For us, discourse organisation is a more general term than *genre*, *rhetorical organisation* and *text structure*.)

discourse structure (p. 44) See *discourse organisation*.

executive control processing/processor (p. 28) Operation of working memory that attends to priority tasks, allocates task operations strategically, sets goals for reading, monitors comprehension and repairs comprehension problems.

exposure to print (p. 21) Total amount of reading done by learners over a long period of time.

extensive reading (p. 73) Approach to the teaching and learning of reading in which learners read large quantities of material that are within their linguistic competence.

fluency (p. 40) Fluency in reading involves a combination of speed, accuracy and fluidity of processing. Fluency is a relative concept that must take into consideration reading task, reading topic, reader's age and amount of L2 exposure.

free-recall measure (p. 112) Measure of a person's ability to reconstruct information from a text at some point after having read the text. No specific ordering is required for the recall and supporting cues for recall are provided.

genre (p. 28) Means for organising formal aspects of a text to reflect specific functional intentions of a group, discipline or culture. Genres (e.g. poetry, mysteries, want ads, letters of recommendation, academic journal articles, sermons) have specific aims, expectations and defining characteristics.

given and new information (p. 112) Way of classifying elements of a sentence according to their presentation of information. Most sentences are written to connect what has previously been said (that which is known to the reader) with something new. The given part of a sentence, the part which is already familiar to the reader, is typically toward the beginning of the sentence; the new information, the main contribution of the sentence, tends to come toward the end of the sentence.

graphic organiser (p. 142) Visual frame used to represent and organise information (e.g. Venn diagrams, time line, pie chart).

graphic representation (p. 81) See *graphic organiser*.

headword (p. 134) Word from which common, formal variants of a word originate. For example, one headword (e.g. educate) would include all these variants: education, educated, educating, educator, educational.

incidental learning (p. 108) Learning that occurs without focusing on specific information. It may or may not require some level of conscious attention. In discussions of reading, readers read to understand the text, not to learn the words in the text. Nonetheless, readers notice and attend to words as they move through texts, even if only for very short periods of time. Some of these words are learned through incidental learning.

inconsiderate texts (p. 113) Texts that are difficult to understand because of poor organisation, difficult vocabulary, abstract imagery, new conceptual information, unfamiliar cultural assumptions, grammatical complexity, etc.

inferencing (p. 14) Ability to draw a logical conclusion based on explicit information in a text and *background knowledge*.

interactive models of reading (p. 33) Metaphorical depictions of reading as some combination of bottom–up and top–down processes, though typically not a full combination of all aspects of *top–down* and *bottom–up models*.

jigsaw reading activities (p. 227) Instructional technique in which subgroups of learners in a class are asked to read different parts of a text. The full picture is then pieced together, like a jigsaw, when members of different groups come together to complete a task.

language experience approach (p. 144) Approach to teaching reading whereby students and teacher prepare reading materials together. A typical sequence of activities is as follows: Students dictate a story to the teacher about a topic of interest, the teacher writes the story down, the students copy the story and the students read the story.

language threshold (p. 50) General level of second language ability that allows a reader to understand a text fluently according to the reader's purpose. Above the threshold, a reader is able to call on strategic reading processes (both first language and second language) effectively. The threshold varies with specific tasks, topics and reader purposes, but at some point with continuous practice in reading, the reader is able to read most texts at a level above the language threshold.

letter–sound knowledge (p. 98) Ability to relate letters and sounds. Note that a sound may have more than one spelling (/f/→f, ff, gh); and a spelling may have more than one sound (a→/a/ [have], /ae/ [mad], /e/ [made]).

letter–sound relationships (p. 47) Consistent relations between a given letter and its phonemic variants, and a given sound and its orthographic variants.

lexical access (p. 20) Rapid and automatic activation of word meanings in the lexicon. It is possible in second language contexts to recognise a word (word recognition), but not have any useful meaning entry for that word stored in the lexicon.

lexical decision task (p. 132) Task in which a participant in a study sits at a computer, decides if a word form that appears on the computer screen is a real word or not and presses one button if it is a word, another if it is a non-word. The time it takes from word appearance to pressing the button is typically what is measured.

lexical sets (p. 174) Sets of words that have semantic or grammatical similarities (e.g. words for food, classroom terms, words related to botany, words for hedging, nouns, transition words, adverbs).

longitudinal study (p. 131) Research that involves the study of the same learners over a period of time, usually for at least 5–6 months but often longer, sometimes up to several years.

matched groups (p. 118) Groups (or words) in a study that are matched for certain factors to help control the study (e.g. for people: proficiency level, time studying the second language, age, task knowledge, gender; for words: frequency, length, number of visually similar words, number of obviously different meanings).

metacognitive awareness (p. 45) See *metacognitive knowledge*.

metacognitive knowledge (p. 146) Conscious awareness of one's knowledge. More specifically, the ability to reflect on what one knows (e.g. language awareness). Such knowledge allows a reader to plan, regulate and monitor learning and (in the context of this book) reading.

metalinguistic awareness (p. 44)   See *metalinguistic knowledge*.

metalinguistic knowledge (p. 45)   Conscious awareness of language that allows one to recognise and discuss linguistic categories such as nouns, verbs, subordinate clauses, word meanings, etc.

models of reading (p. 31)   Theories of the component skills, processes and knowledge bases involved in reading. Formal models are based on the results of empirical evidence and are typically confirmed by additional independent studies. Descriptive models attempt to synthesise existing research comprehensively. Metaphorical models attempt to interpret more generally the reading processes involved in comprehension.

multiple case-study approach (p. 115)   Research method that involves gathering and analysing data about more than one individual example as a way of studying a broader phenomenon. In such studies, the researcher may look at multiple students, multiple groups of learners, multiple classes, etc.

multiplier effect (p. 180)   Possible outcome of training by which the learners of a skill, in turn, teach additional learners. For example, when teachers who learn a new teaching technique at a professional conference return to their schools and train other teachers, that multiplies the effect of the original training.

non-linear text (p. 227)   Text that is not organised by sequences of sentences and paragraphs. Examples of non-linear text include charts, diagrams, figures, graphs, maps and tables.

orthography (p. 47)   Graphic representations of a written language; these graphic representations may be alphabetic, syllabic or logographic in nature.

paced reading (p. 79)   Rate-development activity during which students read at a fixed rate determined by the teacher (e.g. 100 wpm). In an ideal paced-reading programme, students read at a rate that is challenging but not overly frustrating and that gets progressively faster over time.

paired readings (p. 109)   Activity in which students work in pairs on a variety of reading tasks. One possibility is for students to take turns reading segments of the text aloud to each other, with the 'listener' monitoring and helping out with reading problems.

parsing (p. 23) Act of breaking clauses down into their smaller constituent units. See *syntactic parsing*.

phoneme-identification ability (p. 100) Ability to identify phonemic sounds in words. This could mean identifying the first sound of a word, the last sound of a word or segmenting words into component sounds.

phonemic awareness (p. 98) Ability to recognise sounds in words (cf. *phonological awareness*).

phonological awareness (p. 118) General ability of learners to recognise phonemic sounds in a word, syllables in a word or syllable parts within a syllable.

previewing (p. 142) A pre-reading activity that introduces students to key features of a text so that students can establish their own expectations about what information they will find in the text and the way the information is organised.

pseudoword identification (p. 101) Usually the ability to look at a non-word and pronounce it using the phonological rules of the language, or the ability to see a non-word and press a button indicating that the form is a non-word (*lexical decision task*).

qualitative analysis (p. 113) Analysis of qualitative data, data which is not counted (e.g. student interviews), but can be reviewed for noticeable patterns and insights. It typically involves the interpretation of data in non-quantitative ways: categorising responses, highlighting key parts of verbal records, noting interesting patterns in responses.

qualitative data (p. 164) Data relating to or concerning some quality (cf. *quantitative data*).

quantitative analysis (p. 123) Analysis of quantitative data (numerical data such as reading rates, number of words learned, number of pages read). The data can be counted, categorised and compared in numerous ways.

quantitative data (p. 164) Data that can be counted, measured, expressed as a quantity (cf. *qualitative data*).

rauding (p. 12) A term that 'comes from the combination of two words, reading and auding. It refers to the frequently occurring situation where individuals are reading or listening, and they are understanding most of the thoughts that they are encountering as they read or aud the sentences involved. Rauding focuses on the idea that reading prose and listening to prose generally involve the same comprehension processes' (Carver, 1997, p. 6).

read alouds (p. 79) Classroom procedure in which the teacher reads aloud to students and students follow along, often reading silently along with the teacher.

reading efficiency (p. 122) Ability, often seen as the essence of general reading comprehension, that is formally understood as the interaction of strong reading rate abilities (decoding and speed of processing) and reading accuracy skills (decoding and comprehension skills) (see Carver, 1997).

reading guide (p. 227) An exercise handout, distributed to students before a reading assignment, that 'walks' students through a reading passage, modelling the steps taken and the strategies used to comprehend a passage. It gives students one or two pre-reading tasks, some during-reading tasks and post-reading tasks as follow-up. All tasks are tailored to the assigned passage.

reading to integrate information (p. 14) A purpose for reading that requires the same detailed level of comprehension as *reading to learn*; it also requires decisions about the relative importance of select information and the reorganisation of information from multiple sources. The critical evaluation of information being read is required so that the reader can decide what and how information is to be integrated.

reading to learn (p. 13) A purpose for reading. Reading-to-learn tasks are typical of academic and professional settings where readers need to learn information (i.e. main ideas as well as details that elaborate the main ideas) from the text and link the text to their own knowledge bases.

reading to search (p. 13) A purpose for reading in which readers combine scanning for a word or phrase with minimal sampling of sentence meaning to determine if they are in the right areas of the text for targeted information.

reading-to-write task (p. 227) Classroom activity in which students read to gather information that they can use in a subsequent writing task.

recall measure (p. 119) See *recall task.*

recall task (p. 113) Task that requires a reader to reconstruct information from a text after reading it, by either speaking, writing or completing some formal guide or outline.

regression methodology (p. 107) Statistical procedure that looks for the best fit between a measure (dependent variable) and other variables. Other variables that 'fit' well are referred to as 'predictors' of the key (dependent) measure. The predictors that are significant account for (overlap with) a non-random amount of the variability that can be observed in the key measure. The independent contributions of significant predictors can be measured with this methodology.

rereading (p. 79) Activity in which students reread the same passage or text. Rereading may involve a search for new information, an effort to repair comprehension, the completion of a post-reading activity, or one of a number of fluency-development exercises.

rhetorical frame (p. 13) The patterns of organisation that writers use to present expository information and that readers construct mentally to learn relevant information. Possible frames include cause-effect relations, classification, comparison and contrast, linear sequences and problem–solution relations (cf. *rhetorical organization*).

rhetorical organisation (p. 81) Pattern of organisation used in expository and persuasive texts where information is presented as analysis, cause and effect, classification, comparison and contrast, definition, loose description or problem-solution.

scan (p. 13) Specialised type of reading in which the reader searches quickly for a specific piece of information or a specific word (cf. *skim*).

script (p. 210) Portion of a lesson plan that specifies the exact words that will be used by the teacher. Often used in lessons where the teacher is modelling strategic behaviours while reading aloud to his/her students.

self-reporting survey (p. 106) Survey in which respondents report on what they, themselves, do or know (e.g. how much they read each week).

semantic feature analysis (p. 174) A vocabulary-learning method that requires students to relate terms associated with a topic or some concept. For example, students could be asked to categorise various energy terms (e.g. thermal energy, nuclear energy, hydroelectric energy, solar energy, wind) according to whether the words have certain properties (e.g. organic, natural, polluting, non-polluting).

semantic proposition formation (p. 23) Process of combining word meanings and structural information into basic clause-level meaning units.

shared reading approach (p. 144) Activity in which the teacher shares a book with a group of students or the whole class by reading the book to them. It is typically used with young students and with large books.

shared variance (p. 147) Amount (expressed as a percentage) of overlap between two measures, based on the variation that is shared between the two measures.

situation model of reader interpretation (p. 27) Reader's elaborated interpretation of information from the text in terms of his or her own goals, expectations, feelings and *background knowledge*.

skills (p. 15) Linguistic processing abilities that are relatively automatic in their use and their combinations (e.g. choosing the correct meaning of words with multiple meanings, *semantic proposition formation*, slower reading rate with different texts).

skim (p. 13) Specialised type of reading in which the reader reads quickly for a general understanding of the text, for the gist of a passage. The process typically involves the strategic skipping of segments of the text and the reading of key parts (cf. *scan*).

SSR (p. 177) See *sustained silent reading*.

story previews (p. 109) Technique that involves giving students background information about the story, author, characters and key episodes before students are asked to read. Previews can be used to highlight key vocabulary and important concepts needed for full understanding.

strategies (p. 15) Abilities that are potentially open to conscious reflection and use (e.g. establishing a purpose for reading, taking steps to repair faulty comprehension, previewing a text).

sustained silent reading (SSR) (p. 109) Classroom time devoted to silent reading, when teacher and students are reading materials of their own choice. Typically SSR sessions occur on a regular basis, without instruction, evaluation or interruptions. Also referred to as DEAR: Drop Everything And Read.

syntactic parsing (p. 22) Reader's ability to take in and process words as larger units of structure so that basic grammatical information can be extracted to support clause-level meaning.

text model of reading comprehension (p. 25) Fundamental higher-level comprehension process involving the coordination of ideas from a text that represent the main points and supporting ideas.

text structure (p. 40) Language features that mark text information and writers' intentions (e.g. new versus given information, paragraphing, sequence markers, signalled rhetorical patterns, transition phrases and sentences).

think alouds (p. 114) Classroom (and research) technique that requires learners (or teacher) to report on what they are doing as they complete a task (e.g. reading). They speak their inner thoughts aloud. Practice is always required before being used for data collection purposes.

timed reading (p. 79) Rate-development activity during which students time their reading (in words per minute) and calculate comprehension scores. The goal is to improve reading rate and comprehension over time.

title-recognition checklist test (p. 106) Evaluation technique that requires participants to check off all the book titles that they recognise on a long list of about 60 to 80 titles. Some titles are not real; they are included on the test to find out if participants are overstating what they know.

top–down models of reading (p. 32) Metaphorical depiction of reading that characterises the reader as someone who has a set of expectations about text information, directs the eyes where to look on the page and samples enough information from the text to confirm or reject the hypothesised expectations.

training study (p. 100) Research that involves training a group of participants in some skill or set of tasks.

transactional models of reading (p. 34) See *constructivist models of reading*.

Transactional strategy instruction (p. 113) Approach to reading instruction that leads students to become strategic readers (rather than learners of individual strategies).

transfer (p. 41) Use of L1 knowledge (e.g. phonological, syntactic, strategic) in L2 tasks.

treatment (p. 102) The training, instruction, or resources that are given to an experimental group but not to a *control group*.

treatment group (p. 100) Group of students that is subject to researcher's *treatment*.

working memory (p. 18) Active component of memory processes in cognition. It is limited in capacity, retains active information for a relatively short period of time and integrates information and processes to construct comprehension. It is not a separate part of brain functioning but is a network of currently active information and related processes being used at a given moment.

working memory activation (p. 24) Process in which information that is sufficiently excited (electrically and chemically in the brain) becomes part of the working network of information being used actively in cognitive processing.

Index of studies summarized in Chapters 4–5 and model action research projects presented in Chapters 6–9 – Organized by general theme

General theme	Studies summarized in Chapters 4–5		Model action research projects in Chapters 6–9	
	Chapter, section	page	Model no.	page
Attitudes toward reading	Ch 4, section 4.2.8	119	9.1.9	242
Background knowledge	Ch 5, section 5.2.7	142		·
Comprehension	Ch 4, section 4.2.5	113	7.1.4	190
	Ch 4, section 4.2.7	117	7.1.7	196
	Ch 4, section 4.2.8	119	8.1.6	216
	Ch 5, section 5.2.4	136	8.1.8	220
	Ch 5, section 5.2.6	140	9.1.3	232
	Ch 5, section 5.2.7	142		
Demands of reading passages			9.1.5	236
Dictionaries, student use of			7.1.3	188
Discourse organisation	Ch 4, section 4.2.4	111	8.1.6	216
	Ch 5, section 5.2.4	136	8.1.7	219
			8.1.8	220
Exposure to print	Ch 4, section 4.2.1	105		
	Ch 4, section 4.2.8	119		

General theme	Studies summarized in Chapters 4–5		Model action research projects in Chapters 6–9	
	Chapter, section	page	Model no.	page
Extensive reading	Ch 4, section 4.2.3 Ch 5, section 5.2.8	109 144	6–2	161–181
Fluency	Ch 4, section 4.2.3	109		
Glosses, effectiveness of			7.1.4	190
Graphic organisers			8.1.6 8.1.8	216 220
Incidental learning	Ch 4, section 4.2.2	108		
Language threshold	Ch 5, section 5.2.9	145		
Mandated reading materials			7.1.1 9.1.4 9.1.5 9.1.6	186 233 236 238
Mental translation	Ch 5, section 5.2.6	140		
Metacognitive knowledge	Ch 5, section 5.2.9	145		
Metacognitive strategies			8.1.5	214
Modelling reading strategies			8.1.3	210
Motivation	Ch 4, section 4.2.8	119	9.1.7	239
Non-linear text			9.1.6	238
Paced reading			7.1.8	197
Paired re-readings			7.1.9	199
Pre- and post-reading	Ch 5, section 5.2.7	142	8.1.7 9.1.2 9.1.4	219 230 233
Previews	Ch 5, section 5.2.7	142		
Purposes for reading			9.1.1	230
Rate			7.1.7 7.1.8	196 197
Reading activities			8.1.7 8.1.9 9.1.2	219 222 230
Reading efficiency	Ch 4, section 4.2.9	122		

General theme	Studies summarized in Chapters 4–5		Model action research projects in Chapters 6–9	
	Chapter, section	page	Model no.	page
Text structure	Ch 4, section 4.2.4 Ch 5, section 5.2.4	111 136	8.1.7	219
Topics of interest/readings			9.1.7	239
Vocabulary	Ch 4, section 4.2.2 Ch 5, section 5.2.1 Ch 5, section 5.2.3 Ch 5, section 5.2.9	108 130 134 145	6–1 7.1.1 7.1.2 7.1.3 7.1.4 7.1.5	161–180 186 188 188 190 191
Word recognition	Ch 4, section 4.2.7 Ch 5, section 5.2.2	117 132	7.1.6	194

References

Adams, M. (1990) *Beginning to read: Thinking and learning about print*. Cambridge, MA: MIT Press.

Aebersold, J.A. and Field, M.L. (1997) *From reader to reading teacher: Issues and strategies for second language classrooms*. New York: Cambridge University Press.

Alderson, J.C. (2000) *Assessing reading*. New York: Cambridge University Press.

Alexander, P.A. and Jetton, T.L. (2000) Learning from text: A multidimensional and developmental perspective. In M.L. Kamil, P.B. Mosenthal, P.D. Pearson and R. Barr (eds), *Handbook of reading research*, Volume III (pp. 285–310). Mahwah, NJ: Lawrence Erlbaum.

Anderson, J.R. (1995) *Cognitive psychology and its implications* (4th edn). New York: W.H. Freeman.

Anderson, N.J. (1991) Individual differences in strategy use in second language reading and testing. *The Modern Language Journal*, 75: 460–72.

Anderson, N.J. (1999) *Exploring second language reading: Issues and strategies*. Boston, MA: Heinle & Heinle.

Anderson, R.C. (1996) Research foundations to support wide reading. In V. Greaney (ed.), *Promoting reading: Views on making reading materials accessible to increase literacy levels* (pp. 55–77). Newark, DE: International Reading Association.

Baumann, J.F. and Duffy-Hester, A.M. (2000) Making sense of classroom worlds: Methodology in teacher research. In M.L. Kamil, P.B. Mosenthal, P.D. Pearson and R. Barr (eds), *Handbook of reading research*, Volume III (pp. 77–98). Mahwah, NJ: Lawrence Erlbaum.

Beck, I., McKeown, M., Hamilton, R. and Kucan, L. (1997) *Questioning the author: An approach for enhancing student engagement with text*. Newark, DE: International Reading Association.

Beck, I., McKeown, M., Sinatra, G. and Loxterman, J. (1991) Revising social studies text from a text-processing perspective: Evidence of improved comprehensibility. *Reading Research Quarterly*, 26: 251–76.

Beck, I., McKeown, M., Worthy, J., Sandora, C. and Kucan, L. (1996) Questioning the author: A year-long classroom implementation to engage students with texts. *Elementary School Journal*, 96: 385–481.

Bell, J.S. (1995) The relationship between L1 and L2 literacy: Some complicating factors. *TESOL Quarterly*, 29: 687–704.

Bellanca, J. (1990) *The cooperative think tank: Graphic organizers to teach thinking in the cooperative classroom*. Palatine, IL: IRI/Skylight Training.

Bellanca, J. (1992) The *cooperative think tank II: Graphic organizers to teach thinking in the cooperative classroom*. Palatine, IL: IRI/Skylight Training.

Bernhardt, E. (1991) A psycholinguistic perspective on second language literacy. *Reading in Two Languages. AILA Review*, 8: 31–44.

Bernhardt, E. (2000) Second-language reading as a case study of reading scholarship in the 20th century. In M.L. Kamil, P.B. Mosenthal, P.D. Pearson and R. Barr (eds), *Handbook of reading research*, Volume III (pp. 791–811). Mahwah, NJ: Lawrence Erlbaum.

Bernhardt, E. and Kamil, M. (1995) Interpreting relationships between L1 and L2 reading: Consolidating the linguistic threshold and the linguistic interdependence hypothesis. *Applied Linguistics*, 16: 15–34.

Bialystok, E. (2001) Metalinguistic aspects of bilingual processing. In M. McGroarty *et al.* (eds), *Annual Review of Applied Linguistics*, 21: 169–81. New York: Cambridge University Press.

Bossers, B. (1992) *Reading in two languages: A study of reading comprehension in Dutch as a second language and in Turkish as a first language*. Rotterdam: Drukkerij Van Driel.

Brown, R., Pressley, M., Van Meter, P. and Schuder, T. (1996) A quasi-experimental validation of transactional strategy instruction with low-achieving second-grade students. *Journal of Educational Psychology*, 88: 18–37.

Burns, A. (1999) *Collaborative action research for English language teachers*. New York: Cambridge University Press.

Burns, A. and Hammond, J. (forthcoming) *Teaching and researching literacy*. Harlow: Longman.

Burns, A. and Hood, S. (eds) (1995) *Teachers' voices: Exploring course design in a changing curriculum*. Sydney, NSW: National Centre for English Language Teaching and Research.

Byrne, B. (1996) The learnability of the alphabetic principle: Children's initial hypotheses about how print represents spoken language. *Applied Psycholinguistics*, 17: 401–26.

Byrne, B. and Fielding-Barnsley, R. (1989) Phonemic awareness and letter knowledge in the child's acquisition of the alphabetic principle. *Journal of Educational Psychology*, 81: 313–21.

Byrne, B. and Fielding-Barnsley, R. (1991) Evaluation of a program to teach phonemic awareness to young children. *Journal of Educational Psychology*, 83: 451–5.

Byrne, B. and Fielding-Barnsley, R. (1993) Evaluation of a program to teach phonemic awareness to young children: A 1-year follow-up. *Journal of Educational Psychology*, 85: 104–11.

Byrne, B. and Fielding-Barnsley, R. (1995) Evaluation of a program to teach phonemic awareness to young children: A 2- and 3-year follow-up and a new pre-school trial. *Journal of Educational Psychology*, 87: 488–503.

Carpenter, P., Miyake, A. and Just, M. (1994) Working memory constraints in comprehension: Evidence from individual differences, aphasia and aging. In M.A. Gernsbacher (ed.), *Handbook of psycholinguistics* (pp. 1075–1122). San Diego: Academic Press.

Carrell, P.L. (1985) Facilitating ESL reading by teaching text structure. *TESOL Quarterly*, 19: 727–52.

Carrell, P.L. (1991) Second language reading: Reading ability or language proficiency? *Applied Linguistics*, 12: 159–79.

Carrell, P.L. (1992) Awareness of text structure: Effects on recall. *Language Learning*, 42: 1–20.

Carrell, P. (1998) Can reading strategies be successfully taught? *Australian Review of Applied Linguistics*, 21: 1–20.

Carson, J. (1993) Reading for writing: Cognitive perspectives. In J. Carson and I. Leki (eds), *Reading in the composition classroom: Second language perspectives* (pp. 85–104). Boston: Heinle & Heinle.

Carson, J. (2000) Reading and writing for academic purposes. In M. Pally (ed.), *Sustained content teaching in academic ESL/EFL* (pp. 19–34). Boston: Houghton Mifflin.

Carson, J. and Leki, I. (eds) (1993) *Reading in the composition classroom: Second language perspectives*. Boston: Heinle & Heinle.

Carter, R. (1998) *Vocabulary: Applied linguistic perspectives* (2nd edn). New York: Routledge.

Carver, R. (1990) *Reading rate: A review of research and theory*. San Diego: Academic Press.

Carver, R. (1992) Reading rate: Theory, research, and practical implications. *Journal of Reading*, 36: 84–95.

Carver, R. (1993) Merging the simple view of reading with rauding theory. *Journal of Reading Behavior*, 25: 439–55.

Carver, R. (1994) Percentage of unknown vocabulary words in text as a function of the relative difficulty of the text: Implications for instruction. *Journal of Reading Behavior*, 26: 413–37.

Carver, R. (1997) Reading for one second, one minute, or one year from the perspective of rauding theory. *Scientific Studies on Reading*, 1: 3–43.

Carver, R. (1998) Predicting reading level in grades 1 to 6 from listening level and decoding level: Testing theory relevant to the simple view of reading. *Reading and Writing*, 10: 121–54.

Chalhoub-deVille, M. (ed.) (1999) *Issues in computer-adaptive testing of reading proficiency* (Studies in Language Testing 10). Cambridge: Cambridge University Press.

Chall, J.S. and Jacobs, V.A. (1996) The reading, writing, and language connection. In J. Shimron (ed.), *Literacy and education: Essays in memory of Dina Feitelson* (pp. 33–48). Cresskill, NJ: Hampton Press.

Chamot, A.U. and O'Malley, J.M. (1994) *The CALLA handbook: Implementing the cognitive academic language learning approach*. Reading, MA: Addison Wesley.

Chen, H-C. and Graves, M.F. (1995) Effects of previewing and providing background knowledge on Taiwanese college students' comprehension of American short stories. *TESOL Quarterly*, 29: 663–86.

Chen, R-S. and Vellutino, F. (1997) Prediction of reading ability: A cross-validation study of the Simple View of Reading. *Journal of Literacy Research*, 29: 1–24.

Cipielewski, J. and Stanovich, K. (1992) Predicting growth in reading ability from children's exposure to print. *Journal of Experimental Child Psychology*, 54: 74–89.

Coady, J. and Huckin, T. (eds) (1997) *Second language vocabulary acquisition*. New York: Cambridge University Press.

Cohen, A. (1998) *Strategies in learning and using a second language.* London: Longman.

Cohen, A. and Oxford, R. (forthcoming) *Teaching and researching learning strategies.* Harlow: Longman.

Connor, U. (1996) *Contrastive rhetoric.* Cambridge: Cambridge University Press.

Cunningham, A. and Stanovich, K. (1998) The impact of print exposure on word recognition. In J. Metsala and L. Ehri (eds), *Word recognition in beginning literacy* (pp. 235–62). Mahwah, NJ: Lawrence Erlbaum.

Day, R. (ed.) (1993) *New ways in teaching reading.* Alexandria, VA: TESOL.

Day, R. and Bamford, J. (1998) *Extensive reading in the second language classroom.* Cambridge: Cambridge University Press.

Dörnyei, Z. (2001a) New themes and approaches in second language motivation research. In M. McGroarty *et al.* (eds), *Annual Review of Applied Linguistics,* 21: 43–59. New York: Cambridge University Press.

Dörnyei, Z. (2001b) *Teaching and researching motivation.* London: Longman.

Dowhower, S. (1987) Effects of repeated reading on second-grade transitional readers' fluency and comprehension. *Reading Research Quarterly,* 22: 389–406.

Dowhower, S. (1994) Repeated reading revisited: Research into practice. *Reading and Writing Quarterly,* 10: 343–58.

Duffy, G. (1993) Teachers' progress toward becoming expert strategy teachers. *The Elementary School Journal,* 94 (2): 109–20.

Durgunoglu, A. (1997) Bilingual reading: Its components, development, and other issues. In A. deGroot and J. Kroll (eds), *Tutorials in bilingualism: Psycholinguistic perspectives* (pp. 255–76). Mahwah, NJ: Lawrence Erlbaum.

Durgunoglu, A. (1998) Acquiring literacy in English and Spanish in the United States. In A. Durgunoglu and L. Verhoeven (eds), *Literacy development in a multilingual context* (pp. 135–45). Mahwah, NJ: Lawrence Erlbaum.

Dymock, S. (1999) Learning about text structure. In G.B. Thompson and T. Nicholson (eds), *Learning to read: Beyond phonics and whole language* (pp. 174–92). New York: Teachers' College Press.

Edge, J. (ed.) (2001) *Action research: Case studies in TESOL.* Alexandria, VA: TESOL.

Edge, J. and Richards, K. (eds) (1993) *Teachers develop teachers' research: Papers on classroom research and teacher development.* Portsmouth, NH: Heinemann.

Elley, W.B. (1991) Acquiring literacy in a second language: The effect of book-based programs. *Language Learning,* 41: 375–411.

Elley, W.B. (1992) *How in the world do students read?* Hamburg: International Association of the Evaluation of Educational Achievement (distributed through the International Reading Association).

Ellis, N. (1996) Sequencing in SLA. *Studies in Second Language Acquisition,* 18: 91–126.

Ellis, N. (1998) Emergentism, connectionism and language learning. *Language Learning,* 48: 631–64.

Ellis, N. (1999) Cognitive approaches to SLA. In W. Grabe *et al.* (eds), *Annual Review of Applied Linguistics,* 19: 22–42. New York: Cambridge University Press.

Enright, M., Grabe, W., Koda, K., Mosenthal, P., Mulcahy-Ernt, P. and Schedl, M. (2000) *TOEFL 2000 reading framework: A working paper* (TOEFL Monograph Series 17). Princeton, NJ: Educational Testing Service.

Ericsson, K.A. (ed.) (1996) *The road to excellence.* Mahwah, NJ: Lawrence Erlbaum.

Eyraud, K., Giles, G., Koenig, S. and Stoller, F.L. (2000) The word wall approach: Promoting L2 vocabulary learning. *English Teaching Forum,* 38: 2–11.

Feuerstein, T. and Schcolnik, M. (1995) *Enhancing reading comprehension in the language learning classroom*. Burlingame, CA: Alta Book Center.

Freeman, D. (1998) *Doing teacher research: From inquiry to understanding*. Boston, MA: Heinle & Heinle.

Fry, E.B., Kress, J.E. and Fountoukidis, D.L. (1993) *The reading teacher's book of lists* (3rd edn). Englewood Cliffs, NJ: Prentice Hall.

Garcia, G.E. (2000) Bilingual children's reading. In M.L. Kamil, P.B. Mosenthal, P.D. Pearson and R. Barr (eds), *Handbook of reading research*, Volume III (pp. 813–34). Mahwah, NJ: Lawrence Erlbaum.

Gaskins, I. and Elliot, T. (1991) *Implementing cognitive strategy instruction across the school*. Brookline, MA: Brookline Books.

Gathercole, S.E. and Pickering, S.J. (2000) Assessment of working memory in six- and seven-year-old children. *Journal of Educational Psychology*, 92: 377–90.

Geva, E. and Siegel, L. (2000) Orthographic and cognitive factors in the concurrent development of basic reading skills in two languages. *Reading and Writing*, 12: 1–30.

Geva, E. and Wade-Woolley, L. (1998) Component processes in becoming English–Hebrew biliterate. In A. deGroot and J. Kroll (eds), *Tutorials in bilingualism: Psycholinguistic perspectives* (pp. 85–110). Mahwah, NJ: Lawrence Erlbaum.

Geva, E., Wade-Woolley, L. and Shany, M. (1997) Development of reading efficiency in first and second language. *Scientific Studies of Reading*, 1(2): 119–44.

Goldman, S.R. (1997) Learning from text: Reflections on the past and suggestions for the future. *Discourse Processes*, 23: 357–98.

Goldman, S.R. and Rakestraw Jr, J.A. (2000) Structural aspects of constructing meaning from text. In M.L. Kamil, P.B. Mosenthal, P.D. Pearson and R. Barr (eds), *Handbook of reading research*, Volume III (pp. 311–35). Mahwah, NJ: Lawrence Erlbaum.

Goodman, K. (1986) *What's whole in whole language*. Portsmouth, NH: Heinemann.

Goodman, K. (1996) *On reading*. Portsmouth, NH: Heinemann.

Gough, P., Hoover, W. and Peterson, C. (1996) Some observations on the Simple View of Reading. In C. Cornoldi and J. Oakhill (eds), *Reading comprehension difficulties* (pp. 1–13). Mahwah, NJ: Lawrence Erlbaum.

Gough, P. and Wren, S. (1999) Constructing meaning: The role of decoding. In J. Oakhill and S. Beard (eds), *Reading development and the teaching of reading* (pp. 59–78). Malden, MA: Blackwell.

Grabe, W. (1995) Dilemmas for the development of second language reading abilities. *Prospect*, 10: 38–51.

Grabe, W. (1996) Reading in an ESP context: Dilemmas and possible solutions. *ESP Malaysia*, 4: 1–28.

Grabe, W. (1997) Discourse analysis and reading instruction. In T. Miller (ed.), *Functional approaches to written text: Classroom applications* (pp. 2–15). Washington, DC: United States Information Agency.

Grabe, W. (1999) Developments in reading research and their implications for computer-adaptive reading assessment. In M. Chalhoub-deVille (ed.), *Issues in computer-adaptive testing of reading proficiency* (Studies in Language Testing 10, pp. 11–47). Cambridge: Cambridge University Press.

Grabe, W. (2000) Reading research and its implications for reading assessment. In A. Kunnan (ed.), *Fairness and validation in language assessment* (pp. 226–62). Cambridge: Cambridge University Press.

Grabe, W. and Gardner, D. (1995) Discourse analysis, coherence, and reading instruction. *Lenguas Modernas*, 22: 69–88.

Grabe, W. and Kaplan, R.B. (1996) *Theory and practice of writing*. London: Longman.

Grabe, W. and Stoller, F.L. (2001) Reading for academic purposes: Guidelines for the ESL/EFL teacher. In M. Celce-Murcia (ed.), *Teaching English as a second or foreign language* (3rd edn) (pp. 187–203). Boston: Heinle & Heinle.

Graves, M., Watts-Taffe, S. and Graves, B. (1998) *Essentials of elementary reading*. Boston, MA: Allyn & Bacon.

Greaney, V. (1996) Reading in developing countries: Problems and issues. In V. Greaney (ed.), *Promoting reading: Views on making reading materials accessible to increase literacy levels* (pp. 5–38). Newark, DE: International Reading Association.

Guthrie, J., Wigfield, A., Metsala, J. and Cox, K. (1999). Motivational and cognitive predictors of text comprehension and reading amount. *Scientific Studies of Reading*, 3: 231–56.

Guthrie, J., Van Meter, P., Hancock, G.R., Alao, S., Anderson, E. and McCann, A. (1998) Does Concept-Oriented Reading Instruction increase strategy use and conceptual learning from text? *Journal of Educational Psychology*, 90: 261–78.

Guthrie, J.T. and Wigfield, A. (2000) Engagement and motivation in reading. In M.L. Kamil, P.B. Mosenthal, P.D. Pearson and R. Barr (eds), *Handbook of reading research*, Volume III (pp. 403–22). Mahwah, NJ: Lawrence Erlbaum.

Guthrie, J., Wigfield, A. and Von Secker, C. (2000) Effects of integrated instruction on motivation and strategy use in reading. *Journal of Educational Psychology*, 92: 331–41.

Hanley, J.R., Tzeng, O. and Huang, H.S. (1999) Learning to read Chinese. In M. Harris and G. Hatano (eds), *Learning to read and write: A cross-linguistic perspective* (pp. 173–95). Cambridge: Cambridge University Press.

Harris, A.J. and Serwer, B.L. (1966) The CRAFT project: Instructional time in reading research. *Reading Research Quarterly*, 2: 27–57.

Harris, M. and Hatano, G. (1999a) Introduction: A cross-linguistic perspective on learning to read and write. In M. Harris and G. Hatano (eds), *Learning to read and write: A cross-linguistic perspective* (pp. 1–9). Cambridge: Cambridge University Press.

Harris, M. and Hatano, G. (eds) (1999b) *Learning to read and write: A cross-linguistic perspective*. Cambridge: Cambridge University Press.

Hartmann, R.R.K. (2001) *Teaching and researching lexicography*. London: Longman.

Hatch, E. and Brown, C. (1995) *Vocabulary, semantics, and language education*. New York: Cambridge University Press.

Hazenburg, S. and Hulstijn, J.H. (1996) Defining a minimal receptive second-language vocabulary for non-native university students: An empirical investigation. *Applied Linguistics*, 17: 145–63.

Heimlich, J. and Pittelman, S. (1986) *Semantic mapping: Classroom applications*. Newark, DE: International Reading Association.

Hess, N. (1991) *Headstarts: One hundred original pre-text activities*. Reading, MA: Addison Wesley.

Hirvela, A. (2001) Incorporating reading into EAP writing courses. In J. Flowerdew and M. Peacock (eds), *Research perspectives on English for academic purposes* (pp. 330–46). New York: Cambridge University Press.

Hoover, W. and Gough, P. (1990) The Simple View of Reading. *Reading and Writing*, 2: 127–60.

Hyerle, D. (1996) *Visual tools for constructing knowledge.* Alexandria, VA: Association for Supervision and Curriculum Development.

Jacobs, G. (1994) What lurks in the margins: Use of vocabulary glosses as a strategy in second language reading. *Issues in Applied Linguistics*, 5: 115–37.

Janzen, J. (1996) Teaching strategic reading. *TESOL Journal*, 6: 6–9.

Janzen, J. and Stoller, F.L. (1998) Integrating strategic reading in L2 instruction. *Reading in a Foreign Language*, 12: 251–69.

Jones, B.F., Pierce, J. and Hunter, B. (1988/1989) Teaching students to construct graphic representations. *Educational Leadership*, 46: 20–5.

Juel, C. (1999) The messenger may be wrong, but the message may be right. In J. Oakhill and S. Beard (eds), *Reading development and the teaching of reading* (pp. 201–12). Malden, MA: Blackwell.

Just, M. and Carpenter, P. (1992) A capacity theory of comprehension: Individual differences in working memory. *Psychological Review*, 99: 122–49.

Kemmis, S. and McTaggart, R. (1988) *The action research planner* (3rd edn). Geelong, Australia: Deakin University Press.

Kern, R.G. (1994) The role of mental translation in second language reading. *Studies in Second Language Acquisition*, 16: 441–61.

Kintsch, W. (1988) The role of knowledge in discourse comprehension: A construction–integration model. *Psychological Review*, 95: 163–82.

Kintsch, W. (1998) *Comprehension: A framework for cognition.* Cambridge: Cambridge University Press.

Knight, S. (1994) Dictionary use while reading: The effects on comprehension and vocabulary acquisition for students of different verbal abilities. *Modern Language Journal*, 94: 285–99.

Koda, K. (1996) L2 word recognition research: A critical review. *Modern Language Journal*, 80: 450–60.

Koda, K. (1997) Orthographic knowledge in L2 lexical processing. In J. Coady and T. Huckin (eds), *Second language vocabulary acquisition* (pp. 35–52). New York: Cambridge University Press.

Koda, K. (1999) Development of L2 intraword orthographic sensitivity and decoding skills. *Modern Language Journal*, 83: 51–64.

Koda, K. (2000) Cross-linguistic variations in L2 morphological awareness. *Applied Psycholinguistics*, 21: 297–320.

Krashen, S. (1993) *The power of reading: Insights from the research.* Englewood, CO: Libraries Unlimited.

Kroll, J. and deGroot, A. (1997) Lexical and conceptual memory in the bilingual: Mapping form to meaning in two languages. In A. deGroot and J. Kroll (eds), *Tutorials in bilingualism: Psycholinguistic perspectives* (pp. 169–99). Mahwah, NJ: Lawrence Erlbaum.

Kucan, L. and Beck, I. (1997) Thinking aloud and reading comprehension research: Inquiry, instruction, and social interaction. *Review of Educational Research*, 67: 271–99.

Laufer, B. (1997) The lexical plight in second language reading. In J. Coady and T. Huckin (eds), *Second language vocabulary acquisition* (pp. 20–34). New York: Cambridge University Press.

Lee, J.W. and Schallert, D.L. (1997) The relative contribution of L2 language proficiency and L1 reading ability to L2 reading performance: A test of the threshold hypothesis in an EFL context. *TESOL Quarterly*, 31: 713–39.

Leki, I. (1992) *Understanding ESL writers: A guide for teachers*. Portsmouth, NH: Heinemann.

Li, S. and Munby, H. (1996) Metacognitive strategies in second language academic reading: A qualitative investigation. *English for Specific Purposes*, 15: 199–216.

Liow, S. (1999) Reading skill development in bilingual Singaporean children. In M. Harris and G. Hatano (eds), *Learning to read and write: A cross-linguistic perspective* (pp. 196–213). Cambridge: Cambridge University Press.

Lundberg, I. (1999) Learning to read in Scandinavia. In M. Harris and G. Hatano (eds), *Learning to read and write: A cross-linguistic perspective* (pp. 157–72). Cambridge: Cambridge University Press.

Luppescu, S. and Day, R. (1993) Reading, dictionaries, and vocabulary learning. *Language Learning*, 43: 263–87.

MacWhinney, B. (1997) Second language acquisition and the competition model. In A. deGroot and J. Kroll (eds), *Tutorials in bilingualism: Psycholinguistic perspectives* (pp. 113–42). Mahwah, NJ: Lawrence Erlbaum.

Mandel Glazer, S. (1992) *Reading comprehension: Self-monitoring strategies to develop independent readers*. New York: Scholastic.

Martin, J. (1989) *Factual writing: Exploring and challenging social reality*. New York: Oxford University Press.

McCarthy, M. (1990) *Vocabulary*. New York: Oxford University Press.

McGuinness, D. (1997) *Why our children can't read and what we can do about it*. New York: Free Press.

McKay, S. (1993) *Agendas for second language literacy*. New York: Cambridge University Press.

McKenna, M.C., Kear, D.J. and Ellsworth, R.A. (1995) Children's attitudes toward reading: A national survey. *Reading Research Quarterly*, 30: 934–56.

McKenna, M.C. and Robinson, R.D. (1997) *Teaching through text: A content literacy approach to content area reading* (2nd edn). New York: Longman.

Mikulecky, B. (1990) *A short course in teaching reading skills*. Reading, MA: Addison-Wesley.

Mikulecky, L. (1990) Literacy for what purpose? In R.L. Venezky, D.A. Wagner and D.S. Cilberti (eds), *Towards defining literacy* (pp. 24–34). Newark, DE: International Reading Association.

Miller, W.M. and Steeber de Orozco, S. (1990a) *Reading faster and understanding more*, Book 1 (3rd edn). Glenview, IL: Scott, Foresman/Little Brown.

Miller, W.M. and Steeber de Orozco, S. (1990b) *Reading faster and understanding more*, Book 2 (3rd edn). Glenview, IL: Scott, Foresman/Little Brown.

Miyake, A. and Friedman, N. (1998) Individual differences in second language proficiency: Working memory as language aptitude. In A. Healy and L. Bourne Jr (eds), *Foreign language learning: Psycholinguistic studies on training and retention* (pp. 339–64). Mahwah, NJ: Lawrence Erlbaum.

Mohan, B. (1986) *Language and content*. Reading, MA: Addison Wesley.

Morgan, J. and Rinvolucri, M. (1986) *Vocabulary*. New York: Oxford University Press.

Muljani, D., Koda, K. and Moates, D.R. (1998) The development of word recognition in a second language. *Applied Psycholinguistics*, 19: 99–113.

Nagy, W. (1988) *Teaching vocabulary to improve reading comprehension*. Newark, DE: International Reading Association.

Nagy, W., Anderson, R.C. and Herman, P. (1987) Learning word meanings from context during normal reading. *American Educational Research Journal*, 24: 262–82.

Nagy, W., Garcia, G., Durgunoglu, A. and Hancin-Bhatt, B. (1993) Spanish-English bilingual students' use of cognates in English reading. *Journal of Reading Behavior*, 25: 241–59.

Nagy, W., Herman, P. and Anderson, R.C. (1985) Learning words from contexts. *Reading Research Quarterly*, 20: 233–53.

Nagy, W.E. and Scott, J.A. (2000) Vocabulary processes. In M.L. Kamil, P.B. Mosenthal, P.D. Pearson and R. Barr (eds), *Handbook of reading research*, Volume III (pp. 269–310). Mahwah, NJ: Lawrence Erlbaum.

Nation, I.S.P. (ed.) (1994) *New ways in teaching vocabulary*. Alexandria, VA: TESOL.

Nation, I.S.P. (2001) *Learning vocabulary in another language*. New York: Cambridge University Press.

Nelson, G. and Burns, J. (2000) Managing information for writing university exams in American history. In M. Pally (ed.), *Sustained content teaching in academic ESL/EFL* (pp. 132–57). Boston: Houghton Mifflin.

Nicholson, T. (1991) Do children learn words better in context or in lists? A classic study revisited. *Journal of Educational Psychology*, 83: 444–50.

Nicholson, T. (1993) The case against context. In G. Thompson, W. Tunmer and T. Nicholson (eds), *Reading acquisition processes* (pp. 91–104). Clevedon, UK: Multilingual Matters.

Nist, S. and Simpson, M. (2000) College studying. In M.L. Kamil, P.B. Mosenthal, P.D. Pearson and R. Barr (eds), *Handbook of reading research*, Volume III (pp. 645–66). Mahwah, NJ: Lawrence Erlbaum.

Nunan, D. (1990) Action research in the language classroom. In J.C. Richards and D. Nunan (eds), *Second language teacher education* (pp. 62–81). New York: Cambridge University Press.

Nunan, D. (1993) Action research in language education. In J. Edge and K. Richards (eds), *Teachers develop teachers' research: Papers on classroom research and teacher development* (pp. 39–50). Oxford: Heinemann.

Nuttall, C. (1996) *Teaching reading skills in a foreign language* (new edn). Oxford: Heinemann.

Ogbu, J.U. (1987) Opportunity structure, cultural boundaries, and literacy. In J.A. Langer (ed.), *Language, literacy, and culture: Issues of society and schooling* (pp. 149–77). Norwood, NJ: Ablex.

Oney, B., Peter, M. and Katz, L. (1997) Phonological processing in printed word recognition: Effects of age and writing system. *Scientific Studies of Reading*, 1: 65–83.

Paris, S.G., Wasik, B.A. and Turner, J.C. (1991) The development of strategic readers. In R. Barr, M.L. Kamil, P. Mosenthal and P.D. Pearson (eds), *Handbook of reading research*, Volume II (pp. 609–40). Mahwah, NJ: Lawrence Erlbaum.

Parks, S. and Black, H. (1992) *Organizing Thinking: Graphic organizers*, Book I. Pacific Grove, CA: Critical Thinking Press & Software.

Parks, S. and Black, H. (1990) *Organizing Thinking: Graphic organizers*, Book II. Pacific Grove, CA: Critical Thinking Press & Software.

Parry, K. (1991) Building a vocabulary through academic reading. *TESOL Quarterly*, 25: 629–53.

Pearson, P.D. and Fielding, L. (1991) Comprehension instruction. In R. Barr, M.L. Kamil, P. Mosenthal and P.D. Pearson (eds), *Handbook of reading research*, Volume II (pp. 815–60). Mahwah, NJ: Lawrence Erlbaum.

Perfetti, C. (1985) *Reading ability*. New York: Oxford University Press.

Perfetti, C. (1994) Psycholinguistics and reading ability. In M.A. Gernsbacher (ed.), *Handbook of psycholinguistics* (pp. 849–94). San Diego: Academic Press.

Perfetti, C. (1997) Sentences, individual differences, and multiple texts: Three issues in text comprehension. *Discourse Processes*, 23: 337–55.

Perfetti, C., Britt, M. and Georgi, M. (1995) *Text-based learning and reasoning*. Hillsdale, NJ: Lawrence Erlbaum.

Perfetti, C., Rouet, J.F. and Britt, M. (1999) Toward a theory of documents representation. In H. van Oostendorp and S. Goldman (eds), *The construction of mental representations during reading* (pp. 99–122). Mahwah, NJ: Lawrence Erlbaum.

Perfetti, C.A., van Dyke, J. and Hart, L. (2001) The psycholinguistics of basic literacy. In M. McGroarty *et al.* (eds), *Annual Review of Applied Linguistics*, 21: 127–49. New York: Cambridge University Press.

Pittelman, S., Heimlich, J., Berglund, R. and French, M. (1991) *Semantic feature analysis: Classroom applications*. Newark, DE: International Reading Association.

Plaut, D., McClelland, J., Seidenberg, M. and Patterson, K. (1996) Understanding normal and impaired word reading: Computational principles of quasi-regular domains. *Psychological Review*, 103: 56–115.

Pressley, M. (1995) A transactional strategies instruction Christmas carol. In A. McKeough, J. Lupart and A. Marini (eds), *Teaching for transfer: Fostering generalization in learning* (pp. 177–213). Mahwah, NJ: Lawrence Erlbaum.

Pressley, M. (1998) *Reading instruction that really works*. New York: Guilford Press.

Pressley, M. (2000) What should comprehension instruction be the instruction of? In M.L. Kamil, P.B. Mosenthal, P.D. Pearson and R. Barr (eds), *Handbook of reading research*, Volume III (pp. 545–61). Mahwah, NJ: Lawrence Erlbaum.

Pressley, M., El-Dinary, P., Gaskins, I., Schuder, T., Bergman, J., Almasi, J. and Brown, R. (1992) Beyond direct explanation: Transactional strategy instruction of reading comprehension strategies. *Elementary School Journal*, 92: 513–55.

Pressley, M. and Woloshyn, V. (1995) *Cognitive strategy instruction that really improves children's academic performance* (2nd edn). Cambridge, MA: Brookline Books.

Proctor, R. and Dutta, A. (1995) *Skill acquisition and human performance*. Thousand Oaks, CA: Sage.

Rasinski, T. (1990) Effects of repeated reading and listening-while-reading on reading fluency. *Journal of Educational Research*, 83: 147–50.

Rasinski, T., Padak, N., Linek, W. and Sturtevant, E. (1994) Effects of fluency development on urban second-grade readers. *Journal of Educational Research*, 87: 158–65.

Read, J. (2000) *Assessing vocabulary*. New York: Cambridge University Press.

Readence, J.E., Bean, T.W. and Baldwin, R.S. (1998) *Content area literacy: An integrated approach* (6th edn). Dubuque, IA: Kendall/Hunt.

Reppen, R. (1994/1995) A genre-based approach to content writing instruction. *TESOL Journal*, 4: 32–5.

Richards, J.C. (1998) *Beyond training: Perspectives on language teacher education*. New York: Cambridge University Press.

Richards, J.C. and Lockhart, C. (1994) *Reflective teaching in second language classrooms*. New York: Cambridge University Press.

Rosen, N. and Stoller, F.L. (1994) *Javier arrives in the U.S.: A text for developing readers*. Englewood Cliffs, NJ: Prentice Hall Regents.

Rost, M. (2001) *Teaching and researching listening*. London: Longman.

Samuels, S.J., Schermer, N. and Reinking, D. (1992) Reading fluency: Techniques for making decoding automatic. In S.J. Samuels and A. Farstrup (eds), *What research has to say about reading instruction* (2nd edn, pp. 124–44). Newark, DE: International Reading Association.

Schmitt, N. (2000) *Vocabulary in language teaching*. New York: Cambridge University Press.

Schmitt, N. and McCarthy, M. (eds) (1997) *Vocabulary: Description, acquisition, and pedagogy*. New York: Cambridge University Press.

Schoonen, R., Hulstijn, J. and Bossers, B. (1998) Metacognitive and language-specific knowledge in native and foreign language reading comprehension: An empirical study among Dutch students in grades 6, 8 and 10. *Language Learning*, 48: 71–106.

Schunk, D. (2000) *Learning theories: An educational perspective* (3rd edn). Upper Saddle River, NJ: Merrill.

Segalowitz, N. (1986) Second language reading. In J. Vaid (ed.), *Language processing in bilinguals: Psycholinguistic and neuropsychological perspectives* (pp. 3–19). Hillsdale, NJ: Lawrence Erlbaum.

Segalowitz, N. (2000) Automaticity and attentional skill in fluent performance. In H. Riggenbach (ed.), *Perspectives on fluency* (pp. 200–19). Ann Arbor, MI: University of Michigan Press.

Segalowitz, N., Poulson, C. and Komoda, M. (1991) Lower level components of reading skill in higher level bilinguals: Implications for reading instruction. *Reading in Two Languages. AILA Review*, 8: 15–30.

Segalowitz, S., Segalowitz, N. and Wood, A. (1998) Assessing the development of automaticity in second language word recognition. *Applied Psycholinguistics*, 19: 53–67.

Seidenberg, M. and McClelland, J. (1989) A distributed developmental model of word recognition and naming. *Psychological Review*, 96: 523–68.

Share, D. and Levin, I. (1999) Learning to read and write in Hebrew. In M. Harris and G. Hatano (eds), *Learning to read and write: A cross-linguistic perspective* (pp. 89–111). Cambridge: Cambridge University Press.

Sharon, A.T. (1973) What do adults read? *Reading Research Quarterly*, 9: 148–69.

Shimron, J. and Sivan, T. (1994) Reading proficiency and orthography: Evidence from Hebrew and English. *Language Learning*, 44: 5–27.

Shulman, L.S. (1997) Disciplines of inquiry in education: A new overview. In R.M. Jaeger (ed.), *Complementary methods for research in education* (2nd edn, pp. 3–29). Washington, DC: American Educational Research Association.

Siegel, L. (1994) Working memory and reading: A life-span perspective. *International Journal of Behavioural Development*, 17: 109–24.

Silberstein, S. (1994) *Techniques and resources in teaching reading*. New York: Oxford University Press.

Snow, C., Burns, S. and Griffin, P. (1998) *Preventing reading difficulties in young children*. Washington, DC: National Academy Press.

Somekh, B. (1993) Quality in educational research – The contribution of classroom teachers. In J. Edge and K. Richards (eds), *Teachers develop teachers' research: Papers on classroom research and teacher development* (pp. 26–38). Oxford: Heinemann.

Spargo, E. (1989) *Timed readings: Fifty 400-word passages with questions for building reading speed* (3rd edn) [10-book series]. Lincolnwood, IL: Jamestown.

Spargo, E. (1998) *Timed readings plus: 25 two-part lessons with questions for building reading speed and comprehension* [10-book series]. Lincolnwood, IL: Jamestown.

Stahl, S.A. (1997) Instructional models in reading: An introduction. In S.A. Stahl and D.A. Hayes (eds), *Instructional models in reading* (pp. 1–29). Mahwah, NJ: Lawrence Erlbaum.

Stahl, S.A. (1999) *Vocabulary development*. Cambridge, MA: Brookline Books.

Stahl, S.A., Heubach, K. and Cramond, B. (1997) *Fluency oriented reading instruction* (Reading Research Report no. 79). Athens, GA: National Reading Research Center.

Stanovich, K. (1980) Toward an interactive-compensatory model of individual differences in the acquisition of literacy. *Reading Research Quarterly*, 16: 32–71.

Stanovich, K. (1986) Matthew effects in reading: Some consequences of individual differences in the acquisition of literacy. *Reading Research Quarterly*, 21: 360–407.

Stanovich, K. (2000) *Progress in understanding reading: Scientific foundations and new frontiers*. New York: Guilford Press.

Stanovich, K.E., Cunningham, A.E. and Feeman, D.J. (1984) Intelligence, cognitive skills, and early reading progress. *Reading Research Quarterly*, 19: 278–303.

Stanovich, K.E. and Stanovich, P. (1999) How research might inform the debate about early reading acquisition. In J. Oakhill and R. Beard (eds), *Reading development and the teaching of reading* (pp. 12–41). Oxford: Blackwell.

Stanovich, K., West, R., Cunningham, A., Cipielewski, J. and Siddiqui, S. (1996) The role of inadequate print exposure as a determinant of reading comprehension problems. In C. Cornoldi and J. Oakhill (eds), *Reading comprehension difficulties: Processes and intervention* (pp. 15–32). Mahwah, NJ: Lawrence Erlbaum.

Stoller, F.L. (1993) Developing word and phrase recognition exercises. In R. Day (ed.), *New ways in teaching reading* (pp. 230–3). Alexandria, VA: TESOL.

Stoller, F.L. (1994a) Developing a focused reading lab for L2 students. *Reading in a Foreign Language*, 10: 33–53.

Stoller, F.L. (1994b) Making the most of a newsmagazine passage for reading skills development. *English Teaching Forum*, 32: 2–7.

Stoller, F.L. (1997) Project work: A means to promote language and content. *English Teaching Forum*, 35: 2–9, 37.

Stoller, F.L. (1999) Time for change: A hybrid curriculum for EAP programs. *TESOL Journal*, 8: 9–13.

Stoller, F.L. and Grabe, W. (1997) A six Ts' approach to content-based instruction. In M.A. Snow and D.M. Brinton (eds), *The content-based classroom: Perspectives on integrating language and content* (pp. 78–94). New York: Addison-Wesley Longman.

Stoller, F.L. and Rosen, N. (2000) *Changing generations: A story for developing reading skills*. New York: Longman.

Tan, A. and Nicholson, T. (1997) Flashcards revisited: Training poor readers to read words faster improves their comprehension of texts. *Journal of Educational Psychology*, 89: 276–88.

Tang, G.M. (1992) Teaching content knowledge and ESOL in multicultural classrooms. *TESOL Journal*, 2: 8–12.

Thompson, G. and Nicholson, T. (eds) (1999) *Learning to read: Beyond phonics and whole language*. New York: Teachers' College Press.

Tierney, R.J. and Readence, J.E. (1999) *Reading strategies and practices: A compendium* (5th edn). Boston: Allyn & Bacon.

Treville, M.-C. (1996) Lexical learning and reading in L2 at the beginning level: The advantage of cognates. *The Canadian Modern Language Review*, 53: 173–90.

Tsang, W.K. (1996) Comparing the effects of reading and writing on writing performance. *Applied Linguistics*, 17: 210–33.

Tunmer, W. and Chapman, J. (1999) Teaching strategies for word identification. In G. Thompson and T. Nicholson (eds), *Learning to read: Beyond phonics and whole language* (pp. 74–102). New York: Teachers' College Press.

Urquhart, S. and Weir, C. (1998) *Reading in a second language: Process, product and practice*. New York: Longman.

Vacca, R. and Vacca, J. (1998) *Content area reading* (6th edn). New York: Addison Wesley.

Verhoeven, L. (1994) Linguistic diversity and literacy development. In L. Verhoeven (ed.), *Functional literacy: Theoretical issues and educational implications* (pp. 199–219). Amsterdam: John Benjamins.

Verhoeven, L. and Aarts, R. (1998) Attaining functional biliteracy in the Netherlands. In A. Durgunoglu and L. Verhoeven (eds), *Literacy development in a multilingual context* (pp. 111–33). Mahwah, NJ: Lawrence Erlbaum.

Vygotsky, L.S. (1978) *Mind in society*. Cambridge, MA: Harvard University Press.

Wagner, R. and Stanovich, K. (1996) Expertise in reading. In K.A. Ericsson (ed.), *The road to excellence* (pp. 189–225). Mahwah, NJ: Lawrence Erlbaum.

Wallace, M.J. (1998) *Action research for language teachers*. New York: Cambridge University Press.

Weir, C. (forthcoming) *Teaching and researching testing*, Harlow: Longman.

Wigfield, A. and Guthrie, J.T. (1997) Relations of children's motivation for reading to the amount and breadth of their reading. *Journal of Educational Psychology*, 89: 420–32.

Zamel, V. (1992) Writing one's way into reading. *TESOL Quarterly*, 26: 463–81.

Subject Index

Author Index